W9-AZU-748

Crime and Consequence

CHAIRMAN
Rabbi Moshe Kotlarsky

PRINCIPAL BENEFACTOR
Mr. George Rohr

EXECUTIVE DIRECTOR
Rabbi Efraim Mintz

———

AUTHOR
Rabbi Shmuel Super

EDITOR
Rabbi Mordechai Dinerman

EDITORIAL BOARD
Rabbi Menachem Feldman
Rabbi Yehuda Leib Heber
Rabbi Levi Mendelow
Rabbi Shalom Paltiel
Rabbi Avrohom Sternberg

RESEARCH
Rabbi Yaakov Gershon

COORDINATOR
Mrs. Rivki Mockin

ADMINISTRATOR
Mrs. Chana Dechter

Printed in the United States of America
© Copyrighted and Published 2018
by **THE ROHR JEWISH LEARNING INSTITUTE**
822 Eastern Parkway, Brooklyn, NY 11213

All rights reserved.
No part of the contents of this book may be reproduced or transmitted in
any form or by any means without the written permission of the publisher.

Cover Art: *The Memorable Address of Louis XVI at the Bar of the
National Convention,* Luigi Schiavonetti, printmaker; after William
Miller, Italy. (London: Testolini, 1796) (Rijksmuseum, Amsterdam)

(888) YOUR-JLI/718-221-6900
WWW.MYJLI.COM

Crime and Consequence

JLI
JEWISH LEARNING INSTITUTE

STUDENT TEXTBOOK

The Rohr Jewish Learning Institute acknowledges the generous support of the following individuals and foundations:

PRINCIPAL BENEFACTOR

GEORGE ROHR
New York, NY

ADVISORY BOARD OF GOVERNORS

YAAKOV AND KAREN COHEN
Potomac, MD

YITZCHOK AND JULIE GNIWISCH
Montreal, QC

BARBARA HINES
Aspen, CO

DANIEL B. MARKSON
S. Antonio, TX

DANIEL AND ROSIE MATTIO
Seattle, WA

DAVID MINTZ
Tenafly, NJ

DR. STEPHEN F. SERBIN
Columbia, SC

LEONARD A. WIEN, JR.
Miami Beach, FL

PARTNERING FOUNDATIONS

WILLIAM DAVIDSON FOUNDATION

MEROMIM FOUNDATION

KOHELET FOUNDATION

CRAIN-MALING FOUNDATION

WORLD ZIONIST ORGANIZATION

AVI CHAI FOUNDATION

OLAMI—WOLFSON FOUNDATION

RUDERMAN FAMILY FOUNDATION

ESTATE OF ELLIOT JAMES BELKIN

KOSINS FAMILY FOUNDATION

PILLARS OF JEWISH LITERACY

KEVIN BERMEISTER
Sydney, Australia

PABLO AND SARA BRIMAN
Mexico City, Mexico

ZALMAN AND MIMI FELLIG
Miami Beach, FL

YOSEF GOROWITZ
Redondo Beach, CA

DR. VERA KOCH GROSZMANN
S. Paulo, Brazil

HERSCHEL LAZAROFF
Monsey, NY

JENNY LJUNGBERG
New York, NY

DAVID MAGERMAN
Gladwyne, PA

DR. MICHAEL MALING
Deerfield, IL

YITZCHAK MIRILASHVILI
Herzliya, Israel

BEN NASH
New Jersey

YAIR SHAMIR
Savyon, Israel

LARRY SIFEN
Virginia Beach, VA

SPONSORS

MARK AND REBECCA BOLINSKY
Long Beach, NY

DANIEL AND ETA COTLAR
Houston, TX

GORDON DIAMOND
Vancouver, BC

AMIR AND DAFNA ELYASHAR
Ramat Aviv, Israel

SHMUEL AND SHARONE GOODMAN
Chicago, IL

JOE AND SHIRA LIPSEY
Aspen, CO

ELLEN MARKS
S. Diego, CA

RACHELLE NEDOW
El Paso, TX

PETER AND HAZEL PFLAUM
Newport Beach, CA

FRANK (A"H) AND FRUMETH POLASKY
Saginaw, MI

MOSHE AND YAFFA POPACK
Fisher Island, FL

HERCHEL AND JULIE PORTMAN
Denver, CO

EYAL AND AVIVA POSTELNIK
Marietta, GA

DR. ZE'EV RAV-NOY
Los Angeles, CA

CLIVE AND ZOE ROCK
Irvine, CA

ZVI RYZMAN
Los Angeles, CA

ALAN ZEKELMAN
Bloomfield Hills, MI

MYRNA ZISMAN
Cedarhurst, NY

THE ROHR JEWISH LEARNING INSTITUTE

gratefully acknowledges
the pioneering and ongoing support of

George and Pamela Rohr

Since its inception,
the Rohr JLI has been
a beneficiary of the vision, generosity,
care, and concern
of the Rohr family.

In the merit of
the tens of thousands of hours of Torah study
by JLI students worldwide,
may they be blessed with health,
Yiddishe nachas *from all their loved ones,*
and extraordinary success
in all their endeavors.

Dedicated by

Ralph and Sylvia Heyman

Dayton, Ohio

◟

JLI is indebted and deeply grateful for their partnership in bringing Torah study to all corners of the world, and honors their exemplary commitment to integrity as champions of justice and civility.

In the merit of the Torah study by thousands of students worldwide, may they be blessed with good health, happiness, *nachat* from their loved ones, and success in all their endeavors.

◟

In partnership with Rabbi Nochum Mangel, Chabad of Greater Dayton

The course
CRIME AND CONSEQUENCE

has been approved in these states and provinces for fulfillment of the continuing education requirements for legal and ethics credits:

United States
Alabama
Alaska*
Arkansas
California*
Colorado
Connecticut
Delaware
Florida
Georgia
Idaho
Illinois
Indiana
Iowa
Kansas
Kentucky
Louisiana
Minnesota
Missouri
Nevada
New Jersey

New York*
North Carolina
Ohio
Oklahoma
Oregon
Pennsylvania
Rhode Island
South Carolina
Tennessee
Utah
Virginia*
Washington
Wisconsin

Canada
British Columbia
Ontario*
Saskatchewan*

*Pending approval at the time this book went to print

Endorsements

"One of the great ethical tests facing any democracy is how it handles people who break its laws. The United States has long been an outlier among democracies in the breadth of its use of the criminal justice system to shape the behavior of its citizens. This uniquely American approach to the administration of justice has had momentous political, economic, and social consequences. Frankly confronting the recent history of U.S. criminal justice is one of the most important tasks facing civic society. JLI is to be congratulated for its engagement in this challenging conversation."

DR. TODD CLEAR

University Professor, Rutgers Law School
Former President, American Society of Criminology

"About one percent of the adult population in the U.S. is incarcerated in our nation's prisons and jails—far more than any other country on earth. There is an urgent need to devise and implement policies to reduce the population behind bars without sacrificing public safety. There are policies for achieving this goal, but their adoption requires an educated population. The JLI's course is an exemplar of the type of educational initiative that is needed."

DR. DANIEL S. NAGIN

Teresa and H. John Heinz III University Professor of Public Policy and Statistics, Carnegie Mellon University; Clinical Professor of Law and Vice Dean for Experiential and Clinical Education, Harvard Law School

"Americans today are struggling with how to reform a criminal justice system that sends too many people to prison, retains the death penalty in many states, and seems all too often to take race into account in policing and punishment. While better scientific studies of our policies are surely needed, alone they are not enough. Effective reform requires a searching effort to consider and debate those values that ought to be reflected in criminal justice. In opening up the world of Jewish Talmudic and ethical teachings on criminal justice, *Crime and Consequence* provides a tremendous resource for stimulating that much-needed discussion."

DR. JONATHAN SIMON

Adrian A. Kragen Professor of Law and
Faculty Director, Center for the Study of Law and Society
University of California, Berkeley, School of Law

"It is a profound irony that the United States is a true beacon of democracy, freedom, and the rule of law while it imprisons more of its own citizenry than any other country. Clearly, the American criminal justice system is in need of systematic reform. *Crime and Consequence*, the new course of the Rohr Jewish Learning Institute (JLI), brings rigorous legal analysis, statistical data on incarceration and rehabilitation, and case studies into a uniquely profound dialogue with the values undergirding our entire political tradition. JLI is to be commended for pushing the American political conversation in a more humane and informed direction."

PROFESSOR ALAN DERSHOWITZ

Felix Frankfurter Professor of Law, Emeritus
Harvard University

"JLI's criminal justice/prison reform course focuses needed attention on a vital subject. Most important, by emphasizing Talmudic teachings, JLI's course shows that this is a subject that involves our oldest and most treasured ideas of right and wrong."

SCOTT TUROW
Attorney and best-selling author, including *Presumed Innocent*

"JLI has put together a wonderful course on the causes and consequences of crime. It will help all those who take it reflect hard on one of the hardest questions of all: Why punish?"

PROFESSOR STEPHEN GARVEY
Cornell Law School

"I commend the Rohr Jewish Learning Institute for publishing *Crime and Consequence,* which is a groundbreaking and edifying examination of how to approach modern criminal justice challenges through the lens of the ancient wisdom embodied in Talmudic law. This course and supplementary materials provide valuable insight into key challenges such as promoting effective alternatives to incarceration, improving indigent defense, and expanding opportunities for self-improvement for those who are convicted and even incarcerated so that we can break the cycle of crime."

MARC LEVIN, ESQ.
Vice President, Criminal Justice Policy
Texas Public Policy Foundation

"Questions about the causes of crime and the appropriate governmental response have challenged and bedeviled social thinkers for centuries. Indeed, such big questions have no easy answers. In light of the current bipartisan support for criminal justice reform, especially at the state and local level, your course is timely and important. I am glad to see the Rohr Jewish Learning Institute take on this topic in a thoughtful and productive manner."

DR. JOHN H. LAUB
Distinguished University Professor, Department of Criminology and Criminal Justice
University of Maryland

"We are now at a moment of changing attitudes among policymakers and the general public regarding the world-record prison population in the United States. With increasing calls for a change in our approach to crime and punishment, the JLI course is quite timely in helping to frame these issues for a broad audience."

MARC MAUER
Executive Director
The Sentencing Project

"Despite a bipartisan consensus that reforms are needed, problems such as mass incarceration and lethal policing uniquely plague the American criminal justice system. *Crime and Consequence* acknowledges that American criminal justice is as much a moral and ethical crisis as it is a policy challenge. Through applying Talmudic law to American criminal justice, this course promises to bring a fresh perspective to the most pressing ethical issues and broaden the constituency for reform."

PROFESSOR PAUL HIRSCHFIELD
Department of Sociology
Rutgers University

"That such a large percentage of people—particularly people of color—is incarcerated is one of the great moral scourges of our time. America desperately needs new policies in place that reduce this population, treat people fairly, and live up to our own aspirations for equality for all. For the Jewish Council on Public Affairs, it is a vital priority to get the Jewish community fully engaged in the civil rights movement of our time. There are many good ideas out there. We've seen best practices in action. But we need to make sure that the larger polity understands the challenge and potential solutions. JLI provides precisely such a learning opportunity."

DAVID BERNSTEIN
President and CEO
Jewish Council on Public Affairs

"America remains the only western democratic nation that still has a death penalty. And America also has the most severe and punitive criminal justice system among democracies, as measured by the percentage of the population incarcerated and the severity of sentences. I believe that there's a correlation between these features, which is why a discussion about the death penalty is essential to any discussion about criminal justice reform. I therefore applaud the Rohr Jewish Learning Institute for including a lesson on this subject in its course, *Crime and Consequence,* bringing this important matter to a wide audience."

STEPHEN GREENWALD
President
American Association of Jewish Lawyers and Jurists

"Criminal justice is at a crossroads, and there has never been a better time for people to come together to debate the issues and think hard about whether we are getting it right."

BRANDON GARRETT
L. Neil Williams Professor of Law
Duke University

"The issues raised go to the heart of the dilemmas facing our society, and are in the minds of every judge and every thoughtful person living under the rule of law in our great democratic country."

HON. JACK B. WEINSTEIN
Senior United States District Judge
U.S. District Court, Eastern District of New York

"The need for criminal justice reform has been acknowledged by Americans across the political spectrum. While there is a wide consensus on the need for action in this area, there is little consensus on guiding principles and suggested reforms. The Rohr Jewish Learning Institute (JLI) has once again performed an important communal service by drawing on the wisdom of millennia of Jewish thinking and scholarship in examination of a vital contemporary question. I have found previous JLI sourcebooks to be enjoyable reading and academically valuable resources at the same time."

PROFESSOR DAVID LUCHINS
Chair, Political Science Department
Touro College and University System

"This course serves an incredibly important purpose: taking a source—the Talmud—that has remained relevant to law and policy for thousands of years, and demonstrating that continued relevance to today's modern audience. It also tackles one of the most important and hotly contested issues in society today: how the criminal justice system can or should be reformed. In so doing, it utilizes some of the most timely and relatable criminal cases and examples, which is really in keeping with the tradition of Talmudic learning itself. So many audiences, both secular and religious, would benefit from this unique, insightful, and informative program."

PROFESSOR MARTIN PRITIKIN
Dean
Concord Law School, Purdue University

"As an observant Jew and academic, I am interested in the Jewish perspective on criminal justice. Indeed, I would like to present a course with this focus and believe it would be welcomed by both the criminal justice and theology departments at my university."

PROFESSOR HOWARD ABADINSKY
Professor of Criminal Justice
St. John's University

"The Jewish community needs this new course to examine the problems of the American criminal justice system. Today we have 2.4 million people in jailor prison and over seven million in correctional custody, including lock-ups, probation, parole, or community supervision. A majority of these people are first-offenders, and the population is disproportionately poor, young, male, and black or brown. We desperately need fresh intellectual ideals to penetrate and illuminate the social, political, economic, and legal issues related to societal failures with the way we perceive and process crime in our country."

STEPHEN C. RICHARDS
Professor Emeritus
Department of Criminal Justice, University of
Wisconsin Oshkosh

Contents

Lesson

1

LOCK AND KEY
WHAT'S THE POINT OF PRISON?

A quick glance at the statistics suggests an uncomfortable truth: modern-day societies imprison people at a rate unparalleled, and indeed unimaginable, in past times. Why is this so? Why do we lock people up, and what do we hope to achieve by doing so? Does the purpose of prison always outweigh the cons of conviction? This lesson considers and contrasts secular and Talmudic theories of criminal justice, before suggesting how to ensure a more just justice system.

Lá dedans tu pourras gueuleur! (Inside you'll be able to heal!), from the series *Crimes et Châtiments (Crimes and Punishments)* from *L'Assiette au Beurre*, no. 48, Félix Emile-Jean Vallotton, 1902. (The Museum of Fine Arts, Houston)

QUESTION FOR DISCUSSION

If you were on a parole board, would you give Anthony Rolon and juvenile murderers like him a second chance?

Man in een gevangenis (Man in jail), Jan Wandelaar, etching, Netherlands, c. 1722–1723. (Rijksmuseum, Amsterdam)

*Watch **Professor Steven Drizin**, cofounder of the **Center on Wrong-ful Convictions of Youth**, discuss how the science of adolescent brain development relates to our view of juvenile offenders:*

MYJLI.COM/CRIME

Figure 1.1

Four Theories of Punishment

1 Retribution

2 Incapacitation

3 Deterrence

4 Rehabilitation

*Watch as **Professor Robert Blecker**, an advocate of the retributive theory of punishment, argues that our criminal justice system needs more retribution:*

MYJLI.COM/CRIME

QUESTION FOR DISCUSSION

Which of these theories of punishment do you think guides the justice system in your country?

TEXT 1a

MARTIN H. PRITIKIN, "PUNISHMENT, PRISONS, AND THE BIBLE"
CARDOZO LAW REVIEW, 28:2, P. 721

When the penitentiary system in the United States began in the late eighteenth century, it was specifically designed for the purpose of rehabilitating the prisoner.... Rehabilitation continued to be the dominant goal of the American penitentiary system for nearly two centuries....

Views about how inmates were to be rehabilitated changed over time. Originally, the offender was separated from his former life and made to reflect—through isolation, work, fasting, and/or Bible study—in order to change his ways. But the results of solitary confinement and starvation diets were sorely disappointing, and as the Industrial Revolution gained steam, "vocational and academic training came to replace remorse and discipline as the principal instrument for rehabilitation." This was not an abandonment of rehabilitation as a goal, but rather a shift in approach regarding how to achieve it.

MARTIN H. PRITIKIN

Law professor. Martin Pritikin graduated magna cum laude from Harvard Law School and spent several years litigating before entering academia full time, teaching advanced litigation and criminal law. Pritikin currently serves as the dean of Concord Law School.

By the 1960s, a growing optimism about science in general, and psychiatry in particular, led some to view criminal behavior as a manifestation of mental illness that, with proper supervision within the criminal justice system, could be "cured." Indeterminate sentencing was widespread, and parole boards were effectively given the role of determining when a prisoner was "cured" and thus fit to be released. This was, effectively, a medical model of criminal justice.

TEXT **1b**

MARTIN H. PRITIKIN, IBID., P. 722

The medical model—and the rehabilitative model in general—came under increasing attack in the late 1960s and 1970s. . . .

Scholarly critiques of rehabilitation—and corollary support for retribution—abounded, and the critics were emboldened by research indicating that rehabilitation, did not, in fact, work. Sociologist Robert Martinson's influential 1974 paper, *What Works? Questions and Answers About Prison Reform* [THE PUBLIC INTEREST, Issue 35, Spring, 1974, pp. 22–54], was widely relied on for its perceived conclusion that "nothing works" to reduce recidivism.

Figure 1.2

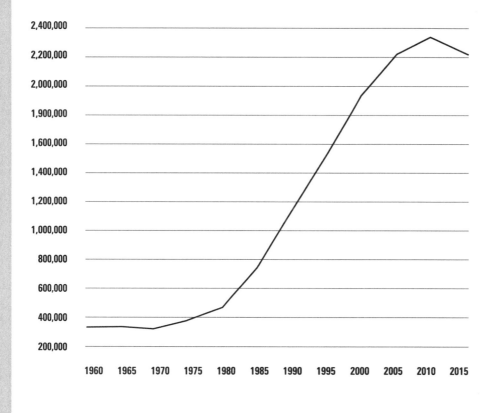

**NUMBER OF PEOPLE
INCARCERATED IN THE U.S.**

BUREAU OF JUSTICE STATISTICS, AND PRISONPOLICY.ORG

*Are you up to date with
important facts about crime
and criminal justice in the
U.S? Take a **quick quiz**
to find out:*

MYJLI.COM/CRIME

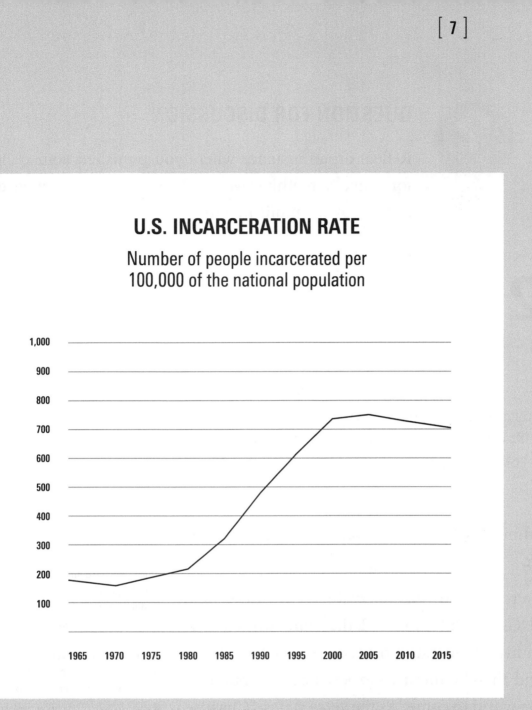

U.S. INCARCERATION RATE

Number of people incarcerated per
100,000 of the national population

BUREAU OF JUSTICE STATISTICS, AND PRISONPOLICY.ORG

QUESTION FOR DISCUSSION

Reflect on an instance where you punished your child for doing something wrong. What were you trying to achieve by the punishment?

TEXT 2

SEFER HACHINUCH, MITZVAH 594

תקצד. מִצְוָה לְהַלְקוֹת לָרָשָׁע

מִשׁוֹרְשֵׁי הַמִּצְוָה: לְפִי שֶׁיִּשְׂרָאֵל נִקְרָאִים בָּנָיו שֶׁל מָקוֹם, וְרָצָה בָּרוּךְ הוּא לְיַסְּרָם עַל הָעֲבֵירוֹת, כְּדֵי שֶׁיָּשׁוּבוּ אֵלָיו וְיִזְכּוּ בָּאַחֲרוֹנָה בָּעוֹלָם שֶׁכֻּלּוֹ טוֹב, וּכְעִנְיָן שֶׁכָּתוּב (מִשְׁלֵי יט, יח) יַסֵּר בִּנְךָ כִּי יֵשׁ תִּקְוָה וְאֶל הֲמִיתוֹ אַל תִּשָּׂא נַפְשֶׁךָ.

Commandment 594 is the mitzvah to give lashes to a sinner.

One of the reasons for this mitzvah: The Jewish people are called G-d's* children. G-d therefore wished that they be punished, to cause them to repent and return to Him and thereby merit to experience the abundant good of the world to come. As the verse states, "Chastise your son for there is hope—do not set your heart on his destruction" (PROVERBS 19:18).

SEFER HACHINUCH

A work on the biblical commandments. Four aspects of every mitzvah are discussed in this work: the definition of the mitzvah; ethical lessons that can be deduced from the mitzvah; basic laws pertaining to the observance of the mitzvah; and who is obligated to perform the mitzvah, and when. The work was composed in the 13th century by an anonymous author who refers to himself as "the Levite of Barcelona." It has been widely thought that this referred to Rabbi Aharon Halevi of Barcelona (Re'ah); however, this view has been contested.

---

* Throughout this book, "G-d" and "L-rd" are written with a hyphen instead of an "o" (both in our own translations and when quoting others). This is one way we accord reverence to the sacred divine name. This also reminds us that, even as we seek G-d, He transcends any human effort to describe His reality.

TEXT 3

RABBI SHNE'UR ZALMAN OF LIADI, *LIKUTEI TORAH*, *MATOT* 86B

כָּל עוֹנְשֵׁי הַתּוֹרָה עִם הֱיוֹתָן בְּחִינַת גְבוּרוֹת מִכָּל מָקוֹם הֵן כְּלוּלוֹת בַּחֲסָדִים שֶׁהָעוֹנֶשׁ הוּא שֶׁעַל יְדֵי זֶה זֶה נַעֲשֶׂה תִּיקוּן לְנֶפֶשׁ הַחוֹטֵא.

While the punishments of the Torah are expressed as severity, their core identity is kindness—because through them the soul of the sinner achieves its rectification.

RABBI SHNE'UR ZALMAN OF LIADI (ALTER REBBE) 1745–1812

Chasidic rebbe, halachic authority, and founder of the Chabad movement. The Alter Rebbe was born in Liozna, Belarus, and was among the principal students of the Magid of Mezeritch. His numerous works include the *Tanya*, an early classic containing the fundamentals of Chabad Chasidism, and *Shulchan Aruch HaRav*, an expanded and reworked code of Jewish law.

TEXT 4a

DEUTERONOMY 21:22–23

לֹא תָלִין נִבְלָתוֹ עַל הָעֵץ כִּי קָבוֹר תִּקְבְּרֶנּוּ בַּיּוֹם הַהוּא כִּי קִלְלַת אֱלֹקִים תָּלוּי; וְלֹא תְטַמֵּא אֶת אַדְמָתְךָ אֲשֶׁר ה' אֱלֹקֶיךָ נֹתֵן לְךָ נַחֲלָה.

But you shall not leave his body on the pole overnight. Rather, you must bury him on that same day, for a hanging body is an insult to G-d. You shall not thereby defile your land that G-d gives you as an inheritance.

TEXT 4b

RASHI, AD LOC.

> זִלְזוּלוֹ שֶׁל מֶלֶךְ הוּא, שֶׁאָדָם עָשׂוּי בִּדְמוּת דְּיוּקְנוֹ, וְיִשְׂרָאֵל הֵם בָּנָיו. מָשָׁל
> לִשְׁנֵי אַחִים תְּאוֹמִים שֶׁהָיוּ דוֹמִין זֶה לָזֶה, אֶחָד נַעֲשָׂה מֶלֶךְ וְאֶחָד נִתְפַּס
> לִלְסְטִיּוּת וְנִתְלָה. כָּל הָרוֹאֶה אוֹתוֹ אוֹמֵר "הַמֶּלֶךְ תָּלוּי".

It is a degradation of the King [G-d] because man is made in the likeness of His image, and the people of Israel are His children. This can be compared to identical twin brothers, one of whom became a king while the other became an outlaw and was hanged. Whoever would see the outlaw hanging would say, "The king is hanging."

RABBI SHLOMO YITSCHAKI (RASHI) 1040–1105

Most noted biblical and Talmudic commentator. Born in Troyes, France, Rashi studied in the famed *yeshivot* of Mainz and Worms. His commentaries on the Pentateuch and the Talmud, which focus on the straightforward meaning of the text, appear in virtually every edition of the Talmud and Bible.

Man voorgeleid voor een rechtbank (Man Being Brought before a Court), Arnold Houbraken, etching, Northern Netherlands, 1682. (Rijksmuseum, Amsterdam)

TEXT 5

JEFFREY IAN ROSS, PHD AND STEPHEN C. RICHARDS, PHD, *BEHIND BARS: SURVIVING PRISON* (INDIANAPOLIS: ALPHA BOOKS, 2002), PP. 106, 109–110

The education programs are always inadequate. Prisons are filled with men and women who desperately need to upgrade their formal education. In some joints a majority of the men are high school dropouts. While we know that this lack of education may have contributed to their attraction to crime, the prison education curriculum will do little to alleviate this problem. Unfortunately, very little resources, staff, and space are devoted to so-called "inmate education." . . .

A mountain of academic research clearly demonstrates that higher education is the single most effective means to lower criminal recidivism rates. Simply stated, prisoners who complete a year or more of college courses while incarcerated are far less likely to violate parole or be returned to prison on a new conviction. Still, most prison systems have no post-secondary education offerings at all.

Occasionally, a local college might offer one or two intro level courses, but these are few and far between, dependent as they are on the institution and the whims of the warden. In any event, they only serve up to a few dozen prisoners at a time who can somehow scrounge

JEFFREY IAN ROSS, PHD

Criminologist and author. Ross specializes in policing and corrections. He has worked in a correctional facility and for the U.S. Department of Justice, and is currently a professor at the University of Baltimore's School of Criminal Justice.

STEPHEN C. RICHARDS, PHD

Criminologist and author. Stephen Richards served a nine-year sentence in federal prison for drug distribution. After his release, Richards earned a PhD in sociology from Iowa State University, and is currently a professor of criminal justice at the University of Wisconsin-Oshkosh.

Richard Bernstein, a Michigan State Supreme Court justice, overcame overwhelming odds to achieve his position: he was born blind. Find out why he visited a state prison and what he learned there:

MYJLI.COM/CRIME

up the funds to pay the tuition. The college may pull the plug on the program when they discover the convicts can't afford the courses and/or when they lose patience with the bureaucrats who manage the penitentiary.

Prison administrators, despite their program propaganda, usually don't actively support higher education. They're jailers, not educators. Most wardens, even those who publicly portray themselves as dedicated to rehabilitation, see outside university instructors as potentially subversive threats to the security and smooth running of the institution.

Convicts taking college classes also may be subject to frequent cell shakedowns and disciplinary transfers to administrative detention (solitary confinement) or other institutions. Wardens may consider educated convicts to be a threat to their authority, because they have the ability to write letters to the media to report inhumane conditions and corruption. Convict students may also be regarded as dangerous because they use the mail and phones to communicate with outside university personnel and other people who have influence with the press or political system.

Prior to 1992, prisoners could apply for Federal Pell grants, which paid college tuition for courses taught inside prison walls or by correspondence. Some convicts were able to access this program, receive funding, and pay for college credits. Filling out the applications was always a hassle, particularly for federal prisoners, who were more likely to get transferred and thus have to reapply several times. Prisoners no longer have to worry about the hassle, because the grants aren't available anymore.

Classroom in an American jail, c. 1920.

TEXT

JEFFREY IAN ROSS, PHD AND STEPHEN C. RICHARDS, PHD, IBID., PP. 127–128

You might assume that when you go to prison you'll be allowed to "do your own time" and, if you stay out of the way of gangs, they'll leave you alone. Unfortunately, your ability to be left to your own devices depends on the prison that you are sent to. Some penitentiaries are literally run by gangs. In those pens, if you don't join one faction or another, you may not be able to defend yourself.

What bothers many convicts, in fact one of their biggest fears, is that once they've decided that they can "do their time," situations arise where they have to defend themselves, and this will inevitably put them in a position where they'll catch another case and never go home. For example, gang bangers (members) may try to extort cigarettes from you or do a cell invasion in which they simply run into your house and grab your stuff. If you don't retaliate, they'll continue to do it to you. In this case, you may think that it's in your best interest to either join another gang for self-protection or "strap up" . . . and hunt down your perpetrators and stick and cut them.

TEXT 7

BERNARD KERIK, *FROM JAILER TO JAILED: MY JOURNEY FROM CORRECTION AND POLICE COMMISSIONER TO INMATE #84888-054* (NEW YORK: THRESHOLD EDITIONS, 2015), PP. 250–251

While the inmates . . . aren't chained to the wall and beaten, the noise, the filth, and the lack of basic amenities are collateral forms of punishment designed to break a man's spirit and institutionalize him. Being herded like cattle into the mess hall three times a day and then rushed through substandard meals. Having your cubicle torn apart by officers and all your worldly possessions, as meager as they may be, ripped out of your locker and strewn around the area. Washing with cold water because the water heater broke and wasn't replaced for months. Unnecessary additional punishments and degradation imposed on the inmate. For what purpose? Revenge?

There is a culture among certain correction staffs—imagine this across the country—where it is acceptable to inflict as much punishment on the inmates as the staff can get away with. Not physical punishment, but psychological. I witnessed a constant, ever-present reliance on a systematic form of psychological punishment. Day in and day out, men in prison are treated like children and then expected to act like men. Humiliation and degradation are all too common. Inmates are verbally abused, harassed, and belittled by staff. They didn't really do it to me, but I watched them do it to others—our unit manager standing there telling

BERNARD KERIK
1955–

Former New York City police commissioner and convicted felon. After concluding military service, Bernard Kerik joined the NYPD, rising to the position of commissioner of the New York City Department of Corrections, and then NYC police commissioner. In 2010, Kerik was sentenced to four years in federal prison for charges including tax fraud and false statements. Since his release, Kerik has become a vocal advocate for criminal justice reform.

an inmate he's "scum," holding his thumb and index fingers an inch apart, saying to the inmate, "You're this big. This is all you are to me." This is the unit manager who sets an example for the other staff members.

TEXT **8**

U.S. NATIONAL INSTITUTE OF JUSTICE, "RECIDIVISM," WWW.NIJ.GOV

Bureau of Justice Statistics studies have found high rates of recidivism among released prisoners. One study tracked 404,638 prisoners in 30 states after their release from prison in 2005. The researchers found that:

- Within three years of release, about two-thirds (67.8 percent) of released prisoners were rearrested.

- Within five years of release, about three-quarters (76.6 percent) of released prisoners were rearrested.

U.S. NATIONAL INSTITUTE OF JUSTICE
Research, development, and evaluation agency of the U.S. Department of Justice. The NIJ provides knowledge and tools to the criminal justice community to reduce crime and advance justice.

TEXT 9

THE REBBE, RABBI MENACHEM MENDEL SCHNEERSON, *SICHOT KODESH* 5736, VOL. 1, PP. 614–615

וואָס בְּנוֹגֵעַ צוּ בְּרִיאַת הָאָדָם וואָס עֶר אִיז בּאַשאַפֿן גֶעוואָרן "בְּצַלְמֵינוּ כִּדְמוּתֵינוּ", זאָגט מֶען אוֹיף דֶערוֹיף "אָדָם לְעָמָל יוּלָד" (אִיוֹב ה, ז), אוּן "אֲנִי נִבְרֵאתִי לְשַׁמֵּשׁ אֶת קוֹנִי" (קִידּוּשִׁין פב, ב). דאָס הֵייסט, אַז אַ מֶענטשׁ אִיז בּאַשאַפֿן גֶעוואָרן ניט אוֹיף צוּ זַיין אַ הוֹלֵךְ בָּטֵל, נאָר עֶר אִיז בּאַשאַפֿן גֶעוואָרן אוֹיף אוֹיפֿטאָן, אוּן אִין אַן אוֹפֿן אַז סʼוועט זַיין "לְשַׁמֵּשׁ אֶת קוֹנִי" - אוֹיפֿטאָן אִין טוֹב, אִין קְדוּשָׁה אוּן אִין רוּחָנִיּוּת וְכוּלֵי ...

אָבֶּער בְּשַׁעַת אַז עֶר זיצט אִין בֵּית הָאֲסוּרִים, נֶעמט מֶען בּאַ אִים צוּ די מֶעגלֶעכקֵייט אַז עֶר זאָל עֶפֶּעס טאָן ... מʼזאָל אִים אָבֶּער האַלטן אִין עוֹלָם הַזֶה, אוּן תּוֹרַת חֶסֶד זאָל זאָגן זֶען אִים אַרַיין אִין בֵּית הָאֲסוּרִים, אוּן נֶעם בּאַ אִים צוּ די מֶעגלֶעכקֵייט פֿוּן מְקַיֵּים זַיין די שְׁלִיחוּת פֿוּן "אָדָם לְעָמָל יוּלָד" - דאָס אִיז הֵיפֶּךְ הַחֶסֶד, אוּן אָן קֵיין תּוֹעֶלֶת.

אוּן דֶערפֿאַר אִיז אוֹיך ניטאָ אִין תּוֹרָה קֵיין עוֹנְשִׁים פֿאַר עַיִן תַּחַת עַיִן כִּפְשׁוּטוֹ, יָד תַּחַת יָד כִּפְשׁוּטוֹ וְכוּלֵי, וואָס בּאַ עַמֵי הָאָרֶץ, בּא די גרֶעסטֶע אוּן בֶּעסטֶע פֿוּן זֵיי, אִיז בּזְמַן מַתַּן תּוֹרָה גֶעוועֶן אַ דָבָר הָרָגִיל אַז מֶען האָט מַעֲנִישׁ גֶעוועֶן יָד תַּחַת יָד כִּפְשׁוּטוֹ, ווי סʼאִיז גֶעוועֶן זֵייעֶרֶע דִינִים אַז אַ גַנָב וואָס עֶר האָט גֶעגַנבʼעט בּאַ אִים די יָד, אָבֶּער אִין תּוֹרַת חֶסֶד קֶען ניט זַיין אַזוֹינֶע עוֹנְשִׁים, וואָרוּם דֶעמאָלט קֶען עֶר טאָן מֶערניט ווי מיט אַיין האַנט, מֶערניט ווי מיט אַיין אוֹיג, מֶערניט ווי מיט אַיין שֶׁן, אָדֶער ווייניקֶער מיט אַיין שֶׁן, וואָרוּם סʼפֿעלט בּאַ אִים אַ שֶׁן.

אִיז אִין תּוֹרָה קֶען ניט זַיין נאָר אַזאַ מִין עוֹנֶשׁ וואָס שטֶערט ניט צוּ מְמַלֵּא זַיין אָט די שְׁלִיחוּת.

RABBI MENACHEM MENDEL SCHNEERSON 1902–1994

The towering Jewish leader of the 20th century, known as "the Lubavitcher Rebbe," or simply as "the Rebbe." Born in southern Ukraine, the Rebbe escaped Nazi-occupied Europe, arriving in the U.S. in June 1941. The Rebbe inspired and guided the revival of traditional Judaism after the European devastation, impacting virtually every Jewish community the world over. The Rebbe often emphasized that the performance of just one additional good deed could usher in the era of Mashiach. The Rebbe's scholarly talks and writings have been printed in more than 200 volumes.

Man was created in the divine image and "was born to toil" (JOB 5:7) and to "serve his Creator" (TALMUD, KIDUSHIN 82B). Man was not created to be idle, but to work and achieve positive things—to "serve his Creator," in holy and spiritual pursuits. . . .

When a person is in prison they are denied the ability to do anything. . . . Placing a living person in a prison and denying them the ability to fulfill their life mission of "man was born to toil" is contrary to the Torah of kindness. This is cruel and does not benefit anyone.

For the same reason, the Torah does not have punishments like an "eye for an eye, a hand for a hand" in the literal sense. Other nations, including the greatest and best of them, used such punishments as a matter of course. Some had a law that a thief that stole with his hand should have his hand cut off. But ours is a Torah of kindness and doesn't include such punishments because this would restrict the person to the use of only one hand, eye, tooth, etc.

Torah can only have punishments that do not interfere with man's ability to achieve his or her divine mission.

Learn more about the **Lubavitcher Rebbe's** *views on incarceration:*

MYJLI.COM/CRIME

TEXT 10

DEUTERONOMY 19:1–5

שָׁלוֹשׁ עָרִים תַּבְדִּיל לָךְ בְּתוֹךְ אַרְצֶךָ אֲשֶׁר ה' אֱלֹקֶיךָ נֹתֵן לְךָ לְרִשְׁתָּהּ.
תָּכִין לְךָ הַדֶּרֶךְ, וְשִׁלַּשְׁתָּ אֶת גְּבוּל אַרְצְךָ אֲשֶׁר יַנְחִילְךָ ה' אֱלֹקֶיךָ, וְהָיָה
לָנוּס שָׁמָּה כָּל רֹצֵחַ.

וְזֶה דְּבַר הָרֹצֵחַ אֲשֶׁר יָנוּס שָׁמָּה וָחָי; אֲשֶׁר יַכֶּה אֶת רֵעֵהוּ בִּבְלִי דַעַת וְהוּא
לֹא שֹׂנֵא לוֹ מִתְּמֹל שִׁלְשֹׁם. וַאֲשֶׁר יָבֹא אֶת רֵעֵהוּ בַיַּעַר לַחְטֹב עֵצִים,
וְנִדְּחָה יָדוֹ בַגַּרְזֶן לִכְרֹת הָעֵץ וְנָשַׁל הַבַּרְזֶל מִן הָעֵץ וּמָצָא אֶת רֵעֵהוּ וָמֵת.
הוּא יָנוּס אֶל אַחַת הֶעָרִים הָאֵלֶּה וָחָי.

You shall set aside for yourselves three cities in the land your G-d is giving you to possess. Prepare the roads and divide the land that G-d is giving you as an inheritance into three parts, so that a person who kills someone may flee for refuge to one of these cities.

This is the type of killer who should flee there, so that he may live: anyone who strikes his fellow unintentionally, someone he didn't hate previously. For instance, when a man goes with his fellow into the forest to chop wood, and as he swings his ax to cut down the tree, the iron flies off the handle, hitting his fellow and killing him. Such a person should flee to one of these cities and live.

TEXT **11a**

NUMBERS 35:6

וְאֵת הֶעָרִים אֲשֶׁר תִּתְּנוּ לַלְוִיִּם אֵת שֵׁשׁ עָרֵי הַמִּקְלָט אֲשֶׁר תִּתְּנוּ לָנֻס שָׁמָּה הָרֹצֵחַ.

Six of the cities that you give the Levites will be cities of refuge, to which a killer may flee.

TEXT **11b**

MAIMONIDES, *MISHNEH TORAH*, LAWS OF THE SABBATICAL AND JUBILEE YEARS 13:12

וְלָמָּה לֹא זָכָה לֵוִי בְּנַחֲלַת אֶרֶץ יִשְׂרָאֵל וּבְבִזָּתָהּ עִם אֶחָיו מִפְּנֵי שֶׁהֻבְדַּל לַעֲבוֹד אֶת ה' לְשָׁרְתוֹ וּלְהוֹרוֹת דְּרָכָיו הַיְשָׁרִים וּמִשְׁפָּטָיו הַצַּדִּיקִים לָרַבִּים שֶׁנֶּאֱמַר, "יוֹרוּ מִשְׁפָּטֶיךָ לְיַעֲקֹב וְתוֹרָתְךָ" (דְּבָרִים כג, י).

The Levites did not receive a portion in the Land of Israel and in the spoils of war like their brethren. This is because they were designated to serve G-d and to instruct the people in G-d's just ways and righteous laws. As it says, "They will teach Your judgments to Jacob and Your Torah to Israel" (DEUTERONOMY 33:10).

RABBI MOSHE BEN MAIMON (MAIMONIDES, RAMBAM) 1135–1204

Halachist, philosopher, author, and physician. Maimonides was born in Córdoba, Spain. After the conquest of Córdoba by the Almohads, he fled Spain and eventually settled in Cairo, Egypt. There, he became the leader of the Jewish community and served as court physician to the vizier of Egypt. He is most noted for authoring the *Mishneh Torah,* an encyclopedic arrangement of Jewish law, and for his philosophical work, *Guide for the Perplexed.* His rulings on Jewish law are integral to the formation of halachic consensus.

TEXT **11c**

MAIMONIDES, *MISHNEH TORAH*, LAWS OF MURDERERS
AND THE PROTECTION OF LIFE 7:6

עִיר מִקְלָט שֶׁרוּבָּה רַצְחָנִים אֵינָהּ קוֹלֶטֶת . . .
וְכֵן עִיר שֶׁאֵין בָּהּ זְקֵנִים אֵינָהּ קוֹלֶטֶת.

If the majority of the inhabitants of a city of refuge are
killers, it can no longer serve as a haven. . . .

Similarly, a city that does not have elders cannot serve
as a haven.

Rabbis Studying, anonymous, Paris, 1935

TEXT **12**

MAIMONIDES, *MISHNEH TORAH*, LAWS OF THE SANHEDRIN, 24:9–10

וְכֵן יֵשׁ לוֹ לִכְפּוֹת יָדַיִם וְרַגְלַיִם וְלֶאֱסוֹר בְּבֵית הָאֲסוּרִים . . . שֶׁנֶּאֱמַר, "הֵן
לְמוֹת הֵן לִשְׁרֹשִׁי הֵן לַעֲנָשׁ נִכְסִין וְלֶאֱסוּרִין" (עֶזְרָא ז, כו).

כָּל אֵלּוּ הַדְּבָרִים לְפִי מַה שֶׁיִּרְאֶה הַדַּיָּין שֶׁזֶּה רָאוּי לְכָךְ וְשֶׁהַשָּׁעָה צְרִיכָה.

The judge may have a person's hands and feet bound. He may also imprison him . . . as the verse states: "[Judgment will be speedily administered to him,] whether to be executed, uprooted, financially penalized, or imprisoned" (EZRA 7:26).

All of the above measures should be applied according to the judge's determination that it is appropriate that the violator be punished in this manner and that the needs of the time require it.

TEXT 13

REGULATIONS OF THE JEWISH COMMUNITIES OF CASTILE, 1432 (CITED IN SIMCHA ASSAF, *HA'ONASHIM ACHAREI CHATIMAT HATALMUD*, P. 90)

אֲנַחְנוּ מְתַקְּנִים שֶׁשּׁוּם דַּיָּן לֹא יוֹשִׁיב יְהוּדִי אוֹ יְהוּדִית בְּמַאֲסָר מִבְּלִי שֶׁיִּכְתּוֹב פְּקֻדָּתוֹ זוֹ בִּכְתָב וְעֵדִים יַחְתְּמוּ עַל זֶה גַם הוּא מְחוּיָב לְהוֹדִיעַ אֶת הַטַּעַם וְהַיְסוֹד לִפְקֻדָּה זוֹ.

We legislate that no judge may imprison a Jewish man or woman without issuing a written order notarized by witnesses. He must also notify of the reason and basis for the order.

REGULATIONS OF THE JEWISH COMMUNITIES OF CASTILE

The 1432 Regulations of the Jewish Communities of Castile were the product of a synod of representatives of the Jewish communities of Castile that convened in Valladolid, Spain, under the leadership of court Rabbi Avraham Benveniste. The regulations cover Jewish education, the justice system, and taxation.

*Watch **Professor Glenn Dynner** discuss how autonomous Jewish communities in Eastern Europe dealt with criminals:*

MYJLI.COM/CRIME

La Justice (Justice),
Igor Pose, watercolor
on paper, 2004.

TEXT 14

BERNARD KERIK, *FROM JAILER TO JAILED: MY JOURNEY FROM CORRECTION AND POLICE COMMISSIONER TO INMATE #84888-054* (NEW YORK: THRESHOLD EDITIONS, 2015), P. 244

I've met good men—yes, good men—in prison who made mistakes out of stupidity or ignorance, greed, or just bad judgment, but they did not need to be sent to prison to be punished: eighteen months for catching too many fish; two years for inflating income on a mortgage application; three months for selling a whale's tooth on eBay; fifteen years for a first-time nonviolent drug conspiracy in which no drugs were found or seized. There are thousands of people like these in our prisons today, costing American taxpayers billions of dollars when these individuals could be punished in smarter, alternative ways.

KEY POINTS

1 There are four major theories of punishment in legal thought: retribution, incapacitation, deterrence, and rehabilitation.

2 Historically, in the American legal system, the emphasis was on rehabilitation. But this changed in the 1970s, and retribution and incapacitation became the dominant goals of punishment. This shift in emphasis fueled an explosion in the number of people being incarcerated.

3 The Torah's primary theory of punishment is rehabilitation of the sinner—for their own sake. Even the worst criminal was created in G-d's image, and is therefore worthy of our help to rehabilitate themselves.

4 The reality of the contemporary prison system is that educational opportunities are woefully inadequate, violence is endemic, and prisoners are subjected to dehumanization and abuse.

5 The Bible does not prescribe an incarceration system because it maintains that every human being has a G-d-given mission in life and requires freedom in order to pursue it.

6 Jewish law tolerates prisons only when absolutely necessary to protect society.

*Watch as **Professor Jonathan Sarna**, prominent historian of American Judaism, discuss how Jews fare in U.S. prisons:*

MYJLI.COM/CRIME

7 On the policy level, the Torah teaches us that (a) prisons should be used much less, only when absolutely necessary; (b) the prison system must be completely overhauled, protecting the dignity of the prisoners and focusing on rehabilitation; and (c) convicted criminals should be granted second chances if they are no longer a threat to society.

8 Criminals are human beings, deserving our concern, respect, and assistance. The families of the incarcerated also suffer greatly, and are in need of our help.

What are your views regarding "life without the possibility of parole"? Take a poll at:

MYJLI.COM/CRIME

Appendix

TEXT **15a**

LEVITICUS 24:19–20

וְאִישׁ כִּי יִתֵּן מוּם בַּעֲמִיתוֹ, כַּאֲשֶׁר עָשָׂה כֵּן יֵעָשֶׂה לּוֹ. שֶׁבֶר תַּחַת שֶׁבֶר, עַיִן תַּחַת עַיִן, שֵׁן תַּחַת שֵׁן. כַּאֲשֶׁר יִתֵּן מוּם בָּאָדָם, כֵּן יִנָּתֶן בּוֹ.

Anyone who injures his fellow should be injured in the same manner: A fracture for fracture, eye for eye, tooth for tooth. Just as he inflicted an injury upon a person, so shall it be inflicted upon him.

TEXT **15b**

MAIMONIDES, *MISHNEH TORAH*, LAWS OF INJURY AND DAMAGES 1:3

זֶה שֶׁנֶּאֱמַר בַּתּוֹרָה, "כַּאֲשֶׁר יִתֵּן מוּם בָּאָדָם כֵּן יִנָּתֶן בּוֹ" (וַיִּקְרָא כד, כ), אֵינוֹ לַחֲבוֹל בָּזֶה כְּמוֹ שֶׁחָבַל בַּחֲבֵרוֹ, אֶלָּא שֶׁהוּא רָאוּי לְחַסְרוֹ אֵבֶר אוֹ לַחֲבוֹל בּוֹ כְּמוֹ שֶׁעָשָׂה וּלְפִיכָךְ מְשַׁלֵּם נִזְקוֹ.

The Torah's statement, "Just as he inflicted an injury upon a person, so shall it be inflicted upon him" (LEVITICUS 24:20), does not mean that the person who caused the injury should actually be subjected to a similar physical punishment. Instead, the intent is to state that he *deserves* to lose a limb or to be injured in the same manner as his fellow was and therefore must pay proportionate financial restitution.

TEXT 16

RABBI SAADIA GA'ON, *EMUNOT VEDE'OT* 4:2

וְהִתְבּוֹנַנְתִּי בְּמַה שֶּׁכְּבָר לְפָנֵי כֵן צִיוָּוה בָּעוֹלָם הַזֶּה לַהֲרוֹג בְּסוּגֵּי אַרְבַּע מִיתוֹת.

וְהִתְבָּרֵר לִי כִּי זֶה לְטוֹבָתוֹ, וְאֵינָם מְחוּץ לְמַה שֶּׁמְחַיֵּיב הַשֵּׂכֶל, לְפִי שֶׁהַשֵּׂכֶל מְחַיֵּיב כְּמוֹ שֶׁנִּרְאֶה לָאָדָם עַצְמוֹ שֶׁכְּרִיתַת מִקְצָת אֲבָרָיו אִם נִיזוֹקוּ בְּרַעַל אוֹ בְּמַחֲלָה, טוֹבָה הִיא לוֹ לְהַצִּיל שְׁאָר גּוּפוֹ, כַּךְ נִרְאֶה לְמִין הָאָדָם שֶׁהֲרִיגַת מִי שֶׁהוּשְׁחַת מֵהֶם וְהִשְׁחִית בָּאָרֶץ, דָּבָר נָכוֹן כְּדֵי לְהַצִּיל שְׁאָר בְּנֵי אָדָם.

RABBI SAADIA GA'ON (RASAG) 882–942 CE

Rabbinic scholar, philosopher, and exegete. Rabbi Saadia Ga'on was born in Egypt and came to the forefront of the rabbinic scene through his active opposition to Karaism, a divergent sect that denied the divinity of the Oral Law. In 928, the exilarch David ben Zakai invited him to head the illustrious yeshiva in Sura, Babylonia, thereby bestowing upon him the honorific title "Ga'on." He is renowned for his works on the Torah, Hebrew linguistics, Jewish philosophy, and his redaction of a *siddur*.

I have contemplated G-d's command to physically execute certain criminals with one of the four methods of execution.

My analysis is that it is for the benefit of mankind and not illogical at all. Regarding an individual, amputating a limb that is damaged due to an infection or illness is appropriate in order to save the rest of the body. Similarly, it follows logically that the same can be said for mankind in general: executing a degenerate person who has committed destructive crimes is appropriate in order to save the rest of mankind.

TEXT **17**a

DEUTERONOMY 19:16–20

כִּי יָקוּם עֵד חָמָס בְּאִישׁ לַעֲנוֹת בּוֹ סָרָה, וְעָמְדוּ שְׁנֵי הָאֲנָשִׁים אֲשֶׁר לָהֶם הָרִיב לִפְנֵי ה', לִפְנֵי הַכֹּהֲנִים וְהַשֹּׁפְטִים אֲשֶׁר יִהְיוּ בַּיָּמִים הָהֵם. וְדָרְשׁוּ הַשֹּׁפְטִים הֵיטֵב, וְהִנֵּה עֵד שֶׁקֶר הָעֵד, שֶׁקֶר עָנָה בְאָחִיו. וַעֲשִׂיתֶם לוֹ כַּאֲשֶׁר זָמַם לַעֲשׂוֹת לְאָחִיו, וּבִעַרְתָּ הָרָע מִקִּרְבֶּךָ. וְהַנִּשְׁאָרִים יִשְׁמְעוּ וְיִרָאוּ וְלֹא יֹסִפוּ לַעֲשׂוֹת עוֹד כַּדָּבָר הָרָע הַזֶּה בְּקִרְבֶּךָ.

If a false witness accuses someone of a crime, the two people involved in the dispute should stand in the presence of G-d, before the priests and the judges who are in office at the time. The judges must make a thorough investigation, and if the witness proves to be a liar, giving false testimony against his fellow, you should do to the false witness just as that witness intended to do to the other party. You must purge the evil from your midst. The rest of the people will hear of this and be afraid, and never again will such an evil thing be done among you.

TEXT 17b

MAIMONIDES, *GUIDE FOR THE PERPLEXED* 3:41

כִּי גֹדֶל הָעוֹנֶשׁ וְחוֹמֶר פְּגִיעָתוֹ, אוֹ קַטְנוֹ וְקַלּוּת סְבִילָתוֹ, יִהְיֶה בִּבְחִינַת אַרְבָּעָה דְבָרִים.

הָאֶחָד חוֹמֶר הָעֲבֵרָה, כִּי הַמַּעֲשִׂים אֲשֶׁר תּוֹצָאוֹתֵיהֶם הֶפְסֵד גָּדוֹל עוֹנְשָׁן חָמוּר, וְהַמַּעֲשִׂים אֲשֶׁר תּוֹצָאוֹתֵיהֶן הֶפְסֵד קַל וּמוּעָט עוֹנְשָׁן קַל.

וְהַשֵּׁנִי רִבּוּי מְצִיאוּתָן, שֶׁהַדְּבָרִים הַמְצוּיִּים יוֹתֵר צָרִיךְ לְמָנְעָן בְּעוֹנֶשׁ חָמוּר, אֲבָל מְעַטֵּי הַמְצִיאוּת הֲרֵי עוֹנֶשׁ קַל עִם מִיעוּט מְצִיאוּתָן מַסְפִּיק בִּמְנִיעָתָן.

וְהַשְּׁלִישִׁי גֹדֶל הָהַעֲזָה שֶׁבַּדָּבָר, כִּי הַדָּבָר שֶׁיֵּשׁ לָאָדָם הַעֲזָה לַעֲשׂוֹתוֹ, אִם מִפְּנֵי שֶׁהַתַּאֲוָה מוֹשֶׁכֶת אֵלָיו מְאֹד, אוֹ לְתוֹקֶף הַהֶרְגֵּל, אוֹ לְגֹדֶל הַצַּעַר שֶׁבַּעֲזִיבָתוֹ, הֲרֵי לֹא יִמָּנַע מִמֶּנּוּ כִּי אִם חַשַׁשׁ דָּבָר גָּדוֹל.

וְהָרְבִיעִי קַלּוּת עֲשִׂיַּת אוֹתָהּ הַפְּעוּלָה בְּהֶעְלֵם וּבְהֶסְתֵּר כְּדֵי שֶׁלֹּא יַרְגִּישׁוּ בוֹ אֲחֵרִים, הֲרֵי הַהַרְתָּעָה מִזֶּה לֹא תְהֵא כִּי אִם בַּחַשַׁשׁ עוֹנֶשׁ קָשֶׁה וְחָמוּר.

The severity and intensity of a punishment, or its mildness and manageability, is determined by considering four factors:

The first factor is the severity of the transgression itself. Actions that lead to large losses must result in severe punishments, while those that cause lesser losses should result in more mild punishment.

The second factor is how widespread the particular transgression is. If a certain transgression is fairly common, it requires a severe punishment as a deterrent. But for a more rare transgression, a mild punishment will suffice for deterrence.

The third factor is degree of desire associated with the sin. For something that people have a strong urge toward—either because the temptation for it is very strong, because they have become accustomed to it, or because refraining from it will cause great pain—only the threat of a severe punishment will have an impact.

The fourth factor is the ease with which the particular transgression can be committed in secret without anyone noticing. If it is easy to do this, only a strong and severe punishment will be an effective deterrent.

Additional Readings

INCARCERATION AS A MODALITY OF PUNISHMENT AND REHABILITATION
A TORAH PERSPECTIVE

RABBI SHOLOM D. LIPSKAR

All footnotes have been removed to conserve space. To read the complete article, see www.chabad.org/1125719.

Introduction

Every civilization throughout history has promulgated rules providing for the punishment of those who offend society's norms. The history of criminal justice is replete with societies that have included the practice of "incarceration" as one form of such punishment with—arguably—various degrees of success as a deterrent to crime or as a form of retribution for it.

Under America's criminal justice system, we have incarcerated more than two million of our fellow citizens in federal, state and county facilities. Prison building has been described as one of the "growth" industries of the decade.

Yet, the concept of prison appears nowhere in Judaism. Indeed, while sentencing options as diverse as financial penalties, atonement offerings, corporal punishment, capital punishment and even death directly by the hand of G-d are found in the Torah, the punishment of "incarceration" as we know it is nowhere to be found in traditional Torah-based Jewish law.

This article will first attempt—in a highly-abbreviated form—to explain the various references to imprisonment in the Pentateuch, Prophets, Talmud,

RABBI SHOLOM D. LIPSKAR

Spiritual leader and founder of "The Shul of Bal Harbour" as well as founder of the Landow Yeshiva Center in Miami Beach, the Aleph Institute, and the Educational Academy for the Elderly. Rabbi Lipskar is an internationally recognized leader in Torah education and is known for bringing the values of Torah to people from all walks of life.

Maimonides, Codes of Jewish Law, Halachic Responsa of generally-accepted Rabbinical sources and community edicts.

Second, it will posit a Torah-based philosophical rationale as to why the Torah does not advocate prison.

Finally, recognizing that we now live in a society that increasingly appears to demand longer and "tougher" sentences, it will offer suggestions consistent with the Torah rationale to propose certain programs in prison that should reduce recidivism and improve chances for rehabilitation.

"Prison" in the Torah

A careful reading of Torah sources reveals that where the Torah refers to prisons, they are not sanctioned modes of punitive incarceration. There are prisons established by non-Jewish societies, e.g., Joseph's imprisonment in the jails of Pharaoh's Egypt; prisons created in contravention to Jewish Law, e.g., the jailing of the prophet Jeremiah; prisons utilized as temporary holding cells until trial and sentencing; and a prison environment used solely to execute a sentence of capital punishment.

That is not to say that Jewish law did not condone restrictions on liberty. The Bible itself provides for servitude (involuntary, imposed by the court), as a reparative form of incarceration. Under certain circumstances, the court could order that a perpetrator of larceny or theft be "sold" for a period of time (not to exceed six years) in order to raise the funds necessary to make restitution. Yet such court-imposed servitude could not degenerate into cruel slave labor. The "bondsman" was entitled by law to good nutrition, proper clothing, productive work and food and shelter for his wife and children. Restitution, not punishment, was the goal.

Another form of restrictive liberty—often misunderstood as "prisons" by readers of the Bible—were the "Cities of Refuge," three of which were established by Moses just prior to the Jews' entry into the Holy Land after wandering though the desert for forty years and three others established by Joshua after the Jews settled in the Land of Israel. Those cities were, in effect, the earliest known form of "protective custody." Persons found guilty of unpremeditated murder were given the option of moving into one of what eventually were six cities, thereby escaping the lawful revenge of the victim's surviving relatives.

But the Cities of Refuge cannot—under any stretch of the imagination—be deemed to have functioned in any way similar to today's prisons. For one thing, the offender was not isolated from contact with his loved ones and outside contacts. These environments were penal colonies that had all functions of a community, including productive work. Indeed, once the offender chose to flee to one of the cities, the court would order the inmate's wife, children and teacher to accommodate him. The underlying purpose of the Cities of Refuge was atonement, not isolation.

A clear indication that the Torah does not advocate the use of prisons is the fact that, while the Scriptures deal in minutest detail with all punishments, giving the precise method of their infliction, types of instruments used, amount of fines, etc., there is absolutely no guidance to be found with respect to punitive incarceration.

Prison Contrary to Creation's Purpose

The Jewish tradition teaches that everything in this universe was created by G-d with a positive purpose—to be utilized completely without waste. Accordingly, in the criminal justice system, punishments should effect direct results and benefits for all parties involved: the perpetrator, victim and society in general.

For the criminal, the consequential punishment of crime brings penance, atonement, rehabilitation and ultimate purging. After being punished, one starts with a fresh slate; Jewish law dictates that the community must accept the wrongdoer as before and he

regains a place in the World to Come. For the victim and society, punishment must serve goals such as restitution, deterrence, retribution and protection.

Imprisonment does not serve these functions. It certainly brings no benefit (short- or long-term) to the victim. It appears to offer only temporary benefit to society (taking into account the high percentage of recidivism and the increasing numbers of people being sent "away"). And it obviously does no good for the inmate. On the contrary, prison inhibits and limits man's potential, destroys families and breeds bitterness, anger, insensitivity and eventual recidivism.

Man is understood in the Jewish tradition to play the central role in fulfilling G-d's creation, charged with making this world into a "dwelling place for Almighty G-d" and using each of his moments to accomplish this purpose by serving his Maker. Accordingly, man must use all resources available to fulfill this obligation. Imprisonment inherently limits a person's mobility and ability to function. Accordingly, it appears inconsistent for G-d to charge man with obligations and at the same time prevent him from fulfilling them.

Reconciling Torah with the Reality of Present-Day Incarceration in America

Although the Torah does not endorse the use of prisons as a viable punishment, Torah law imposes an obligation on Jews to obey the law of the land in which they reside, particularly when the government of that land respects human rights and believes in the betterment, freedom and growth of their inhabitants. Accordingly, following the axiom that everything in creation is for a purpose, we must find meaning and purpose in prison to the extent possible.

Examining the extant forms of imprisonment in the Torah, one that most closely parallels the concept of punitive incarceration is the penal colonies established in the Cities of Refuge. We may find and develop some humane and beneficial aspects of imprisonment from the Torah's rules and regulations for this environment.

First, Torah law specifies that such penal colonies must be designed to provide a proper human habitat, required to be located near market towns and fresh water.

Second, the sentencing court was obligated to send the inmate's teacher and mentor into these penal colonies together with the offender. Addressing the most important needs of the inmate, the Torah insists that his rabbi/teacher be placed in the prisoner's environment, too. The detriment of limiting the teacher's freedom is balanced against benefit of giving the incarcerated an opportunity for life through rehabilitation. A Torah-true life—introduced and administered by a competent rabbi/teacher—can be the foremost force in this rehabilitative process.

In his compendium of the Laws of *Rotze'ach*, Maimonides expounds on the Biblical verse: "and he should run to one of these cities (of refuge) and live," by noting that "a student who is exiled to a penal colony has his teacher exiled together with him so that he should live." Having one's teacher present gives the inmate an opportunity for life, for those who seek wisdom without the study of Torah are considered as dead.

Making the Best of Prison Time

When imprisonment affords the opportunity for rehabilitation and restructuring of the offender's values, priorities and lifestyle, then a valid purpose can be established and realized.

For serious and proper rehabilitation—called *Teshuvah*, or return, in the Jewish tradition—there are two necessary prerequisites. First, one must gain a true understanding and acceptance of one's present state of being as undesirable. Second, one must develop a firm and disciplined resolve to change and improve. Both remorse for the past and resolutions for the future are required. In the prison environment—where one is separated from society and sheds much of the externalities of societal pressures and facades—one may begin a realistic and objective evaluation of self and structure a pattern for improvement.

The disciplining forces of Jewishness—the commandments referred to as *mitzvot*—give a person: (1) the mechanism to create control devices for his actions, even to the extent of affecting habit; and (2) regulation in structuring balanced living patterns.

These benefits not only prepare a person for a personal life of righteousness and decency, but can extend outward to be an example to others of how not to act and how one can change. The guidelines of Jewish living, through the study of Torah and performance of its mitzvot, allow the prison environment to be utilized in this positive manner.

Indeed, as the Torah teaches, from the darkest moments and deepest loss can come the greatest light and ultimate gain. Consequently, it is of utmost importance to make it possible for inmates in physical confinements to transform a period of suspended death to vibrant life, thus fulfilling their purpose in the universe.

The proven way for a Jew to attain this freedom is by involving himself in a life of Torah study and observance. Non-Jews can obtain this same type of spiritual development through the study of, and commitment to abide by, the Seven Noahide Laws.

Our prison systems spend much time and money on vocational, academic and psychological programs. To really accomplish the rehabilitation that is possible in prison, we should also focus on emancipating and structuring the soul—maximizing the human potential even while temporarily incarcerating the body.

The above discussion is based, in great part, on public discourses given by Rabbi Menachem Mendel Schneerson, The Lubavitcher Rebbe, of righteous memory, on Purim 5736 (Spring, 1976), Shabbos Nasso and Shabbos Korach 5745 (Summer, 1985).

Reprinted with permission of Chabad.org

PUNISHMENT, PRISONS, AND THE BIBLE

MARTIN H. PRITIKIN

All footnotes have been removed to conserve space. To read the complete article, visit www.myjli.com/crime.

I. THE PURPOSES OF IMPRISONMENT AS A FORM OF PUNISHMENT IN THE UNITED STATES

A. Justificatory Theories of Imprisonment

The purposes of punishment are commonly divided between the deontological—inflicting punishment for its own sake, i.e., retribution—and the teleological or utilitarian—inflicting punishment to achieve some benefit, i.e., deterrence, incapacitation and rehabilitation. Restitution is also sometimes included, although some contend it is more properly characterized as a civil remedy, or that it is really just a means of promoting the other utilitarian goals.

When discussing theories of punishment, at least four different questions may be involved. First, why punish at all? Second, whom should we punish? Third, how much punishment is appropriate? And fourth, which mode of punishment should we employ?

The fourth question regarding the mode of punishment is related to, but analytically distinct from, the third question regarding the amount of punishment. Punishment could be inflicted by means of monetary penalties, imprisonment, exile, or physical torture, to name a few possibilities. Just as one could vary the amounts of different kinds of goods, so that a consumer would be indifferent between them (in that he would be willing to pay an equal price for any of them), one could, in theory, vary the amounts of different modes of punishment so that a criminal offender would be indifferent between them. For

MARTIN H. PRITIKIN

Law professor. Martin Pritikin graduated magna cum laude from Harvard Law School and spent several years litigating before entering academia full time, teaching advanced litigation and criminal law. Pritikin currently serves as the dean of Concord Law School.

example, assuming one wanted to inflict X "units" of punishment, one might determine that a $5000 fine, thirty days in jail, or eight lashes with a whip all achieve an equivalent "amount" of punishment. Thus, deciding how much punishment to inflict does not dictate which modality of punishment is appropriate.

As will be discussed below, although prevailing American views regarding the first three questions—why we punish, who should be punished, and how much they should be punished—have shifted over time, the primary mode of punishment employed—imprisonment—has remained virtually unchanged since the country's early history. The question is, why prisons?

One could offer either negative or positive justifications for using prisons. Negative justifications involve theoretical or pragmatic problems with the alternatives. For example, capital punishment is deemed too severe for most offenses. Torture would violate the constitutional prohibition against cruel and unusual punishment, and would likely be deemed too barbaric today regardless of the constitutional ban. And exile, given the required cooperation of other nations and the sophistication of modern transportation, would likely be difficult to enforce. As for monetary penalties, most criminals probably lack the means to compensate their victims, and garnishing their wages would take years to yield results. Prison is arguably justifiable in that it lacks many of these drawbacks.

But drawbacks to the alternatives do not dictate that prison—as opposed to some more creative alternative—is the best solution. We need positive justifications: a showing that incarceration serves some penological goal more effectively than other modes of punishment.

Prison cannot be justified on the ground that it better serves deterrence or retribution than other punishments. After all, any unpleasant experience—be it prison, torture, exile, etc.—will promote deterrence (because both the offender and third parties will want to avoid the unpleasantness in the future) and retribution (because any harm inflicted upon the offender "squares up" the wrong he committed). Assuming one could calibrate the amounts correctly, any mode of punishment serves these goals equally well.

Nor is prison an effective means of promoting restitution. The work available to prison inmates does not pay the type of wages that would provide any significant compensation to a victim or his family.

Thus, prison is justifiable only if it serves the remaining goals of incapacitation or rehabilitation. Prison undoubtedly does incapacitate, and does so more effectively than other means of punishment (except, obviously, for capital punishment, which is inappropriate for most offenses). Corporal punishment does not incapacitate at all (unless the offender is injured). Nor do monetary penalties. By contrast, an offender is usually completely incapacitated for the duration of his confinement.

Although incarceration necessarily incapacitates, it does not necessarily rehabilitate. One cannot tell, as a theoretical matter, whether spending time in confinement will make offenders more likely, equally likely, or less likely to commit crimes upon release. The conditions of the offender's confinement, with whom he interacts, and the activities in which he engages during his confinement, will likely impact its rehabilitative effect.

As the next section demonstrates, however, many now see retribution, not rehabilitation, as the purpose of prisons. As a result, much attention is paid to sending more people to prison for longer periods, with little paid to whether the time they spend there is productive.

B. History of the Purposes of Imprisonment in the United States

1. 1700s—1960s: The Predominance of Rehabilitation

When the penitentiary system in the United States began in the late eighteenth century, it was specifically designed for the purpose of rehabilitating the prisoner. With the exception of post-Civil War Southern prisons (which emphasized exploitative servitude, until the judicial decisions of the civil rights era put an end to such practices), rehabilitation continued to be the dominant goal of the American penitentiary system for nearly two centuries—that is, until the last several decades.

Although rehabilitation remained the goal until recently, views about how inmates were to be rehabilitated changed over time. Originally, the offender was separated from his former life and made to reflect—through isolation, work, fasting, and/or Bible study—in order to change his ways. But the results of solitary confinement and starvation diets were sorely disappointing, and as the Industrial Revolution gained steam, "vocational and academic training came to replace remorse and discipline as the princip[al] instrument for rehabilitation." This was not an abandonment of rehabilitation as a goal, but rather a shift in approach regarding how to achieve it.

By the 1960s, a growing optimism about science in general, and psychiatry in particular, led some to view criminal behavior as a manifestation of mental illness that, with proper supervision within the criminal justice system, could be "cured." Indeterminate sentencing was widespread, and parole boards were effectively given the role of determining when a prisoner was "cured" and thus fit to be released. This was, effectively, a medical model of criminal justice.

2. The 1960s and Beyond: The Transition to Retribution and Incapacitation

The medical model—and the rehabilitative model in general—came under increasing attack in the late 1960s and 1970s, from both the right and the left. First, there was a concern that, because the medical model is deterministic, explaining all behavior without regard to the individual's will, it threatened to undermine notions of moral accountability at the heart of criminal law. Second, some believed that the medical model operated to the detriment of the "patient:" the prisoner ran the risk that he would never be found "cured" and remain incarcerated indefinitely. Third, the assumptions that most criminals were amenable to treatment, or that treatments ever would exist, were questioned. Fourth, arguably too much discretion was vested in institutions that lacked the requisite authority or moral legitimacy. Said Judge Marvin Frankel: "The almost wholly unchecked and sweeping powers we give to judges in the fashioning of sentences are intolerable for a society that professes devotion to the rule of law." Frankel doubted that judges and parole boards had the time or training needed to make meaningful sentencing decisions. More radical liberals condemned the system of indeterminate sentencing as a "tool of institutional control" that was used to perpetuate class and race biases by oppressing those who "challenge . . . the cultural norm."

Scholarly critiques of rehabilitation—and corollary support for retribution—abounded, and the critics were emboldened by research indicating that rehabilitation, did not, in fact, work. Sociologist Robert Martinson's influential 1974 paper, What Works? Questions and Answers About Prison Reform, was widely relied on for its perceived conclusion that "nothing works" to reduce recidivism.

Martinson himself later denounced the "nothing works" label attributed to his writings, and empirical research conducted by him and others in the late 1970s, 1980s and 1990s countered the pessimism regarding rehabilitative programs. Gradually, more and more scholars concluded that flawed methodology—and not flaws in rehabilitative programs—was largely responsible for their poor reported results.

But by that point, the political tides had already turned. The framework of indeterminate sentencing was rapidly dismantled. By 1983, every state but Wisconsin had adopted mandatory minimum sentencing laws. In 1984, Congress passed the Sentencing Reform Act, which eliminated parole and established a complex system of determinate or presumptive sentences. Congress and many state legislatures also provided for harsher penalties in a number of other ways. They imposed life sentences for a variety of crimes, and created sentence enhancement provisions such as three-strikes laws. They made it easier to try and sentence juveniles as adults. They also reduced resources available for programs to rehabilitate prisoners. The "war on drugs" also led to an increase in resources allocated to criminalizing a pervasive social problem, and fewer resources dedicated to counteracting it.

The combination of these factors has led to a ballooning prison population. Between 1925 and 1972, the national prison population remained fairly stable. But between 1972 and 1997, the number of state and federal inmates rose from 196,000 to 1,159,000—a nearly sixfold increase. In the next decade, the number behind bars nearly doubled again, and now exceeds two million. Our rate of incarceration—approximately one out of every 150 Americans—is the highest in the Western world by at least a factor of five, and has even surpassed the world's previous leader, Russia. It is estimated that the United States has a quarter of the entire world's prison population.

The explosion of the prison population has also meant an explosion in prisons and prison costs. Between 1985 and 1995, the federal and state governments opened an average of one new prison per week. Between 1982 and 1993, government spending on corrections increased over 250%, far outstripping inflation. The rate of spending on prisons also grew to exceed spending on other social services. For example, in 1991, the federal government spent $26.2 billion on corrections to deal with 1.1 million prisoners and about five million probationers; at the same time, it spent only $22.9 billion on its main welfare program, Aid to Families with Dependent Children, which serviced 13.5 million people. Critics argue that spending billions of dollars on prisons diverts funds from social services that might prevent crime, and is thus counterproductive.

As would be expected given the retributivist mood, the growth of prisons was accompanied by a reduction in resources and programming for rehabilitation. (Amenities not directly related to rehabilitation have also been scaled back considerably.) In 1994, Congress eliminated higher education grants for state and federal prisoners. Following this, at least half the states reduced prisoner vocational and technical training programs. By 2002, only nine percent of inmates were enrolled in full time job training or education programs. In 1991, then governor of Massachusetts William Weld put it succinctly: "[inmates] are in prison to be punished, not to receive free education." Some scholars have echoed this sentiment. What seldom gets asked is whether the savings in crime reduction resulting from educating inmates offsets the costs of the "free education."

Nor is this trend away from investing in rehabilitation likely to change. Government prisons face political pressures against allocating resources to rehabilitation, and private prisons not only find expenditures on rehabilitation programs (or any non-essential programs) unprofitable, but may have a perverse incentive not to rehabilitate, since it would decrease the demand for prisons.

Despite the growth of prisons and the worsening of prison conditions, the public still believes not enough is being done to be "tough on crime." In a poll conducted in 1996, 67% of Americans thought that "too little" money was being spent on stopping "the rising crime rate," and 78% said that the courts in their area treated criminals "not harshly enough." Another poll conducted in 1996 found that 75% of Americans favored the death penalty—twice as many as supported it in 1965.

This obsession with cracking down on crime exists despite empirical evidence both that crime rates are not that high, and that "tough on crime" policies are not responsible for making them lower. Our overall crime rates are not that different from other Western countries, undercutting the argument that we need more prisons because we have more criminals to deal with. Similarly, although it was widely believed that "zero tolerance" policing implemented in New York City in 1993, and the Three Strikes Laws adopted in California in 1994, were the reasons for their declining crime rates, violent crime rates were already beginning to decline in those locales in 1990 and 1991. Moreover, crime rates declined by similar amounts during the same period in places that did not adopt or enforce such policies. There is no general demonstrable connection between increasing the severity of criminal penalties and the reduction in overall crime rates.

In fact, just the opposite is true: the evidence indicates that incarceration actually increases crime. A 1989 California study matched comparable felons sentenced to either prison or probation, and found that seventy-two percent of the former group was rearrested within three years of release, compared to sixty-three percent of the latter. Likewise, recidivism rates in a New York juvenile detention center were ten to twenty percentage points higher than those observed in a community-based alternative-to-detention

program. A federal study drew the same conclusion: each instance of incarceration rendered the next more likely.

The correlation between the ideological shift toward retribution and incapacitation, and the increased reliance upon—and worsening conditions within—prisons, is no coincidence. If criminals are monsters who are either undeserving of help or are by nature incapable of reform, it is sensible to lock them up and throw away the key. By contrast, we will see that Jewish law neither views criminals as monsters, nor treats them that way.

II. THE LIMITED ROLE OF RETRIBUTION IN JEWISH LAW
Challenging the Popular Linkage of Retribution with the Hebrew Bible

As discussed above, those who favor prisons often invoke retribution as a justificatory rationale. And advocates of retribution often claim that the Hebrew Bible supports their position. Is their reliance justified?

At first glance, it would seem so. The phrase people most often associate with retribution is likely "an eye for an eye," which appears several times in the Torah. Prosecutors (particularly in the heavily religious South) have often used it in closing arguments to induce juries to return the harshest possible verdict: the death penalty. In large part because of the prominent use of this phrase, the very term "Old Testament justice" is popularly understood to mean harsh vengeance. Legal scholarship, both liberal and conservative, also perpetuates this understanding. So do the media and the public. The Old Testament's "eye for an eye" is often contrasted with the "turn-the-other-cheek" compassion and benevolence of the New Testament.

But how does one determine what the phrase "eye for an eye" really means? This is not unlike the situation one faces whenever engaging in statutory construction. Should one hew closely to the "plain meaning" of the text—which here suggests literal like-kind retaliation? Or should one look to the legislative history (whatever that would mean in the context of theocratic law) or other extrinsic evidence to aid in interpretation?

This Article asserts that because the society in which the Hebrew Bible originated, and for whom it was originally intended, looked outside the text's "plain meaning" to discern what the law "was," so should we. Although one might counter that any such "original" interpretation is not conclusive or binding on our understanding of the Bible today, only the most ardent post-modernist would contend that it is irrelevant.

1. Issues in Interpreting the Hebrew Bible Generally

According to Jewish tradition, Moses received the Torah—the first five books of the Hebrew Bible—from G-d at Mount Sinai in 1313 B.C.E. Although many are familiar with this claim, fewer are aware that the Jewish tradition holds that Moses also received from G-d a more detailed Oral Law, which was then passed down from teacher to student for generations. Between about 200 and 500 C.E., major portions of this oral tradition were reduced to writing in what is now known as the Talmud.

The relationship between the written Torah and the Oral Law is a rich and complex one. One might analogize the written Torah to a lecture outline, and the Oral Law to the lecture itself. The outline is a shorthand, not intended to be read—and perhaps not coherent if read—independent of the oral presentation. Indeed, if the Oral Law appears to contradict or vary from the written Torah, then, according to the traditional Jewish view, "it is the former that governs." The Oral Law is not a secondary source whose purpose is to illuminate a primary text. It is the primary source.

That the Jewish tradition does not embrace a literal interpretation of the written Torah is not surprising, given that the Torah is not a text that lends itself to any "plain meaning." First, the Torah is written in Hebrew, a language that inherently allows for ambiguities regarding sentence structure, verb conjugation, and so on. Second, the biblical variant of Hebrew contains additional ambiguities that are not present in modern Hebrew. Third, Torah scrolls are written with no punctuation or vowels; lack of punctuation can create opportunities for ambiguity in any language, but the meaning of Hebrew words is particularly prone to change depending on changes in vowelization.

Thus, when one reads the Torah, one is necessarily accessing a highly ambiguous text. Unfortunately, translations of the Bible into other languages "often resolve rather than preserve ambiguities, and thus favor one interpretation over another." The linguistic problem rapidly becomes a substantive one, because one cannot coherently understand either the philosophy of Jewish law or the dictates of Jewish practice—known as halacha (literally, "the way" or "path")—without turning to the Oral Law.

2. Interpreting "An Eye for an Eye" in Jewish Law

These challenges to interpreting the Torah directly impact the modern (mis)interpretation of the phrase "eye for an eye." As one prominent contemporary biblical scholar has stated: "Few are the verses of the Bible which have been so frequently and glaringly misunderstood." In Jewish law, the phrase in fact refers to monetary compensation for the value of the lost eye (in terms of pain and suffering, medical bills, lost earnings, and mental suffering), not literal retributive maiming.

The arguments supporting this monetary compensation interpretation are numerous and varied. First, note that the words "eye for an eye" are ambiguous enough to permit the inference of compensation. If one wanted to lay down a rule of literal maiming, as distinguished from compensation, one could have done so far more explicitly. This is precisely what was done in Hammurabi's Code of ancient Babylonia:

> If a man put out the eye of another man, his eye shall be put out. If he break another man's bone, his bone shall be broken. . . . If he put out the eye of a man's slave, or break the bone of a man's slave, he shall pay one-half of its value.

Second, the phrase first appears in a section of the Torah dealing exclusively with how victims of an injury are to be compensated by a tortfeasor. Third, the Torah often prioritizes making restitution to the victim over punishing the offender; putting out the eye of the wrongdoer does not benefit the victim in any tangible sense. Fourth, the only forms of judicially imposed corporal punishment provided for by the Torah are capital punishment and lashes, not maiming. Fifth, given how the "*tachat*" in "*ayin tachat ayin*" (the Hebrew for "eye for eye") is used in other places in the Torah, the use of this word suggests compensation, not literal blinding. Sixth, the Talmud offers a number of additional textual and logical proofs, too detailed to examine here, directed specifically to show that "eye for an eye" requires only compensation.

If the Torah does not literally demand an eye for an eye, why does it use language that implies it does? One explanation rests on the distinction between the punishment the offender deserves, and the punishment that courts are authorized to impose:

> [I]n the Heavenly scales, the perpetrator deserves to lose his own eye—and for this reason he cannot find atonement for his sin merely by making the required monetary payments; he must also beg his victim's forgiveness—but the human courts have no authority to do more than require the responsible party to make monetary restitution.

Thus, "an eye for eye" is an instance where the "plain meaning" of the text of the Torah will lead one to the opposite conclusion from what the halacha actually mandates.

Even if a modern reader were not persuaded by these arguments, the fact remains that this is the understanding that the Torah's primary audience—Torah observant Jews—always had of "eye for an eye." Moreover, not only does no instance of exacting such physical retribution appear anywhere within the Hebrew Bible, but apparently "there is no instance in Jewish history of its literal application ever having been carried out.". . .

III. INCARCERATION IN JEWISH LAW

So far, we have identified the link between retributivism and the increased reliance on prisons. We then challenged the link between the Jewish law and retribution. This Part now examines the role of prisons in Jewish law. It demonstrates that prisons are not a prominent feature in Jewish law, and that Jewish law's alternatives to prison are designed to promote rehabilitation, restitution and atonement, not retribution.

A. Prison in Jewish Law

Jewish criminal law provided for a variety of forms of punishment—including capital punishment, flogging, fines, atonement offerings, and karet (spiritual death)—but prisons as we know them are "nowhere to be found in traditional Torah-based Jewish law." This is not to say that there is no mention of prisons in the Hebrew Bible. But in the relatively rare instances in which they do appear, they are either not sanctioned by Jewish law, serve some function other than as a modality of punishment, or are tolerated as a second-best alternative to other forms of punishment.

1. Prisons Not Sanctioned by Jewish Law

The narratives of the Hebrew Bible relate a few isolated instances where people are placed in prisons as a punishment for alleged crimes. When Joseph, after having been sold into slavery to the Egyptians, spurned the advances of his wife's master, she falsely accused him of assaulting her, and he was imprisoned in Pharaoh's dungeon. Likewise, when Jeremiah prophesized unfavorably, officers of the king, ostensibly because they suspected him of defecting to the Chaldeans, imprisoned him in a dungeon in one of the officer's homes. Neither of these instances, however, shows that Jewish law endorses imprisonment. Joseph was imprisoned by Egypt, a non-Jewish society, and Jeremiah was imprisoned without trial, without factual basis, and in contravention of Jewish judicial procedure. Thus, the mere fact that Bible narratives refer to prisons does not mean that Jewish law sanctioned their use.

2. Prison as a Means to Enforce Other Punishments

Incarceration was used in Jewish law to detain the accused pending trial or a convicted defendant pending sentencing. Where a potentially capital crime was committed, the offender could be imprisoned until the court could determine if a case could be made, or which form of penalty was appropriate. Although this pre-trial or pre-sentencing detention served to incapacitate, its purpose was not to punish, but to detain the offender until an appropriate punishment could be determined.

Prison also served as a civil coercion mechanism. Imprisonment could be used as a method to compel compliance with a court order to divorce a woman to whom it was impermissible to marry, or, according to some sources, to pay a debt. Here, again, although coercive confinement served to inflict unpleasantness on the prisoner, the purpose of the imprisonment was not to punish him for criminal conduct, but rather to induce him to comply with a pre-existing court order which itself delineated the appropriate judicial response to his conduct.

In very limited circumstances, incarceration could be used as a means to carry out an execution. The Talmud discusses the case of someone who commits the same crime punishable by karet—premature death at the hands of G-d—three times. By willfully committing the same offense on three separate occasions, the offender has demonstrated that he has not repented, and in fact desires a premature death. After the third transgression, the offender is placed in a cramped cell precisely his height, so that there is no room to stretch out or lie down. He is fed scant amounts of bread and water so that his stomach shrinks, and he is then fed barley—which expands inside the stomach—until his stomach bursts and he dies. Similarly, one who kills another but is not liable to execution, either because of certain technicalities unrelated to his factual guilt, or because he is sophisticated in criminal laws and knows how to avoid liability—for example, by refusing to explicitly acknowledge the witnesses' warning—may also be subjected to this procedure.

In both of these cases, the court is not authorized to execute the offender according to the halachic judicial formalities, yet it is clear that the offender deserves to die. Since the court cannot execute him directly, it uses incarceration to kill him indirectly. However, like the use of imprisonment as a means of compelling compliance with a court order to divorce or pay a debt, prison is used only as a means to carry out another penalty. Strapping the offender to a chair, bed, or wall, as opposed to confining him in a cell, and implementing the forced barley diet would have the same effect.

3. Prison as a Lesser Alternative Punishment

Rambam, in his classic codification of Jewish law, the Mishneh Torah, discusses several instances where prison may be used in lieu of a more serious punishment.

First, if the king declines to have a murderer killed (which he could do under his royal authority to protect the public welfare), he may nevertheless have him "beaten with severe blows—so that he is on the verge of death—imprisoned, deprived and afflicted with all types of discomfort . . . ." But this is weak evidence that Jewish law endorses prisons. The source for Rambam's position is questionable— nothing in the Torah or the Oral Law itself mentions such authority. Perhaps since imprisonment is permitted as a lesser punishment where execution itself is already permitted, it is intended as a form of clemency. Moreover, Rambam is discussing the king's authority to punish, which, as mentioned above, is independent of the courts' authority to punish, and is not in accordance with the Sinaitic ideal of judicial procedure.

Rambam also discusses a case where one or more murderers sentenced to execution become intermingled among one or more murderers who are not liable for execution, and those liable for execution cannot be identified. Rambam states that the entire group should be imprisoned, since all are potentially dangerous to society, and this contains that threat while avoiding the risk that an individual not subject to the death penalty is executed. But again, here prison is not the prescribed form of punishment for the crime; rather, it is a second-best alternative when individually tailored punishments are not practicable. Moreover, the factual scenario is so unusual that the ruling is not likely to have much practical application.

4. Use of Prisons During the Diaspora

Some Jewish communities during the Diaspora— the period following the Roman expulsion of the Jews from Israel in 70 C.E.—did sanction a broader use of prison as a form of punishment than was prescribed under the Torah-based judicial criminal justice system. During this period, the Jews no longer had an autonomous government (at least until the establishment of the modern state of Israel in 1948), and accordingly, a Torah-based judicial system could not be enforced. But a number of host countries did, to varying degrees, grant Jewish communities living within their borders a limited form of self-rule. Some of these communities permitted prison as a form of criminal punishment.

Two rationales were invoked to justify the use of prison in these circumstances. The first reason given was to deter crime and keep society safe, under the directive in Deuteronomy to "eradicate the evil from your midst" that applies above and apart from the enforcement of specific Torah criminal justice procedures. The second reason was to maintain good relations with the host society, under the dictate dina demalkuta dina (Aramaic for "the law of the land is the law").

But even in these circumstances, there were important Jewish authorities that refused to permit the use of prisons. Moreover, although the leaders who instituted these procedures may have been authorized to establish prisons, there was no disputing that this was a departure from the ideal.

Although prisons are not prominent in Jewish law, there are at least two notable examples of restrictive confinement in Jewish law. The first is cities of refuge, to which accidental killers would be sent. The second is involuntary servitude, which could be used as a penalty for theft. These alternatives to imprisonment reveal the Jewish view of the purposes of restrictive confinement. But a disclaimer is in order. Some of the specific practices regarding these punishments may seem incomprehensible or distasteful to the modern reader living in a secular society. I will attempt to explain, albeit superficially, the rationale behind some of these. But more importantly, the reader should remember that the purpose of discussing these Biblical punishments is not to advocate adoption of, or criticize the use of, particular details of the Biblical legal system. Rather, the purpose is to distill—even after having accounted for the cultural and historical differences—core principles still relevant in our time.

B. Cities of Refuge
1. Which Killers Were Sent to Cities of Refuge
a. Homicide Classifications in Jewish Law

Much like modern law, Jewish law distinguishes between different grades of homicide, and provides for different punishments for each grade. The Torah distinguishes between intentional killers—who are liable to execution by the court—and unintentional killers, who are not. It then further differentiates between three categories of unintentional killers.

First is the inadvertent or negligent killer. He is exiled to a city of refuge in order to atone for the harm he has caused. The city of refuge serves as a haven for the negligent killer, and his time in exile provides him atonement. As long as he remains there, he is immune from retribution at the hands of the go-al ha'dam, or "blood redeemer"—usually the nearest relative of the slain victim. But if the killer is found outside the city of refuge, the blood redeemer may kill him without liability. Because leaving the city of refuge exposes the killer to the possibility of death, he is effectively confined there by threat, if not by physical restraints. Assuming a killer is judged liable to exile, he is required to remain in the city of refuge until the death of the Kohen Gadol, the High Priest. At this point, the slayer is deemed to have gained atonement and may return home. He is now considered an ordinary citizen, and if the blood redeemer kills him, the blood redeemer is liable to be executed.

Second is the killer who acts "unintentionally [but] whose acts resemble those willfully perpetrated"—i.e., who acts with gross negligence or recklessness. He is not liable to execution because he did not act intentionally; but his crime is too severe to be atoned for through exile in a city of refuge. Accordingly, he suffers no punishment at the hands of the court, and is subject to death at the hands of the blood redeemer wherever he finds him.

Third is the killer "whose acts resemble those caused by forces beyond [his] control"—i.e., he acts with virtually no culpability because the killing is a freak accident that no amount of reasonable care could prevent. He is not punished at all. Because such a killer is deemed not liable, if the blood redeemer slays him he is liable for execution, just as if he had executed any other innocent person.

Thus, Jewish law essentially distinguishes between intentional, reckless, negligent, and non-culpable killings. Intentional killers are subject to the most severe penalty, execution. Reckless killers are considered highly culpable, albeit less culpable than intentional killers; they are subject to the risk of execution at the hands of the blood redeemer, but their death is not guaranteed, as it is with intentional killers. Negligent killers are not liable to death, so long as they submit to the punishment of exile in a city of refuge. And non-culpable killers are not liable for any criminal penalty whatsoever.

b. American Law Compared:

The Jewish law classification of homicides, of course, looks much like our own. Under a typical modern statutory scheme, intentional killings are considered murder, and are subject to the most severe penalties—the longest prison sentences or execution; reckless killings are also often considered to be murder, but may be treated somewhat less severely; unintentional but negligent homicides (often called involuntary manslaughter) may still be criminal, although the penalties are often much less harsh; and those whose culpability in causing death does not even rise to the level of negligence are not punished criminally at all.

Jewish law, like American law, makes the level of culpability a significant factor in deciding what punishment is warranted. Jewish law recognized a dividing line between those who were beyond rehabilitating in this world, and who thus needed to die to achieve atonement, and those who could be reformed through some lesser means of punishment, such as exile in a city of refuge. It is also telling that the primary purpose of exile (the closest Biblical analog to the modern institution of prisons) was reformation of the soul (the closest religious analog to the modern concept of rehabilitation).

But there are noteworthy differences. In Jewish law, one who causes the death of another through ordinary negligence is exiled. But, in modern American law, something more than ordinary negligence—"gross negligence"—is usually required to trigger criminal liability. Furthermore, the ostensible purpose of sending the accidental killer to a city of refuge is atonement. If atonement is a religious concept akin to rehabilitation—the "correction" of the offender's soul—how can we say that someone who did not intentionally cause harm (indeed, did not even consciously disregarded a risk of harm) is in need of rehabilitation?

Again, the rationale for punishing the negligent killer, and for viewing him as in need of atonement, can only be understood in the context of religious law. According to Jewish philosophy, there are no true accidents. The physical word is a manifestation of the spiritual world. An accidental mishap in the physical world necessarily reflects some disruption in the spiritual:

> A person can only sin even accidentally if he can imagine himself being able to exist as separate from G-d. . . . [W]hoever is insensitive to the Divine Image in others must also lack any awareness of this attribute in himself and leads to the conclusion that the murderer must have lost the awareness of his own spirituality long before he confronted the situation that resulted in his crime.

The "accidental" killer, although he did not consciously disregard a risk in the instant he caused the victim's death, is still culpable because it is only by virtue of his sin that G-d would lead him to a situation where he would cause another's death. It is the sin that led the killer to commit the "accident" for which he must atone.

There is, of course, no analog to this in American law. Human actions are considered to be the result solely of humans' will, not G-d's. Accordingly, people are punished criminally based on the consequences they intend or on the risks they disregarded or should have regarded, not on their level of "sin."

Another feature that defies comparison is the rule in Jewish law that a killer remains exiled until the death of the High Priest. There is no apparent connection between the lifespan of one individual and the appropriate duration of punishment of another. This rule, too, can only be understood on a spiritual level. One explanation for it is that since the High Priest causes the shechinah, or Divine Presence, to rest upon the land, and the killer removes the Divine Presence by shortening the lives of others, it would be unfitting for the killer to remain free while the High Priest lives.

Other commentators state that the rule is actually a punishment for the High Priest himself. Since it was his duty to pray that Israel would not commit the sin of murder, inadvertent killings show he neglected that duty. Thus, the killers' terms of exile were tied to the High Priest's lifespan so that they would pray for his death, since he failed to prevent their victims' death through his own prayer. While these explanations for the duration of the sentence may hold sway in a religious context, they could never serve as justifications in a secular society.

While it may be neither feasible nor desirable for our secular legal system to borrow from Jewish law's rubric of how to measure offenders' culpability, or how long to punish them, we can still learn lessons from the cities of refuge. Given that the primary goal of exile in the cities of refuge was reformation of the offender, we can examine the conditions of the cities of refuge to see how Jewish law viewed the best way to accomplish this goal.

2. Conditions in the Cities of Refuge
   a. Fostering Exposure to Positive Influences

All cities of refuge were Levite cities—cities of priests. Given that the purpose of sending the manslayer to exile was reformation of the offender, cities of priests were an ideal environment for him:

> The fact that he was responsible for the death of another person requires him to closely inspect his spiritual standing. . . . The [cities of refuge] not only provide physical protection from the avenger of blood but also serve as a spiritual rehabilitation center for the murderer.

Not only were killers sent to live among priests, but the cities of refuge could not be dominated by a criminal population who drowned out the influence of the "good eggs." Rather, killers could not make up a majority of the inhabitants. A city also could not serve as a city of refuge if it lacked elders—distinguished leaders who could educate and serve as role models to the city's residents.

Just as the presence of spiritual role models helps make the city of refuge a "spiritual rehabilitation center," the presence of positive role models can help

make American prisons function as rehabilitation centers as well. Most prisoners today lack such role models; they are exposed primarily to fellow criminals and to prison staff who are usually either indifferent or hostile to them. Studies have shown that, in the absence of close supervision by adult role models, juvenile corrections programs are not only ineffective, but actually serve to increase deviant behavior. Adults may not be as impressionable as juveniles, but whom they associate with cannot help but influence them.

b. Limiting Exposure to Negative Influences

The laws regarding who cannot go to a city of refuge also serve to make the time of confinement conducive to reformation.

Although all killers may flee to a city of refuge pending trial, once a trial has been conducted, only the negligent killer may return to the city of refuge: the intentional killer is executed, and the sin of the reckless killer is considered too severe to be atoned for by exile. The net result of these rules is to segregate killers according to their differing levels of mens rea. Negligent killers in a city of refuge might end up associating with other negligent killers who have been exiled there, but no one within this pool of negligent killers will associate with any intentional or reckless killers.

Empirical studies have confirmed the beneficial effect on recidivism rates of segregating less serious criminals from more serious ones. According to one study, low risk offenders "'show a shift in procriminal attitudes and behavior upon exposure to higher-risk offenders in institutions.' Low-risk offenders placed in institutions ended up with higher re-incarceration rates than similar low-risk offenders who were placed in halfway houses." John Martinson, the author of the study originally cited by retributivists for the view that "nothing works" when it comes to rehabilitation, later refined his position and argued that the success of rehabilitative programs depends on distinguishing offenders who are amenable to rehabilitation from those who are not. Jewish law was already making such distinctions at least two thousand years ago.

c. Humane Environment

Not only was a manslayer's exile designed so that the people he encountered would facilitate his rehabilitation, but the physical surroundings themselves helped maintain a sense of dignity and foster his spiritual growth. Cities of refuge were required to possess all the basic needs for the slayer, including a source of water and marketplaces for provisions. If a city of refuge did not have a natural water supply, it was a public responsibility to provide it with one. The trading of weapons, or of activity that might lead to the introduction of weapons, was forbidden.

In our prisons, by contrast, prisoners often face degrading living conditions. Overcrowding and a general atmosphere of brutality both between inmates and staff and among inmates prevail. These conditions create stress, fear, and anger, promote anti-social and violent behavior, and inhibit what potential for rehabilitation might otherwise exist. According to Michel Foucault, given the isolation, boredom, and violence, "the prison cannot fail to produce delinquents." Even scholars who identify positive deterrent effects of unpleasant prison conditions acknowledge that these benefits may be more than offset by the dehumanizing environs' tendency to inhibit reassimilation of the offender into society.

d. Facilitating Community Reintegration and Identity-Building

Although the manslayer was removed from his former community, he was not isolated from the community within the city of refuge itself. Consider the following fascinating rule:

> When a killer was exiled to a city of refuge, and the inhabitants of the city desire to show him honor, he should tell them, "I am a killer." If they say, "[We desire to honor you] regardless," he may accept the honor from them.

This suggests several things. First, the inhabitants of the city of refuge could interact with the manslayer such that they would be aware of his conduct. Second, the manslayer could be engaged in socially beneficial activity—useful work, charitable deeds, etc.—for which the residents would wish to honor him. Third, he would have to state that he was a killer, indicating that the inhabitants may not otherwise have known that fact; he is not necessarily "branded" as a killer during his confinement. Fourth, even his status as a killer would not necessarily result in total ostracization, as the inhabitants might choose to honor him despite knowing that he has killed.

The possibility that a criminal might not only overcome the stigma of his crime, but even be recognized for distinction, is an important factor in his rehabilitation. "Most important for controlling crime . . . is that shameful expressions of disapproval of criminal or deviant acts be 'followed by efforts to reintegrate the offender back into the community of law-abiding or respectable citizens . . . .'"

Our prison system often does precisely the opposite. Prisoners are given few opportunities to earn the respect of the outside community, because they rarely interact with it. This is understandable, given the security risks. But given that most prisoners—especially those convicted of less serious crimes—will be returning to society sooner or later, the risk may be worth it. If re-exposing them to elements of the outside world makes them less likely to re-offend upon release, it may reduce the overall threat the prisoner presents to society.

Indeed, many of today's prisoners are not only deprived of opportunities for distinction, but every effort is made to make them literally indistinguishable:

> Prisons are . . . institutions of depersonalization and dehumanization. This is due to the prisons' emphasis on uniformity . . . . Life inside the penitentiary is very routine and can be numbingly monotonous. Prisoners are known as often by their numbers as by their names. Commonly adopted expressions of individuality such as dress and hairstyles . . . are limited . . . .

By destroying their sense of self-identity, prisons make it that much more difficult for inmates to develop the strength of character to resist the pressures to reoffend when, as is usually the case, they return to society. Although there are valid security and prison management reasons for the totalitarian approach, there are alternatives. Delaware, for example, has enjoyed great success reducing recidivism of drug offenders by using their time in prison to reintegrate them through "therapeutic communities," which are focused not merely on addiction but on a holistic approach to identity-building and social interaction. "The therapeutic community focuses upon the 'resocialization' of the individual and uses the program's entire community, including staff and residents, as active components of treatment." Similarly, one medium-security federal prison in Pennsylvania that adopted a philosophy of treating inmates humanely and incentivizing them to engage in pro-social behavior has yielded dramatic reductions in violence rates— while actually reducing administrative costs. Common sense suggests that using the period of incarceration as a "training ground" for coping upon release will yield more positive social behavior upon release.

e. Vocational Rehabilitation

The manslayer was to be gainfully employed within the city of refuge. The cities of refuge had to be larger than small villages, so that it would not be too difficult for a newcomer such as the slayer to earn a living. Obviously, there would be no concern with his ability to earn a living if it was not anticipated that he would do so. Similarly, although the manslayer need not pay his landlord rent in one of the six cities of refuge designated by Moses and Aaron, he would have to pay rent in any of the forty-two other Levite cities. The obligation to pay rent is a moot point unless he is gainfully employed.

Modern studies have shown that vocational training for inmates is crucial both to helping them develop the skills they will need to be productive citizens when they return to society, and to helping them develop the motivation to want to become such citizens in the first place. Unfortunately, this is what many modern American prisons are lacking, and such opportunities have grown even more scarce since the retribution movement has taken hold.

f. Educational Rehabilitation

According to the Oral Law, if a Torah scholar commits manslaughter and is exiled to a city of refuge, his teacher is to go with him. Interpreting the passage in Deuteronomy that states that a manslayer shall flee to the city of refuge "and he shall live," the rabbis concluded that "the life of one who possesses knowledge without Torah study is considered to be death." Thus, the manslayer is not left to merely while away his time in exile in a meaningless existence. Indeed,

not only is the offender's education not interrupted by his confinement, his focus on learning can be that much more intense and concentrated while in the city of refuge.

Modern studies emphasize the importance of education during incarceration as an element of rehabilitation. Indeed, opportunities for social reintegration, vocational rehabilitation and education have all been cited as key components in some of the more empirically successful correctional and rehabilitative programs.

Our society would not tolerate requiring a teacher who had committed no crime to accompany his student to prison. There are rationales for the rule: that the teacher himself needs to atone for some spiritual fault that must have somehow contributed to the offender's killing; or that the teacher would be so absorbed in studying Torah that he would not mind leaving his community in order to continue his studies with his student. But these explanations do not make the rule palatable to us. Nevertheless, we must once again be careful not to ignore the important lesson regarding the importance of rehabilitation in punishment, even if we eschew the particular manifestation of the principle.

g. Shielding Offenders from Violence

The enforcement mechanism of the cities of refuge was not iron bars or electrified fences, but simply the knowledge that if the killer leaves the city, he may be slain by the blood redeemer. An obvious initial question is: why does the Torah sanction this form of seeming vigilante justice?

The simple answer is a practical one: the blood redeemer was a quasi-state agent. Ancient Israelite society had no formal police force, no corrections officers, and no court executioners. If a criminal defendant was sentenced to death by the court, the blood redeemer carried out the execution on the court's behalf. That the blood redeemer was acting in an official capacity, and not merely to avenge a private wrong, is further evidenced by the fact that the Torah explicitly forbade the blood redeemer from accepting a ransom from the killer in lieu of his exile. Moreover, since the city of refuge was not designed to physically restrain the manslayer, and had no personnel designated to enforce his captivity, a credible threat of death upon leaving (like the revenge of the victim's relative) may have been necessary to induce him to remain.

But the blood redeemer did not go unchecked. Numerous protective measures minimized the chance that the blood redeemer would kill the slayer on his way to a city of refuge. This made sense, given that any killer traveling to a city of refuge was either seeking asylum pending trial (and thus the court had not yet decided whether he was liable to death); or else had already been sentenced to exile following a trial (and thus the court had affirmatively judged him not liable to death). To reduce the likelihood that someone not sentenced to die would be killed, the six original cities of refuge were spaced roughly equally throughout the land, so that no slayer would need to travel too far to reach any of them. In order to further facilitate rapid passage to the cities of refuge, the court was obligated to construct roads leading to each of them. The roads were to be twice as wide as regular roads. They were to be direct paths, without detours, and free of obstacles. The court was to inspect the roads annually and repair any defects. Signs stating "Refuge, Refuge," were to be posted at intersections to ensure that slayers would know the proper path. Once the court adjudged a defendant liable to exile, he was escorted back to the city of refuge by two Torah sages, because they would have the wisdom to choose words that would calm down the blood redeemer, and because he would be reluctant to act violently out of respect for them.

The slayer's safety was further assured once inside the city of refuge. The blood redeemer was subject to execution if he killed the slayer within the city of refuge. Despite this prohibition, additional measures guarded against the risk that a blood redeemer might nevertheless try to attack the slayer within the city. Cities of refuge could not be large cities, such that the blood redeemer would have reason to frequent the place, and could blend in with the crowd while he sought his prey. They had to be near populated areas, and populous enough themselves, to defend against multiple blood redeemers should they attempt a mass attack on slayers within the city. Hunting and trapping were prohibited in the cities of refuge, since this could lead to the sale of weapons, which might be purchased by the blood redeemer. This ensured that, if the blood redeemer wanted to use a weapon within the city, he would be forced to bring his own, which would be detected upon his entry into the city gates.

In the American penal system, victims' relatives do not usually pose a threat to a convict's physical safety (excluding perhaps participants in retaliatory gang warfare); but his fellow inmate often do. As Judge Frank Easterbrook succinctly put it, "Prisons are dangerous places." Indeed, a quarter-century ago, the executive branch of the federal government conceded the dangerousness of prisons in a brief before the Supreme Court: "In light of prison conditions that even now prevail in the United States, it would be the rare inmate who could not convince himself that continued incarceration would be harmful to his health or safety." Inmates also face the threat of sexual violence. Although accurate statistics on prison rape are difficult to obtain, given victims' reluctance to self-identify, a 2001 Human Rights Watch report concluded that the problem was "much more pervasive than correctional authorities acknowledge."

Obviously, immersing offenders in violence does nothing to make them less violent when they return to society, and likely has the opposite effect. Moreover, if inmates must be at a constant state of attention to guard against assaults, they will have less time, attention, or willingness to devote themselves to more productive endeavors.

We have thus seen that the primary purpose of the cities of refuge was to provide atonement and rehabilitation for the slayer, and that its features were well suited toward promoting those goals.

C. Involuntary Servitude
1. Servitude as a Sanctioned Form of Punishment in Jewish Law

The Torah provides that a thief is obligated to make restitution to his victim in the amount of the thing stolen, and in addition must pay a penalty (usually equal to the amount stolen). If the thief cannot pay the penalty, it becomes a debt he owes to his victim. But if he cannot pay the principal value of the goods stolen, he is sold as an eved—translated as "slave" or "servant"—and lives in his master's home for a period of six years. It was hoped that by dwelling in the home of a law-abiding family, the thief would learn from his master's positive example, and reform his character so as not to steal in the future. Thus, the two primary purposes of this form of punishment were to make restitution to the victim and to rehabilitate the offender.

The selling of a thief into slavery is a form of punishment only loosely related to prison. The eved or slave is not confined to a separate facility designated for the purpose of housing criminals, as prisoners are. Nevertheless, as a necessary incident of his obligation to serve his master, the thief's right of unrestricted movement was abridged. Given that prisons were not generally employed under the Jewish criminal justice system, servitude, like the cities of refuge, is one of the closest analog to prison.

Of course, any proposal to "sell" someone into the service of another private individual would neither be embraced nor tolerated in the United States today. The very word "slavery" is, thankfully, anathema. However, the "slavery" into which the Jewish thief was sold was "more like indentured servitude for a term of years than slavery." Not that one even needs to make this distinction in order to defend servitude as a mode of criminal punishment. The Thirteenth Amendment specifically permits the use of slavery and involuntary servitude "as a punishment for crime whereof the party shall have been duly convicted." Indeed, challenges to "chain gangs" and to other aspects of the post-Civil War plantation model of Southern prisons were sustained under the Eighth Amendment's ban on cruel and unusual punishment, not on Thirteenth Amendment grounds. It is quite common for prisons today to require prisoners to do work in order to maintain the institution. Thus, the question is not whether it is permissible to punish criminals by requiring them to do work, but rather what type of work will it be, and under what conditions will it take place.

2. The Relative Humaneness of Jewish Servitude

It is difficult to suggest that any form of servitude could be "humane." Nevertheless, from a comparative standpoint, Jewish thieves sold into slavery were treated more humanely than many modern American prison inmates.

Jewish law explicitly acknowledged that the thief's "self-image is depressed because of his being sold," and accordingly imposed a variety of obligations on the owner designed to preserve his dignity. The thief was to be treated "as a hired laborer," and could not be made to "perform debasing tasks that are relegated only for servants." He was not to be made to perform tasks that were beyond his physical strength. His family was permitted to live with him, and although the master was obligated to provide for the sustenance of his slave's wife and family, the master was not entitled to the proceeds of any work they performed.

Although the slave was required to "conduct himself as a servant with regard to those tasks he performed," the master was not allowed to hold himself above his *eved*:

> A master is obligated to treat any Hebrew servant or maid servant as his equal with regard to food, drink, clothing and living quarters . . . . [The master] should not eat bread from fine flour while [the servant] eats bread from coarse flour. [The master] should not drink aged wine while [the servant] drinks fresh wine. [The master] should not sleep on cushions while [the servant] sleeps on straw. Indeed, the Sages suggested that the slave was to be treated as more than equal, saying: "Whoever purchases a Hebrew servant purchases a master for himself."

These myriad burdens that Jewish law places on the owner of a slave were intended to counteract the exploitative tendencies inherent in the relationship. They were designed to help ensure that the slave's physical needs will be met, and that his psyche will not be unnecessarily damaged by his lowered status. In sheer economic terms, the legal requirements also make it expensive to be a slave owner, and thus discourage those who have neither the resources nor the inclination to treat a slave humanely from entering the slave-owning market.

By contrast, the incentive in modern American prisons is to house as many inmates as cheaply as possible. Not only is the prisoners' dignity or psychological well-being not typically a priority, but one could imagine the public outcry if politicians and corrections officials devoted substantial resources or attention to those ends.

3. Seemingly Objectionable Aspects of Jewish Servitude

Despite the various ways in which Jewish servitude was preferable to modern American incarceration, some features of this form of punishment would seem illogical or downright unfair to the modern sensibility.

First, we may object to letting the infliction of the punishment turn on the offender's ability to pay. Only the thief who cannot repay the value of the goods stolen is sold. By making the imposition of servitude turn on whether the thief can repay the principal, Jewish law effectively makes the servitude a form of debtor's prison.

One possible explanation is that Jewish law values restitution to the victim more highly than it values the criminal's liberty. Another, more generous, explanation is that the servitude serves as a sort of welfare program. In Jewish law, there were two ways a Jew could become a slave. He could be sold into slavery by the court because of his theft, as has been discussed. Or, if he was severely destitute, he could voluntarily sell himself into slavery in order to raise funds to provide for himself and his family. It may be that the thief who cannot repay the principal of the amount he stole is so impoverished that he was in a position to sell himself voluntarily. Since he chose to steal rather than sell himself, the court forces an involuntary sale in order to raise funds both to repay the victim and to provide sustenance to the thief and his family. In this light, even the imposition of servitude is, albeit in a paternalistic sense, humane.

A second difficulty we encounter is accepting the possibility that anyone would be willing to have a convicted criminal—a thief, no less—serve his sentence by living and working in his home, with full access to all his possessions and in close proximity to his family. Such a possibility is only fathomable in a society very different from our own. The Sinaitic code was written for a "covenantal community"—a religiously homogenous society, all of whose members were motivated by a love of and a desire to serve G-d. Moreover, traditional Jewish culture has always been highly communitarian—interaction with other members of society is essential to fulfilling many of a Jew's religious obligations. Thus, it is quite possible that a thief would not have come from a different culture and background, or even from a different neighborhood, than his victim. He may not have been the "other," a presumed monster, as criminals today are usually perceived. Rather, he would have been a member of the victim's own community who—even if he transgressed by committing theft—had quite a lot to lose by committing additional transgressions like stealing from his owner or assaulting the owner's family. He also would not likely have escaped, as almost any modern convict undoubtedly would, because there was not really anywhere for him to escape to. As a member of the victim's community, escape would be tantamount to self-imposed exile.

Third, Jewish law prescribed that the thief should serve as a slave for six years, regardless of the value of the articles he stole. The rationale for this rule was apparently that, since hired laborers would work for a term of three years, then a slave, who was essentially an involuntary hired laborer, should work twice that amount. Although it may seem unfair that a thief who stole a trifle and one who stole valuable goods would receive the same sentence, this is no worse than mandatory minimum sentencing schemes prevalent in today's society. Thus, if it is unfair, it is unfair for the same reasons that modern law is unfair, not for reasons peculiar to Biblical law.

But the rationale for treating all instances of theft seriously, and for punishing them equally, was not a secular one. According to Jewish law, any theft was considered a serious crime—even more serious than robbery, even though the latter involves taking property by physical force. The reason for this is that the robber's brazen act indicates that he fears neither man nor G-d, while the thief who steals in secret suggests that he fears men more than he fears G-d. Thus, even if petty theft was not a major threat to social stability or safety, it was a serious transgression in religious terms.

In any event, there were several ways in which a slave could secure his release prior to the six-year completion date. First, the slave went free if the master died without leaving a male descendant. Second, the slave went free if the Jubilee year (which occurred every fifty years) occurred during the term of his servitude, regardless how much time remained on his sentence. Third, the master could agree to accept the pro-rated value of the remaining services due him under the slave's term, in lieu of receiving the services themselves. Fourth, the master could voluntarily manumit the slave and forgo a release payment altogether by executing a bill of release.

Yet another aspect of Jewish servitude that evidences both its remarkable humaneness and it seeming unfairness simultaneously is the severance gift. Upon the completion of the thief's term of servitude, the master was obligated to provide him with a generous gift of animals and/or produce—things that would perpetuate themselves and thus yield continuous benefit. This was to provide him with financial resources so that he could begin his life anew without the temptation to steal again. To ensure that the ex-slave would use the funds for the purpose of re-establishing himself, the law provided that his severance gift could not be expropriated from him—a provision akin to a "spendthrift" trust for ex-convicts.

The mandatory severance gift is another rule that would never be accepted in our society. Millions of Americans who have committed no crime have difficulty providing for themselves and their families financially; the idea that released prisoners would be given a substantial endowment to begin their new lives (especially one paid for out of the public fisc) would cause an uproar.

Nevertheless, the general principle that we should take concrete steps to help the criminal's transition back into society and reduce the chances that he will reoffend is a sound one. Most convicts have no more money, education or training upon their release from prison than they did upon entering it. This, combined with the difficulty of finding employment due to the stigma of their ex-convict status, makes the temptation to fall back into criminal life considerable. Certainly the notion of facilitating the criminal's re-entry should be given consideration, given the costs of not doing so—higher recidivism rates, more crime, and the attendant added burdens on the police, prosecutors, and courts.

Thus, even aspects that at first seem strange or unjust may at their root be driven be humanitarian impulses. The difficultly, again, lies in translating these practices into measures that make sense in a different society and era.

Despite the challenges of translation, we can discern that Jewish law's imposition of servitude as a penalty for theft stands as another example of a restriction on liberty that primarily served the goals of restitution and rehabilitation, not retribution. Moreover, given the goal of rehabilitation, the manner of punishment was designed to maintain the dignity of the offender and assist him in successfully reentering society. If players in the modern debate over the purposes and forms of punishment want to borrow a page from the Bible, it is these goals and ideas they should be looking to.

D. The Inconsistency Between Imprisonment and Jewish Law

It should come as no surprise that prison is not prominent in Jewish law, because incarceration conflicts with fundamental tenets of Judaism. According to Jewish philosophy, G-d created everything with a positive purpose. This includes every individual human being—even those who commit crimes—each of whose purpose is to love and serve G-d. According to this view, punishments for criminal transgressions should inure to the benefit of everyone involved—the criminal, the victim, and society at large. Prison is not a very good way to benefit any of these parties.

Prison is little help, and likely a hindrance, to the criminal fulfilling his purpose. Because imprisonment isolates the criminal, it undermines his ability to function in and contribute to society. And because serving G-d in Judaism is a highly social endeavor, the isolation that comes with imprisonment impedes his ability to serve G-d. Moreover, unless there is some aspect of the prison experience that facilitates atonement or rehabilitation, it does nothing to better the criminal. On the contrary, to the extent that prison serves to make criminals more likely to commit crimes in the future (as modern statistics suggest), it increases the chances that he will further sin, face additional imprisonment, and be further impeded in his ability to serve G-d. One could counter that we should not be concerned with whether the criminal is able to fulfill his purpose, that he has forfeited his right to do so by committing his crime. But this would be inconsistent with the Jewish worldview that it would have been worth creating the entire universe for any one individual—whether he be a criminal or not.

The victims of crime are also usually not benefited much by isolating and confining the criminal. While imprisoned, it is highly unlikely that offenders will be able to engage in fruitful labor by which they can compensate victims or their relatives. Their incarceration does perhaps satisfy victims' or their families' desire for vengeance; but the drive for personal satisfaction through vengeance is generally not considered a legitimate interest according to Judaism. Moreover, since any form of enforced unpleasantness serves the goal of retribution, vengeance does not explain why prison should be the preferred method of inflicting pain over any other method.

As for society, imprisonment does provide a social benefit by incapacitating the criminal, although only so long as he is incarcerated. However, if prison makes criminals more likely to commit crimes in the future, this is obviously a detriment, not a benefit. Prison does potentially benefit society by deterring prisoners or others from committing crime, although the empirical evidence on this is questionable. In any event, the benefits to society of imprisonment must be weighed against its costs, and against the costs and benefits of alternatives. Studies suggest that alternatives to prison have had better success in reducing recidivism rates, and at a lower cost—in terms of direct outlays, not to mention the avoided costs of futures crimes committed by, and of the arrests, processing and confining of, would-be recidivists. Thus, the notion that prison is an institution that provides an overall benefit to society is questionable at best.

By contrast, Jewish law alternatives to prison serve, to the extent possible, to benefit the criminal, the victim and society.

As for criminals, spending time working and learning in a city of priests provides atonement and rehabilitation for the negligent killer. Similarly, the six years that a thief spends working in the home of a stable family gives him positive role models to emulate. And both punishments permit the offender to interact with society and to engage in productive work and study.

As for victims, having the negligent killer spend time in a city of refuge admittedly cannot benefit the dead; but then again, no punishment could ever directly benefit the victim of a homicide. At least as regards theft, however, the thief's servitude does provide tangible restitution for his victim.

As for society, the threat of death at the hands of the blood redeemer keeps the negligent killer confined to the city of refuge, thus removing him from his native community. The thief's involuntary servitude does not necessarily incapacitate him, although it is not clear how big of a concern incapacitation would be in his case. To the extent that these punishments only provide limited incapacitation benefits, this drawback may be more than offset by the reduction in recidivism that results from their strong emphasis on rehabilitation.

Thus, the punishments of Jewish criminal justice system are tailored to serve the purposes of that system. It is difficult to say the same of our own.

Conclusion

This Article does not suggest that we adopt specific punishments prescribed by Jewish law, such as cities of refuge or involuntary servitude. Jewish law is G-d-based law, written for a G-d-based society. Its punishments, and the rules for how to apply them, do not have practical application in a modern, secular society. (Indeed, it is not clear if they had practical application even in ancient Israel.) But the punishments in Jewish law evidence that system's view of the appropriate purposes of punishment, and of the ways to advance those purposes. On that front, several core ideas stand out.

First, although there is a prevailing perception that Jewish law focused on retribution, our examination of the punishments that Jewish law instituted in lieu of incarceration reveals that rehabilitation and restitution were its priorities. To the extent that modern advocates of retribution invoke "Old Testament justice" to support the increased use of incarceration, they are relying on an incomplete and misleading view of Jewish law. If one wants to contend that the legal system embodied by the Hebrew Bible is so different from our own, in both its premises and operation, that no useful comparison whatsoever can be made of it, so be it. But if one does choose to examine it, one cannot deny that undue emphasis has been placed on the role of retribution.

Second, despite the possibility that Jewish law was not applied in practice, it embodied highly practical and sensible ideas about when rehabilitation was appropriate. Jewish law made a distinction between those criminals who were beyond rehabilitating in this world, and those that were not. For those whose crimes were so heinous there could be no atonement in this world, or who posed an intractable threat to society because of their repetition of serious crimes, Jewish law made incapacitation a priority, and authorized courts or the king to either execute them or possibly imprison them indefinitely. But lower level criminals—like negligent killers or thieves—would, in all likelihood, be returning to society. Both society and the offender would benefit from imposing punishments that improved these criminals' chances for successful reentry into society. The punishments imposed by Jewish law reflected this fact.

Our current approach, by contrast, is to not only lock up the "lifers," but to make more low-level criminal subject to imprisonment for longer periods of time, with little attention paid to what will happen to them once they get out. Thus, we may be giving up on far too many offenders, and doing far too little to help those on whom we are not giving up. Even if we were unwilling to do more to help prisoners for the prisoners' sake, we should at least consider whether doing so is worthwhile for the sake of the protection of society. Given the fact that our current prisons make people more—not less— likely to commit crime, and given the ballooning costs of building and maintaining these prisons, it makes sense to look at legal systems that offer alternatives regarding how to deal with those offenders who will reenter society. In short, Jewish law shows us that we can prioritize rehabilitation without necessarily being "soft on crime."

Third, even if the particular practices of Jewish law are impracticable in our own time, the policies underlying those practices are not. Cities of refuge incorporated notions of surrounding criminals with good influences and removing them from bad ones; of giving them a humane environment in which to serve their time; of allowing them to have community interaction and rebuild their identities following their wrongdoing; of giving them an opportunity to engage in productive work and to further their educations; and of protecting their physical safety so that these other goals could be achieved unimpeded. Similarly, the servitude imposed upon thieves was designed in such a way to ensure that the slave's dignity was not needlessly impaired, and that he had both the psychological and practical wherewithal to avoid repeating his mistake.

We could not replace prisons with cities of refuge or private servitude, but we could adopt measures that embody the rehabilitative and restitutive principles on which those punishments were based. Measures such as increasing vocational and educational training, mentoring, and community service for prisoners, and increased reliance on intermediate forms of confinement for lower level offenders, may be a way of "translating" those Jewish law practices into our modern world.

The tenets on which the Jewish criminal system is based do not dictate that we scrap the prison system altogether. Jewish law seems to see some value in restrictive confinement. However, the value lies not in the fact of confinement itself, but in how we take advantage of that time to impact the person confined.

It may well be that, in order for a period of separation and confinement to be effective in preventing an offender from committing more crimes upon release, it would have to look so different from prisons as we know them today as to not even be called "prison" in the first place. But if reliance on the Bible leads to adoption of measures that prioritize the dignity of individuals and result in the reduction of crime—as opposed to our spiraling cycle of incarceration, more crime, more prisons, and yet more incarcerations—that would not be such a bad thing. Whether one cares about being true to the meaning of the Bible, or about making our own society safer, it is time we discard our outdated notions of what "Old Testament justice" means.

Excerpted from *Cardozo Law Review*, November 2006
Copyright © 2006 Yeshiva University; Martin H. Pritikin

Lesson

2

JUDGE, JEWRY, AND EXECUTION

JUDAISM AND THE DEATH PENALTY

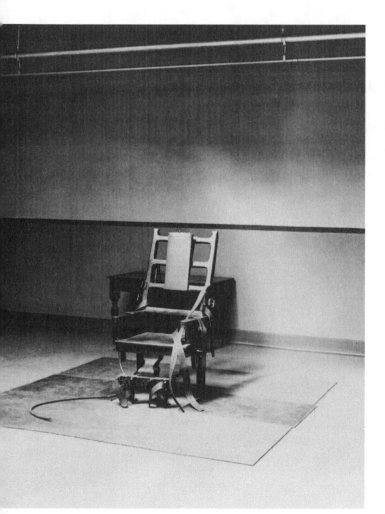

View of the death chamber and electric chair in Sing Sing Prison at Ossining, N.Y., in which Julius and Ethel Rosenberg, convicted of espionage concerning atomic secrets, were electrocuted. Photo dated January 13, 1953.

Some crimes are irreversible. People make mistakes. Taken together, these two propositions suggest both the imperative and impediment for the death penalty and point to its central paradox. Can man have the authority to sentence another man to death? How should we respond to the most serious crimes?

 ### QUESTION FOR DISCUSSION

Should Dzhokhar Tsarnaev receive the death penalty?

 ### QUESTION FOR DISCUSSION

How might one still be in favor of the death penalty, despite learning of the highly questionable execution of Cameron Todd Willingham?

Figure 2.1

The Death Penalty Debate

ARGUMENTS AGAINST THE DEATH PENALTY	ARGUMENTS IN FAVOR OF THE DEATH PENALTY
It is immoral to take a life: it won't bring anyone back. The death penalty is just revenge, a feeling we need to overcome, not indulge.	Some people are so bad they don't deserve to live anymore. The only way to serve justice is to execute them.
The death penalty does not deter murderers.	The death penalty deters murderers.
The costs incurred by the legal process necessary in order to carry out the death penalty are higher than the cost of lifetime imprisonment.	The death penalty saves money from being spent on the lifetime incarceration of terrible people.
The chances of executing innocent people are too great.	The small number of mistakes can be reduced by improving the system. Some chance of error is acceptable considering the positive benefits of the death penalty.
The death penalty is applied unequally based on race. This inequality is ingrained in the system. If the death penalty cannot be applied equitably it should not be used at all.	The racial disparity in the application of the death penalty is not a result of intentional discrimination. Simple changes can be made to the justice system that will eliminate the disparity.

*Does a judge treat a capital case differently? Hear the thoughts of **Justice Richard Bernstein**, of Michigan's Supreme Court:*

MYJLI.COM/CRIME

Exercise 1

Which of these theories of punishment are more compatible with the death penalty and which are less compatible with it?

Fill in the chart with your response.

*Where do U.S. Jews stand on the question of the death penalty? Hear noted historian **Professor Jonathan Sarna** discuss the matter:*

MYJLI.COM/CRIME

THEORY OF PUNISHMENT	COMPATIBILITY WITH THE DEATH PENALTY
Retribution	
Incapacitation	
Deterrence	
Rehabilitation	

TEXT **1a**

EXODUS, 21:12

מַכֵּה אִישׁ וָמֵת, מוֹת יוּמָת.

One who strikes a person with a fatal blow shall be put to death.

*In December 1999, noted attorney **Nathan Lewin** filed an amicus brief before the U.S. Supreme Court with principles of Jewish law that pertain to the death penalty. Watch Mr. Lewin discuss this case and read the brief:*

MYJLI.COM/CRIME

TEXT **1b**

SIFREI, DEVARIM 187

שֶׁמָּא תֹּאמַר הוֹאִיל וְנֶהֱרַג זֶה, לָמָה אָנוּ בָּאִים לָחוּב בְּדָמוֹ שֶׁל זֶה? תַּלְמוּד לוֹמַר, "לֹא תָחוֹס עֵינֶךָ עָלָיו" (דְּבָרִים יט, יג).

One may have argued, "Since one person has already been killed, why should we sentence another person to death?" The verse therefore instructs us, "You shall not pity him" (DEUTERONOMY 19:13).

SIFREI

An early rabbinic Midrash on the biblical books of Numbers and Deuteronomy. *Sifrei* focuses mostly on matters of law, as opposed to narratives and moral principles. According to Maimonides, this halachic Midrash was authored by Rav, a 3rd-century Babylonian Talmudic sage.

TEXT 2

MISHNAH, SANHEDRIN 6:2

אוֹמְרִים לוֹ, הִתְוַדֵּה, שֶׁכֵּן דֶּרֶךְ כָּל הַמּוּמָתִין מִתְוַדִּין שֶׁכָּל הַמִּתְוַדֶּה יֵשׁ לוֹ חֵלֶק לָעוֹלָם הַבָּא.

שֶׁכֵּן מָצִינוּ בְּעָכָן שֶׁאָמַר לוֹ יְהוֹשֻׁעַ "בְּנִי, שִׂים נָא כָבוֹד לַה' אֱלֹקֵי יִשְׂרָאֵל וְתֶן לוֹ תוֹדָה". "וַיַּעַן עָכָן אֶת יְהוֹשֻׁעַ וַיֹּאמַר, אָמְנָה אָנֹכִי חָטָאתִי לַה' אֱלֹקֵי יִשְׂרָאֵל וְכָזֹאת וְכָזֹאת וְגוֹ'" (יְהוֹשֻׁעַ ז, כ-כא).

וּמִנַּיִן שֶׁכִּפֵּר לוֹ וִדּוּיוֹ? שֶׁנֶּאֱמַר "וַיֹּאמֶר יְהוֹשֻׁעַ מֶה עֲכַרְתָּנוּ יַעְכָּרְךָ ה' בַּיּוֹם הַזֶּה" (יְהוֹשֻׁעַ ז, כה). בַּיּוֹם הַזֶּה אַתָּה עָכוּר, וְאִי אַתָּה עָכוּר לָעוֹלָם הַבָּא.

וְאִם אֵינוֹ יוֹדֵעַ לְהִתְוַדּוֹת אוֹמְרִים לוֹ, אֱמוֹר תְּהֵא מִיתָתִי כַּפָּרָה עַל כָּל עֲוֹנוֹתַי.

MISHNAH

The first authoritative work of Jewish law that was codified in writing. The Mishnah contains the oral traditions that were passed down from teacher to student; it supplements, clarifies, and systematizes the commandments of the Torah. Due to the continual persecution of the Jewish people, it became increasingly difficult to guarantee that these traditions would not be forgotten. Rabbi Yehudah Hanasi therefore redacted the Mishnah at the end of the second century. It serves as the foundation for the Talmud.

The condemned person is told, "Confess your transgressions, as it is the practice of all those who are to be executed to confess. Anyone who confesses and regrets his transgressions has a share in the World to Come."

We find this in the case of Achan. Joshua said to him before he was to be executed: "My son, please give honor to the G-d of Israel, and give a confession to Him" (JOSHUA 7:19). The next verse states: "And Achan answered Joshua, and said: 'Indeed, I have sinned against the G-d of Israel, and thus have I done.'" (JOSHUA 7:20)

From where do we derive that Achan's confession achieved atonement for him? A subsequent verse states: "And Joshua said: 'Why have you ruined us? G-d will ruin you on this day'" (JOSHUA 7:25). This implies that on *this* day you are ruined, but you are not ruined in the World to Come.

If the condemned man does not know how to confess, they instruct him to simply say, "Let my death be an atonement for all my sins."

Confession prayer from The Northern French Miscellany, c. 1278–1324. (British Library, London)

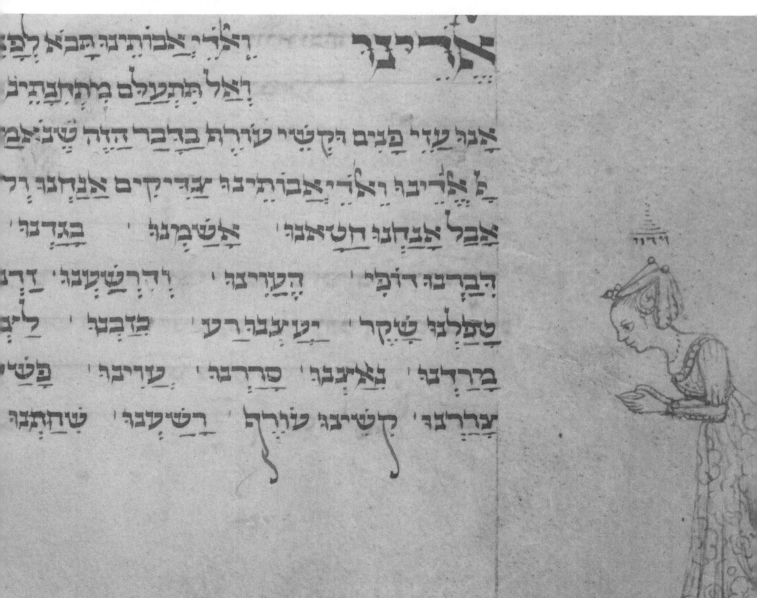

TEXT 3

MAIMONIDES, *MISHNEH TORAH*, LAWS OF THE SANHEDRIN 20:1

אֵין בֵּית דִּין עוֹנְשִׁין בְּאֹמֶד הַדַּעַת אֶלָּא עַל פִּי עֵדִים בִּרְאִיָּה בְּרוּרָה. אֲפִילּוּ רָאוּהוּ הָעֵדִים רוֹדֵף אַחַר חֲבֵירוֹ וְהִתְרוּ בּוֹ וְהֶעֱלִימוּ עֵינֵיהֶם, אוֹ שֶׁנִּכְנַס אַחֲרָיו לְחֻרְבָּה וְנִכְנְסוּ אַחֲרָיו וּמְצָאוּהוּ הָרוּג וּמְפַרְפֵּר וְהַסַּיִּף מְנַטֵּף דָּם בְּיַד הַהוֹרֵג, הוֹאִיל וְלֹא רָאוּהוּ בָּעֵת שֶׁהִכָּהוּ אֵין בֵּית דִּין הוֹרְגִין בְּעֵדוּת זוֹ. וְעַל זֶה וְכַיּוֹצֵא בּוֹ נֶאֱמַר, "וְנָקִי וְצַדִּיק אַל תַּהֲרֹג" (שְׁמוֹת כג, ז).

A court does not punish based on logical estimation, only on the basis of the testimony of witnesses who clearly saw the crime. Even if witnesses saw a person pursuing someone and warned him against committing the crime, if they subsequently diverted their attention and did not see the actual murder, the suspect cannot be executed based on this testimony.

For example, if the pursuer chased the victim into a ruin, and the witnesses followed him and found the victim slain, his body convulsing, and the killer holding a sword dripping blood: since the witnesses did not see the actual fatal blow, the court cannot execute the suspect based on this testimony. Concerning this and similar cases the verse states, "Do not kill an innocent and righteous person" (EXODUS 23:7).

RABBI MOSHE BEN MAIMON (MAIMONIDES, RAMBAM) 1135–1204

Halachist, philosopher, author, and physician. Maimonides was born in Córdoba, Spain. After the conquest of Córdoba by the Almohads, he fled Spain and eventually settled in Cairo, Egypt. There, he became the leader of the Jewish community and served as court physician to the vizier of Egypt. He is most noted for authoring the *Mishneh Torah,* an encyclopedic arrangement of Jewish law, and for his philosophical work, *Guide for the Perplexed.* His rulings on Jewish law are integral to the formation of halachic consensus.

Watch two law professors debate about whether Jewish law supports the abolition of the death penalty:

MYJLI.COM/CRIME

TEXT **4**

MAIMONIDES, IBID., 12:2

אֶחָד תַּלְמִיד חָכָם וְאֶחָד עַם הָאָרֶץ צָרִיךְ הַתְרָאָה, שֶׁלֹּא נִיתְּנָה הַתְרָאָה אֶלָּא לְהַבְחִין בֵּין שׁוֹגֵג לְמֵזִיד שֶׁמָּא שׁוֹגֵג הָיָה.

וְכֵיצַד מַתְרִין בּוֹ, אוֹמְרִין לוֹ פְּרוֹשׁ אוֹ אַל תַּעֲשֶׂה שֶׁזוּ עֲבֵירָה הִיא וְחַיָּיב אַתָּה עָלֶיהָ . . .

אִם פֵּירֵשׁ פָּטוּר. וְכֵן אִם שָׁתַק אוֹ הִרְכִּין בְּרֹאשׁוֹ, פָּטוּר. וַאֲפִילוּ אָמַר יוֹדֵעַ אֲנִי, פָּטוּר. עַד שֶׁיַּתִּיר עַצְמוֹ לְמִיתָה וְיֹאמַר, עַל מְנָת כֵּן אֲנִי עוֹשֶׂה, וְאַחַר כַּךְ יֵהָרֵג.

וְצָרִיךְ שֶׁיַּעֲבוֹר וְיַעֲשֶׂה תֵּיכֶף לַהַתְרָאָה בְּתוֹךְ כְּדֵי דִיבּוּר, אֲבָל אַחַר כְּדֵי דִבּוּר צָרִיךְ הַתְרָאָה אַחֶרֶת.

Both a scholar and a common person need a warning, because the obligation for a warning was instituted to distinguish between an inadvertent and an intentional transgressor.

How is a warning administered? He is told, "Stop!" or, "Do not do it!" [Then he must be told,] "It is a transgression and you are liable to be executed for it." . . .

If he ceases, he is not liable. Even if he remains silent or nods his head, and then commits the murder, he is still not liable for punishment. Even if he responds to the warning saying, "I know," he is still not liable for punishment. To establish liability, he must accept the punishment of death upon himself, saying, "I am doing it with this understanding." Only in such a case is the murderer executed.

The perpetrator must commit the transgression immediately after receiving the warning, within the few seconds it takes to offer a greeting. If this amount of time has passed, a second warning is necessary.

TEXT 5

MISHNAH, SANHEDRIN 4:5 ⚏

כֵּיצַד מְאַיְּמִין אֶת הָעֵדִים עַל עֵדֵי נְפָשׁוֹת, הָיוּ מַכְנִיסִין אוֹתָן וּמְאַיְּמִין
עֲלֵיהֶן. שֶׁמָּא תֹּאמְרוּ מֵאוֹמֶד, וּמִשְּׁמוּעָה, עֵד מִפִּי עֵד וּמִפִּי אָדָם נֶאֱמָן
שָׁמַעְנוּ, אוֹ שֶׁמָּא אִי אַתֶּם יוֹדְעִין שֶׁסּוֹפֵינוּ לִבְדֹּק אֶתְכֶם בִּדְרִישָׁה
וּבַחֲקִירָה.

הֱווּ יוֹדְעִין שֶׁלֹּא כְדִינֵי מָמוֹנוֹת דִּינֵי נְפָשׁוֹת. דִּינֵי מָמוֹנוֹת, אָדָם נוֹתֵן מָמוֹן
וּמִתְכַּפֵּר לוֹ. דִּינֵי נְפָשׁוֹת, דָּמוֹ וְדַם זַרְעִיוֹתָיו תְּלוּיִין בּוֹ עַד סוֹף הָעוֹלָם.
שֶׁכֵּן מָצִינוּ בְּקַיִן שֶׁהָרַג אֶת אָחִיו, שֶׁנֶּאֱמַר, "דְּמֵי אָחִיךָ צוֹעֲקִים" (בְּרֵאשִׁית
ד, י), אֵינוֹ אוֹמֵר דָּם אָחִיךָ אֶלָּא דְמֵי אָחִיךָ, דָּמוֹ וְדַם זַרְעִיוֹתָיו ...

לְפִיכָךְ נִבְרָא אָדָם יְחִידִי, לְלַמֶּדְךָ שֶׁכָּל הַמְאַבֵּד נֶפֶשׁ אַחַת מִיִּשְׂרָאֵל,
מַעֲלֶה עָלָיו הַכָּתוּב כְּאִלּוּ אִבֵּד עוֹלָם מָלֵא. וְכָל הַמְקַיֵּם נֶפֶשׁ אַחַת
מִיִּשְׂרָאֵל, מַעֲלֶה עָלָיו הַכָּתוּב כְּאִלּוּ קִיֵּם עוֹלָם מָלֵא ...

לְפִיכָךְ כָּל אֶחָד וְאֶחָד חַיָּיב לוֹמַר, בִּשְׁבִילִי נִבְרָא הָעוֹלָם.

How do we warn witnesses testifying regarding a capital case? We bring the witnesses in and press them: "Perhaps what you say isn't eyewitness testimony but your own conclusion, or hearsay. Perhaps you heard a different witness testify about this, someone you considered trustworthy. Or, perhaps you are unaware that we will interrogate you, with examination and inquiry.

"Know that capital cases are not like monetary ones. In monetary cases, a false witness can return the money and achieve atonement. But in capital cases, the blood of the victim and all his future offspring hang upon you until the end of time. Thus we find in regard to Cain, who killed his brother, where it says (GENESIS 4:10), 'The bloods of your brother scream out!' The verse does not say blood but bloods, because Cain was responsible for his blood and also the blood of his future offspring. . . .

"It was for this reason that Adam was originally created alone, to teach you that anyone who destroys a life is considered by Scripture to have destroyed an entire world; and anyone who saves a life is considered to have saved an entire world. . . .

"Therefore, every person is obligated to say, 'The world was created for my sake.'"

TEXT **6**

MAIMONIDES, *SEFER HAMITZVOT*, NEGATIVE COMMANDMENT 290

וְאַל יִקְשֶׁה בְּעֵינֶיךָ דָּבָר זֶה וְאַל תַּחְשׁוֹב שֶׁזֶּה דִין עָוֶל, לְפִי שֶׁהַדְּבָרִים הָאֶפְשָׁרִיִּים יֵשׁ מֵהֶם שֶׁאֶפְשָׁרוּתָם קְרוֹבָה מְאֹד, וּמֵהֶם שֶׁאֶפְשָׁרוּתָם רְחוֹקָה מְאֹד, וּמֵהֶם בֵּינוֹנִיִּים בֵּין אֵלּוּ, וְהָאֶפְשָׁר רָחָב מְאֹד.

וְאִילוּ הִרְשָׁתָה תּוֹרָה לְקַיֵּם עוֹנָשִׁים בְּאֶפְשָׁר הַקָּרוֹב מְאֹד, אֲשֶׁר כִּמְעַט קָרוֹב לְמְחֻיָּב הַמְצִיאוּת כְּדֻגְמַת מַה שֶׁהִזְכַּרְנוּ, כִּי אָז הָיוּ מְקַיְּמִים אֶת הָעוֹנָשִׁים בְּמַה שֶׁהוּא יוֹתֵר רָחוֹק מִזֶּה, וּבְמָה שֶׁהוּא עוֹד יוֹתֵר רָחוֹק, עַד שֶׁיְּקַיְּמוּ אֶת הָעוֹנָשִׁים וְיָמִיתוּ בְּנֵי אָדָם בְּעָוֶל בְּאֻמְדָּן קַל לְפִי דִמְיוֹן הַשּׁוֹפֵט.

לְפִיכָךְ סָתַם יִתְעַלֶּה אֶת הַפֶּתַח הַזֶּה וְצִוָּוהוּ שֶׁלֹּא יְקַיֵּם שׁוּם עוֹנֶשׁ אֶלָּא עַד שֶׁיִּהְיוּ שָׁם עֵדִים הַמְעִידִים שֶׁבָּרוּר לָהֶם אוֹתוֹ הַמַּעֲשֶׂה, בְּרוּר שֶׁאֵין בּוֹ שׁוּם סָפֵק, וְאִי אֶפְשָׁר לְהַסְבִּירוֹ אַחֶרֶת בְּשׁוּם אוֹפֶן.

וְאִם לֹא נְקַיֵּם אֶת הָעוֹנָשִׁים בְּאוֹמֶד הֶחָזָק מְאֹד, הֲרֵי לֹא יוּכַל לִקְרוֹת יוֹתֵר מִשֶּׁנִּפְטַר אֶת הַחוֹטֵא. אֲבָל אִם נְקַיֵּם אֶת הָעוֹנָשִׁים בְּאוֹמֶד וּבְדִימוּי, אֶפְשָׁר שֶׁבְּיוֹם מִן הַיָּמִים נַהֲרֹג נָקִי.

וְיוֹתֵר טוֹב וְיוֹתֵר רָצוּי לִפְטוֹר אֶלֶף חוֹטְאִים, מִלַּהֲרֹג נָקִי אֶחָד בְּיוֹם מִן הַיָּמִים.

Do not question this law and consider it unjust. Some possibilities are extremely probable, others are extremely unlikely, and others in between. The realm of "possible" is very broad.

If the Torah would have allowed the court to punish when the offense was very probable and almost definite, then we would eventually come to punish in cases that are less and less probable. Eventually, people would be wrongfully executed based on flimsy indications and the judges' subjective estimation.

G-d therefore closed the door to this possibility and forbade any punishment unless there are witnesses who testify that they are certain about the facts of the case, beyond any possible doubt, and there is no other possible explanation for what transpired.

If we do not inflict punishment even when the offense is most probable, the worst that can happen is that someone who is really guilty will be exonerated. But if punishment is given based on estimation and circumstantial evidence, it is possible that someday an innocent person will be executed.

It is better that even a thousand guilty people be exonerated than to someday execute even one innocent person.

Illustration to Prosper Mérimée's *Carmen*: Carmen's murder, Hugo Steiner-Prag, lithograph, Berlin, 1920. (Leo Black Institute, Center for Jewish History, New York)

TEXT 7

MISHNAH, MAKOT 1:10

סַנְהֶדְרִין הַהוֹרֶגֶת אֶחָד בְּשָׁבוּעַ נִקְרֵאת חַבְלָנִית. רַבִּי אֶלְעָזָר בֶּן עֲזַרְיָה אוֹמֵר, אֶחָד לְשִׁבְעִים שָׁנָה.

A Sanhedrin that executes once every seven years is called a "destructive" court. Rabbi Elazar ben Azaria says once every seventy years.

TEXT 8

MISHNAH, IBID.

רַבִּי טַרְפוֹן וְרַבִּי עֲקִיבָא אוֹמְרִים, אִלּוּ הָיִינוּ בַּסַנְהֶדְרִין לֹא נֶהֱרַג אָדָם מֵעוֹלָם.
רַבָּן שִׁמְעוֹן בֶּן גַּמְלִיאֵל אוֹמֵר, אַף הֵן מַרְבִּין שׁוֹפְכֵי דָמִים בְּיִשְׂרָאֵל.

Rabbi Tarfon and Rabbi Akiva said: "Had we served on the Sanhedrin no one would ever have been executed.

Rabbi Shimon ben Gamliel responded, "You would have caused murder to proliferate."

QUESTION FOR DISCUSSION

How would Rabbi Tarfon and Rabbi Akiva reconcile their statement with the fact that the Torah legislates the death penalty?

QUESTION FOR DISCUSSION

Based on what we have studied to this point, where would the Torah stand regarding the death penalty today?

Vergadering van het Sanhedrin (*Meeting of the Sanhedrin*), Antonie Wierix (II), printmaker; after Bernardino Passeri, engraving, Antwerp, 1593. (Rijksmuseum, Amsterdam)

TEXT 9

MAIMONIDES, *MISHNEH TORAH*, LAWS OF THE SANHEDRIN, 24:4, 10

יֵשׁ לְבֵית דִּין . . . לַהֲרוֹג מִי שֶׁאֵינוֹ מְחוּיָּב מִיתָה. וְלֹא לַעֲבוֹר עַל דִּבְרֵי
תּוֹרָה, אֶלָּא לַעֲשׂוֹת סְיָיג לַתּוֹרָה.

כֵּיוָן שֶׁרוֹאִים בֵּית דִּין שֶׁפָּרְצוּ הָעָם בַּדָּבָר יֵשׁ לָהֶן לִגְדּוֹר וּלְחַזֵּק הַדָּבָר כְּפִי
מַה שֶׁיֵּרָאֶה לָהֶם, הַכֹּל הוֹרָאַת שָׁעָה . . . כָּל אֵלּוּ הַדְּבָרִים לְפִי מַה שֶׁיִּרְאֶה
הַדַּיָּין שֶׁזֶּה רָאוּי לְכָךְ וְשֶׁהַשָּׁעָה צְרִיכָה.

A court has the authority to execute a person who is not liable to be executed under normative Torah law. This is not intended as a violation of Torah law, but rather to create a fence around the words of the Torah.

When the court sees that there is a widespread breach of the law, they may establish safeguards to strengthen the law as they deem necessary, as a temporary measure. . . . These emergency powers should be applied when the judge perceives that this is an appropriate punishment for the offender and that the needs of the time necessitate it.

TEXT 10

RABBI YITSCHAK BEN SHESHET, *RESPONSA* 251 🎧

מִשּׁוּם מִיגְדּוֹר מִלְתָא, כֵּיוָן שֶׁמֵּת מִבֵּינֵיהֶם אִם רוֹאֶה אַתָּה לַהֲמִיתָם . . .
הָרְשׁוּת בְּיָדְךָ . . .

וְאַף לְאוֹתוֹ שֶׁאֵין בּוֹ עֵדִים רַק רְאָיוֹת חֲזָקוֹת וַאֲמַתְלָאוֹת אֲמִתִּיּוֹת.

RABBI YITSCHAK BEN SHESHET (RIVASH) 1326–1408

Halachist. Rivash studied under Rabbeinu Nisim of Gerona (Ran) in Barcelona, and served as rabbi there and in other important Jewish communities in Spain. Because of the eruption of anti-Jewish riots in 1391, he fled to North Africa and settled in Algiers. He was the first to address the halachic status of Marranos. Rivash's halachic responsa are his most important work; they contain sources no longer extant and served, in part, as a basis for the Code of Jewish Law.

Since the victim died as a result of the attack by these two people, you may execute the murderers in order to deter such acts if you see fit to do so. . . .

You may even execute the perpetrator about whom there are no eyewitnesses, based on compelling evidence and truly convincing reasoning.

Medal commemorating the sinking of "U.27" by Royal Navy Q-ship "Baralong," August 19, 1915. Karl Goetz, Munich, 1915.(National Maritime Museum, Greenwich, London)

TEXT **11**

RABBI MEIR OF LUBLIN, *RESPONSA* 138

הִגִּיעַ לְיָדִי הַפְּסַק דִּין אֲשֶׁר תֵּרַצְתָּ עַל דְּבַר הַמַּעֲשֶׂה הַמְכוֹעָר וְהַזָּר, עֲוֹן
הָרְצִיחָה שֶׁעָשָׂה אֶחָד מִפְּרִיצֵי בְּנֵי עַמֵּינוּ כִּנְזְכָּר בְּהָעֵדִיּוֹת אֲשֶׁר שָׁלַח
מַעֲלַת כְּבוֹד תּוֹרָתוֹ לְיָדִי. הֲגַם שֶׁעֵד הַשֵּׁנִי הוּא עֵד מִפִּי עֵד, מִסְּתָמָא
הַמַּעֲשֶׂה הָרַע הוּא יָדוּעַ וּמְפֻרְסָם. וְהַפּוֹשֵׁעַ הָרוֹצֵחַ הוּא בַּמַּאֲסָר
וּבְמִשְׁטָר בְּיַד הַפָּקִד כִּי לֹא פוֹרַשׁ מָה יֵעָשֶׂה לוֹ.

וּבִיקֵּשׁ מַעֲלַת כְּבוֹד תּוֹרָתוֹ מִמֶּנִּי לְחַוּוֹת דַּעְתִּי לְהֲלָכָה לְמַעֲשֶׂה בַּזְּמַן הַזֶּה,
וְאִם יָפֶה דָּנְתָּ וְאִם יָפֶה זִכִּיתָ מִלְהַכּוֹתוֹ נֶפֶשׁ . . .

הָא דְּאָמְרִינָן בְּפֶרֶק זֶה בּוֹרֵר (סַנְהֶדְרִין כז, א) דְּבַר חַמָּא קָטַל נַפְשָׁא . . .
וְלֹא גָזַר לָדוּנוֹ וּלְעוֹנְשׁוֹ בְּמִיתָה . . . כְּבָר כָּתַב הָרִיבַ"שׁ בְּסִימָן רנ"א . . . לְפִי
שֶׁרָאָה לְפִי צוֹרֶךְ הַשָּׁעָה שָׁדֵי בְּסִימוּי כָּזֶה לֹא צִיוָה לְהוֹרְגוֹ . . .

בֶּאֱמֶת הוּא שֶׁצָּרִיךְ כָּל בֵּית דִּין לְהִתְיַישֵּׁב בַּדָּבָר וְלִשְׁקוֹל בְּמֹאזְנֵי שִׂכְלָם
אִם צוֹרֶךְ הַשָּׁעָה הוּא כָּל כַּךְ גָּדוֹל שֶׁכְּדַאי הוּא לְהַעֲנִישׁוֹ בְּעוֹנֶשׁ מִיתָה . . .

אֲבָל נִרְאָה לִי פָּשׁוּט שֶׁלֹּא לְבַד זֶה בִּשְׁכְּבָר רַבִּים מִן כְּלַל הָעָם פְּרוּצִים
בְּאוֹתָהּ עֲבֵירָה הוּא נִקְרָא צוֹרֶךְ שָׁעָה כְּמָה שֶׁעָלָה עַל דַּעְתְּךָ כֵּן כְּמוֹ
שֶׁנִּרְאָה מִדִּבְרֵי מַעֲלָתְךָ . . . וּמִטַּעַם זֶה תֵּרַצְתָּ הַדִּין שֶׁבְּנִדּוֹן זֶה הַנִּזְכָּר לֹא
שַׁיָּךְ לוֹמַר בּוֹ שֶׁהַשָּׁעָה צְרִיכָה לְכָךְ.

וְזֶה אֵינוֹ, אֶלָּא אֲפִילוּ הֵיכִי שֶׁבְּשֶׁעָבַר לֹא הָיוּ הָעָם פְּרוּצִים בַּעֲבֵירָה זוֹ,
אֶלָּא שֶׁרוֹאִים הַבֵּית דִּין שֶׁאִם לֹא יֵעָנְשׁוּ זֶה בְּדִינָא רַבָּה כְּמִיתָה וְכַיּוֹצֵא
בָּזֶה יִהְיֶה שָׂכָר שֶׁמֵּהַיּוֹם וּלְהַבָּא יִהְיוּ הָעָם פְּרוּצִים בַּעֲבֵירָה זוֹ וְיִנְהֲגוּ בָּהּ
קַלּוּת, גַּם זֶה מִיקְרֵי שֶׁהַשָּׁעָה צְרִיכָה לְכָךְ . . .

וְעַתָּה אֲהוּבִי, בְּנִדּוֹן דִּידַן בְּמַעֲשֶׂה הַמְכוֹעָר הַנִּזְכָּר, הֲלֹא אֲנִי מִבַּחוּץ וְאַתֶּם
מִבִּפְנִים, לִשְׁקוֹל בְּמֹאזְנֵי שִׂכְלְכֶם הַזַּךְ גּוֹדֶל צוֹרֶךְ שָׁעָה עַל פִּי הַדְּרָכִים
אֲשֶׁר כָּתַבְתִּי. אֲבָל לְפִי הַנִּרְאֶה כָּל הַנֵּי פְּרָצוֹת שֶׁכָּתַבְתִּי הַשַּׁיָּיכִים לִהְיוֹת
בַּלְהַבָּא שֶׁהַשָּׁעָה צְרִיכִין לְכָךְ, כִּמְעַט כּוּלְהוּ אִיתַנְיֵיהוּ בְּנִדּוֹן הָרַע הַנִּזְכָּר.
וּבְיוֹתֵר שֶׁמִּתּוֹךְ דְּבָרֶיךָ נִזְכָּר שֶׁגַּם בְּאֶשְׁתָּקֵד נַעֲשָׂה בְּאוֹתוֹ גָּבוּל מַעֲשֶׂה
רַע כָּזֶה וְיָצָא וְיָצָא בְּלֹא כְּלוּם וְיִתְרַבּוּ הַמִּתְפָּרְצִים חַס וְשָׁלוֹם . . .

וְאֵינָה הָאֱלֹקִים לְיָדוֹ שֶׁכְּבָר הוּא נִתְפַּשׂ בְּיָדֵי גּוֹיִם, הַצַּד הַיּוֹתֵר טוֹב הָיָה
שֶׁיַּד בֵּית דִּין יִשְׂרָאֵל לֹא יִהְיֶה בּוֹ. רַק גּוֹאֲלֵי הַדָּם יִתְבְּעוּ מִמֶּנוּ נִקְמַת דַּם
הַנִּשְׁפָּךְ עַל יְדֵי הַפָּקִד, שֶׁיְּבַעֲרֶנּוּ מִן הָעוֹלָם וְעַל יְדֵי זֶה יְגַדְרוּ הַפִּרְצָה.

RABBI MEIR OF LUBLIN
1558–1616

Polish rabbi and Talmudist. Rabbi Meir served as rabbi of a number of prestigious Polish communities, most notably the city of Lublin. He is known for his commentary on the Talmud, halachic responsa, and the famous yeshiva he headed in Lublin.

I received your ruling concerning the abhorrent case of murder committed by a renegade member of our people, as evidenced by the records of testimony that you sent me.

Although the second witness in this case did not see the murder himself, and he testifies based on what he heard from an eyewitness, I understand that the facts of the case are clear and well known, and the murderer is currently being held in the custody of the local non-Jewish authorities awaiting sentencing. Your honor ruled that the perpetrator should not be put to death, and you asked for my halachic opinion on whether this is the correct decision.

Regarding the case in the Talmud (SANHEDRIN 27A) that a man by the name of Bar Chama murdered someone . . . and they did not consider the death penalty . . . Rabbi Yitschak ben Sheshet already explained (RESPONSA 251) . . . that the reason why they did not use the death penalty was because they estimated that for the needs of their time it was sufficient to use corporal punishment.

The truth is that every court must carefully consider and weigh whether the needs of the time are so great as to require the death penalty. . . .

In my opinion, it is simple that the "need of the time" is not only assessed on the basis of whether the sin is

*Learn more about this responsa from Rabbi Meir of Lublin. Watch as **Rabbi Shlomo Yaffe** provides a comprehensive overview:*

MYJLI.COM/CRIME

already common amongst the people. I understand from your words that you are of this opinion . . . and therefore you don't consider this case to rise to the level of the "need of the time."

This is incorrect. Even if until now this sin was not prevalent among the people, but the court believes that if it doesn't punish the murderer with a punishment as severe as death, the result will be that, in the future, people will disregard the severity of this sin and it will become common, this too is considered the "need of the time." . . .

Now, my dear colleague, regarding this particular abhorrent case. I am distant, and you are local. It is therefore up to you to evaluate yourself how great the "need of the time" is, based on the criteria I have given.

However, it appears to me that the possible negative ramifications of being lenient that I described are relevant in this terrible case. This is especially so because you mentioned in your letter that a similar horrible incident took place in your area recently, and the offender was not punished. Failing to punish severely will cause murder to proliferate, G-d forbid. . . .

Since by divine providence the murderer is already in the hands of the non-Jewish authorities, it would be best that the Jewish court not execute him themselves.

Rather, the relatives of the victim should demand from the local ruler that he avenge the spilled blood and eliminate the murderer from the world. This will deter future murders.

QUESTION FOR DISCUSSION

What do you find to be noteworthy about this text?

QUESTION FOR DISCUSSION

What practical guidance might Jewish law give us regarding the use of the death penalty today?

KEY POINTS

1 The Torah rejects the argument that the death penalty is immoral.

2 Torah law has many restrictions placed on the use of the death penalty. Two eyewitnesses are required to testify in order to impose the death penalty, and the perpetrator must have received and verbally acknowledged an explicit warning of the consequences of the crime.

3 The logic behind the high standards of Jewish law is the infinite value of human life. The Torah therefore considers it preferable that even a thousand guilty people be exonerated, rather than that one innocent individual be executed.

4 These restrictions would render a death sentence almost impossible to impose. The reason why the Torah has the death penalty on the books is to serve as a didactic statement about the severity of murder and the value of life.

5 Jewish law includes an emergency clause, allowing a court to impose the death penalty based on compelling evidence, even if the prosecution does not meet the normative threshold of eyewitnesses, advance warning, and verbal acknowledgment.

6 This emergency clause can only be invoked if murder has become a societal problem, and can only be deterred through the use of the death penalty. If other forms of punishment can serve as an equally effective deterrent, the death penalty cannot be used.

Have your views on the death penalty changed after this lesson? **Take a poll** *at:*

MYJLI.COM/CRIME

Appendix A

Figure 2.2

Capital Punishment in the United States

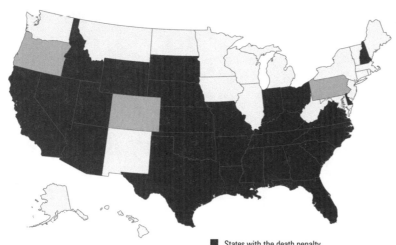

■ States with the death penalty

■ States with a Governor-imposed moratorium

□ States without the death penalty

STATES WITH THE DEATH PENALTY (30)

Alabama	Ohio
Arizona	Oklahoma
Arkansas	Oregon
California	Pennsylvania
Colorado	South Carolina
Florida	South Dakota
Georgia	Tennessee
Idaho	Texas
Indiana	Utah
Kansas	Virginia
Kentucky	Wyoming
Louisiana	
Mississippi	ALSO
Missouri	U.S. Gov't.
Montana	U.S. Military
Nebraska	
Nevada	
New Hampshire	
North Carolina	

STATES WITHOUT THE DEATH PENALTY (20) (YEAR ABOLISHED OR OVERTURNED IN PARENTHESES)

Alaska (1957)	New Mexico (2009)
Connecticut (2012)	New York (2007)
Delaware (2016)	North Dakota (1973)
Hawaii (1957)	Rhode Island (1984)
Illinois (2011)	Vermont (1964)
Iowa (1965)	Washington (2018)
Maine (1887)	West Virginia (1965)
Maryland (2013)	Wisconsin (1853)
Massachusetts (1984)	
Michigan (1846)	
Minnesota (1911)	ALSO
New Jersey (2007)	Dist. of Columbia (1981)

DEATH PENALTY STATES WITH GUBERNATORIAL MORATORIA (3)

Colorado (2013)	Pennsylvania (2015)
Oregon (2011)	

DEATH PENALTY INFORMATION CENTER, "STATES WITH AND WITHOUT THE DEATH PENALTY," DEATHPENALTYINFO.ORG

Figure 2.3

Capital Punishment Worldwide

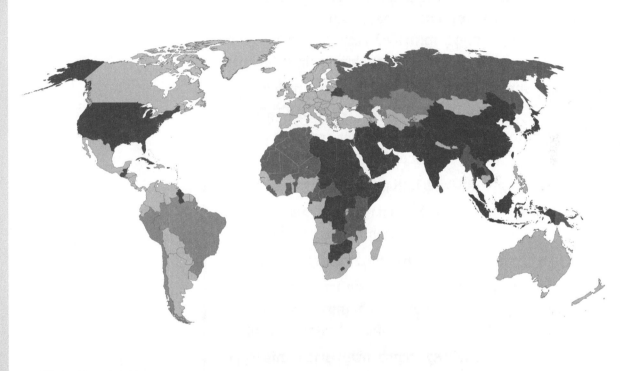

■ Legal form of punishment
■ Legal form of punishment but no executions in the last 10 years
■ Retained only for exceptional crimes
■ Abolished for all crimes

WIKIMEDIA COMMONS, BASED ON AMNESTY INTERNATIONAL STANDARDS

Appendix B

TEXT 12

MAIMONIDES, *MISHNEH TORAH,* LAWS OF THE SANHEDRIN 10

אֶחָד מִן הַדַּיָּנִים בְּדִינֵי נְפָשׁוֹת שֶׁהָיָה מִן הַמְזַכִּין אוֹ מִן הַמְחַיְּיבִין, לֹא מִפְּנֵי שֶׁאָמַר דָּבָר הַנִּרְאָה לוֹ בְּדַעְתּוֹ, אֶלָּא נָטָה אַחַר דִּבְרֵי חֲבֵירוֹ, הֲרֵי זֶה עוֹבֵר בְּלֹא תַעֲשֶׂה. וְעַל זֶה נֶאֱמַר, "וְלֹא תַעֲנֶה עַל רִיב לִנְטוֹת" (שְׁמוֹת כג, ב). מִפִּי הַשְּׁמוּעָה לָמְדוּ, שֶׁלֹּא תֹאמַר בִּשְׁעַת מִנְיָן דַּי שֶׁאֶהְיֶה כְּאִישׁ פְּלוֹנִי, אֶלָּא אֱמוֹר מַה שֶּׁלְּפָנֶיךָ.

וּבִכְלָל לָאו זֶה שֶׁלֹּא יַחֲזוֹר הַמְלַמֵּד זְכוּת בְּדִינֵי נְפָשׁוֹת לְלַמֵּד חוֹבָה, שֶׁנֶּאֱמַר, "לֹא תַעֲנֶה עַל רִיב לִנְטוֹת" (שְׁמוֹת כג, ב).

בַּמֶּה דְּבָרִים אֲמוּרִים, בִּשְׁעַת מַשָּׂא וּמַתָּן. אֲבָל בִּשְׁעַת גְּמַר דִּין יֵשׁ לַמְלַמֵּד זְכוּת לַחֲזוֹר וּלְהִתְמַנּוֹת עִם הַמְחַיְּיבִים.

תַּלְמִיד שֶׁהָיָה מְזַכֶּה וּמֵת, רוֹאִין אוֹתוֹ כְּאִילּוּ הוּא מְזַכֶּה בִּמְקוֹמוֹ.

אָמַר אֶחָד, יֵשׁ לִי לְלַמֵּד עָלָיו זְכוּת, וְנִשְׁתַּתֵּק אוֹ מֵת קוֹדֶם שֶׁיְּלַמֵּד זְכוּת וְיֹאמַר מֵאֵי זֶה טַעַם מְזַכֶּה, הֲרֵי הוּא כְּמִי שֶׁאֵינוֹ.

שְׁנַיִם שֶׁאָמְרוּ טַעַם אֶחָד, אֲפִילּוּ מִשְּׁנֵי מִקְרָאוֹת, אֵין נִמְנִין אֶלָּא כְּאֶחָד.

וּמִפִּי הַשְּׁמוּעָה לָמְדוּ שֶׁאֵין מַתְחִילִין בְּדִינֵי נְפָשׁוֹת מִן הַגָּדוֹל, שֶׁמָּא יִסְמְכוּ הַשְּׁאָר עַל דַּעְתּוֹ וְלֹא יִרְאוּ עַצְמָן כְּדַאִין לַחֲלוֹק עָלָיו. אֶלָּא יֹאמַר כָּל אֶחָד דָּבָר הַנִּרְאֶה לוֹ בְּדַעְתּוֹ.

וְכֵן אֵין פּוֹתְחִין בְּדִינֵי נְפָשׁוֹת לְחוֹבָה אֶלָּא לִזְכוּת.

כֵּיצַד, אוֹמְרִים לָזֶה שֶׁחָטָא, אִם לֹא עָשִׂיתָ דָּבָר זֶה שֶׁהֵעִידוּ בּוֹ עָלֶיךָ אַל תִּירָא מִדִּבְרֵיהֶם.

אָמַר אֶחָד מִן הַתַּלְמִידִים בְּדִינֵי נְפָשׁוֹת, יֵשׁ לִי לְלַמֵּד עָלָיו חוֹבָה, מְשַׁתְּקִין אוֹתוֹ. אָמַר, יֵשׁ לִי לְלַמֵּד עָלָיו זְכוּת, מַעֲלִין אוֹתוֹ עִמָּהֶן לַסַּנְהֶדְרִין. אִם יֵשׁ מַמָּשׁ בִּדְבָרָיו, שׁוֹמְעִין לוֹ וְאֵינוּ יוֹרֵד מִשָּׁם לְעוֹלָם. וְאִם אֵין מַמָּשׁ בִּדְבָרָיו אֵינוּ יוֹרֵד מִשָּׁם כָּל הַיּוֹם כּוּלּוֹ.

אֲפִילּוּ אָמַר הַנִּדּוֹן עַצְמוֹ יֵשׁ לִי לְלַמֵּד עַל עַצְמִי זְכוּת, שׁוֹמְעִין לוֹ וְעוֹלֶה לַמִּנְיָן. וְהוּא שֶׁיִּהְיֶה מַמָּשׁ בִּדְבָרָיו.

בֵּית דִּין שֶׁטָּעוּ בְּדִינֵי נְפָשׁוֹת וְחִיְּיבוּ אֶת הַפָּטוּר וְגָמְרוּ דִּינוֹ לְחוֹבָה, וְנִרְאָה לָהֶם הַטַּעַם שֶׁיִּסְתְּרוּ בּוֹ אֶת דִּינוֹ כְּדֵי לְזַכּוֹתוֹ, סוֹתְרִין וְחוֹזְרִין וְדָנִין אוֹתוֹ.

אֲבָל אִם טָעוּ וּפָטְרוּ אֶת הַמְחֻיָּיב הֲרִיגָה אֵין סוֹתְרִין אֶת דִּינוֹ וְאֵין מַחֲזִירִין אוֹתוֹ.

A judge in a capital case that makes a decision to exonerate or convict not based on his own personal judgment, but following a colleague's opinion, has committed a transgression. This is forbidden by the verse, "You shall not be swayed in judgment" (EXODUS 23:2). The Oral Tradition interprets this verse as prohibiting a judge from saying, "It is sufficient for me to follow so-and-so's opinion." Rather, the judge must express his own opinion.

The same verse also prohibits a judge who had proposed a rationale for exoneration in a capital case to then propose a rationale for conviction. The verse can also be read as stating, "You shall not sway toward conviction."

This rule applies only during the deliberation phase, but a judge who was inclined toward exoneration can vote in favor of conviction at the decision phase.

If a student who is not on the court offers a rationale for exoneration but dies before it could be properly considered, the court continues to deliberate the rationale.

However, if the student had said, "I can offer a rationale to exonerate him," and then dies or loses the power of speech before being able to present the reasoning, the court does not deliberate over what his reasoning may have been.

If two students offered the same reasoning, even if they quoted different proof texts, one of them is allowed to join in the court's deliberations, but not both.

The Oral Tradition teaches that, in capital cases, we do not allow the most senior judge to voice his opinion first, lest the other judges rely on his opinion and consider themselves unworthy to argue against him. Rather, every judge must state his own personal opinion.

Similarly, in capital cases, we do not open with a statement that points to guilt, but rather with one that points toward acquittal.

How is this done? The defendant is told, "If you did not commit the transgression concerning which testimony was given concerning you, do not fear the words of the witnesses."

In a capital case, if one of the students who is not part of the court says that he has an argument in favor of conviction, we silence him. But if he says that he has an argument in favor of exoneration he is included in the deliberations of the court. If his words are of substance, we heed his statements and he continues to participate in the deliberations. If his words are not of substance, he participates in the deliberations only for that day.

Even if the defendant himself says he has an argument in favor of his own exoneration, we heed his words and he is included in the deliberations, provided his words are of substance.

When a court errs with regard to a capital case and convicts an innocent person, and later they discover a rationale that would require that the ruling be nullified and he be vindicated, they nullify the ruling and retry the case.

If, however, the court errs and acquits a person who was actually liable, the judgment is not nullified and the case is not retried.

Additional Readings

CAPITAL PUNISHMENT IN JEWISH LAW AND ITS APPLICATION TO THE AMERICAN LEGAL SYSTEM: A CONCEPTUAL OVERVIEW

SAMUEL J. LEVINE

All footnotes have been removed to conserve space. To read the complete article, visit www.myjli.com/crime.

I. Introduction

In recent years, a growing body of scholarship has developed in the United States that applies concepts in Jewish law to unsettled, controversial, and challenging areas of American legal thought. While some scholars endorse the application of Jewish legal theory to American law, others are more cautious. One area of Jewish legal thought that has found prominence in both American court opinions and American legal scholarship concerns the approach taken by Jewish law to capital punishment.

One aim of this Essay is to discuss the issue of the death penalty in Jewish law as it relates to the question of the death penalty in American law, a discussion that requires the rejection of simplistic conclusions and the confrontation of the complexities of the Jewish legal system. For example, it is not uncommon to find both proponents and opponents of the death penalty attempting to support their respective positions through citations to sources in Jewish law. Such attempts, however, often fail to consider the full range of Jewish legal scholarship, relying instead only on sources that appear superficially to favor one position over the other. Thus, another goal of this Essay is to present a general and balanced overview of Jewish

SAMUEL J. LEVINE

Professor. Levine is a professor of law at Touro Law Center and the director of the Jewish Law Institute. He has published more than forty law review articles in the areas of legal ethics, criminal law, law and religion, Jewish law, and constitutional law.

law with respect to legal and historical attitudes towards the death penalty. More specifically, this Essay focuses on the conceptual underpinnings behind pertinent Jewish law, considering the potential relevance and effect of those conceptualizations on American legal thought.

Part II of this Essay discusses the United States appellate court case of Hayes v. Lockhart which makes reference to the death penalty in Jewish law. This case reflects some of the methods employed by members of the legal community who seek to support their positions on the death penalty by referring to Jewish law. Part III takes a close look at the death penalty in the Written Torah, which is often cited by those favoring capital punishment. Part IV examines the complex position taken by the Oral Torah towards the death penalty as reflected in the Talmud and other rabbinic sources. This Essay concludes that any meaningful application of Jewish law to the death penalty debate is impossible without an accurate and complete analysis and understanding of Jewish law in its proper context.

II. Hayes v. Lockhart—A Case in Point

The 1988 case of Hayes v. Lockhart offers one example of the injection of Jewish Law into the death penalty debate and illustrates how either side can use Jewish Law to support their respective position. This case illustrates the failure of both sides to appreciate fully the complexity of the Jewish legal system with respect to capital punishment.

In Hayes, the United States Court of Appeals for the Eighth Circuit considered the habeas petition of a defendant who had been convicted of capital felony murder and sentenced to death. During his rebuttal argument at the penalty phase of the trial, the prosecutor referred to a Biblical verse stating "he that strikes a man and he dies shall surely be put to death." Although the majority did not "condone the prosecutor's remarks," it found that the defense counsel's failure to object to the remarks did not constitute ineffective assistance of counsel.

In a dissenting opinion, Judge Bright described the case as involving "a prosecutor's overzealous and unprincipled pursuit of the death penalty and defense counsel's passive response." Judge Bright characterized the prosecutor's "selective quoting" from the Bible as "not only incendiary, but also misleading." Judge Bright also asserted that "[i]n fact, the Old Testament does not advocate the death penalty. Rather, ancient Jewish law abhors the death penalty and sets forth such a multitude of procedural barriers as to render execution, in the words of Gerald Blidstein, 'a virtual impossibility.'"

The prosecutor's reliance on the Biblical verse to support the implementation of the death penalty in the United States was indeed problematic and misplaced. As Judge Bright correctly noted, the prosecutor's citation to the Biblical text without further reference to its foundation in Jewish law resulted in an incomplete and inaccurate interpretation. Thus, Judge Bright's emphasis on the need to consult the work of Jewish legal scholars is instructive, but his brief discussion of the issue is incomplete. The Talmud clearly details the painstaking procedural safeguards that were required to be observed before the death penalty could be carried out. Nevertheless, it is evident from Biblical, Talmudic, and post-Talmudic sources that capital punishment was, at times, an actual element of the authority of both the judiciary and the king.

Perhaps more problematic than the failure of both the prosecution and the appellate judges in Hayes to fully investigate the role of the death penalty in Jewish law was the apparently unquestioned notion that the resolution of the religious issue should influence the approach to capital punishment in the United States. One problem is the reliance on an entirely different legal and religious system to help resolve a question of American jurisprudence. The problem arises even though it is not unusual for courts to turn to other legal systems, including the Bible, for guidance in taming unsettled areas of law, particularly those with profound moral implications. Indeed, the inclusion in this Symposium of a panel relating to the approaches taken to the death penalty by Catholic and Jewish law reflects an assumption that these approaches are somehow relevant to American law.

Another deeper problem lies in the apparent attitudes of the prosecution and Judge Bright in Hayes. There seems to be a disturbing lack of sophistication in the supposition that a simple historical determination of the frequency of death penalty sentences in the Jewish legal system should determine how Jewish law would prescribe death sentences in the American legal system. Such a supposition ignores the fact that Jewish laws are premised on diverse underlying conceptual foundations, some of which may be applicable to American law and others which are rooted in religious principles foreign to American jurisprudential thought. Part III and Part IV examine more closely these conceptual foundations in an attempt to arrive at a more nuanced application of the approach to capital punishment in Jewish law.

III. Capital Punishment in the Written Torah

The fundamental source of all Jewish law is the Written Torah—the Five Books of Moses. As the prosecutor in Hayes observed, the Torah does prescribe the death penalty for murder. In fact, those seeking a legal text that incorporates capital punishment as part of the legal system can readily look to the text of the Torah for support, because it contains numerous references to the death penalty. In his Code of Law, Moses Maimonides, the Medieval legal authority, documented the various offenses subject to the death penalty according to the Torah, counting a total of thirty-six such offenses.

Despite the availability of the death penalty for the crimes enumerated in the Torah, reliance on the text of the Torah to support the implementation of the death penalty in the United States is tenuous at best. First, the very fact that the Torah prescribes the death penalty for numerous offenses other than murder represents a fundamental difference between the law of the Torah and American law. Serving as a basic religious document as well as a legal document, the Torah consists not only of civil law but also of ritual law, in addition to historical narrative that pervades and unites the text. The religious nature of the Torah is dramatically illustrated by many of the offenses deemed punishable by death, including for example, various forms of idolatry and violation of the Sabbath. In fact, the majority of capital offenses listed in the Torah relate to purely religious matters, with relatively few involving actions that would be considered criminal in the United States. Thus, the religious objectives of the legal system manifested in the Written Torah make it an unlikely model for American jurisprudence.

One of the central functions of capital punishment in the Biblical justice system was to provide a means for the offender to atone for the capital offense. The concepts of repentance and atonement are central to Jewish religious thought and practice. Even those who commit the most grievous sins have the opportunity and obligation to repent from those sins. Those who commit capital offenses thus receive the harshest of punishments, partly because only such a harsh punishment is considered sufficient to merit complete spiritual atonement. Although the processes of repentance and atonement are inherent parts of Jewish legal system, that is clearly not the case in American penal law. Various rationales have been offered to support the use of the death penalty in the American criminal justice system, none of which justifies the death penalty on the grounds of repentance. The notion of repentance would presumably be regarded as an unacceptable introduction of a purely religious motive into a criminal penalty. Any such theory would likely be discredited as a violation of the Establishment Clause, or as a legally improper reliance on religious concepts that have no proper place in American legal thought.

Second, and perhaps more fundamentally, reliance on the text of the Torah to support the death penalty in American law assumes that the text of the Torah is a complete depiction of the Jewish legal system. Such an assumption overlooks another basic premise of Jewish legal and religious thought, which is that as a written text the Torah must be contextually interpreted in order to be understood and applied to a living society. Under Jewish legal theory, in conjunction with the Written Torah, G-d gave to Moses at Mount Sinai an Oral Torah different from, but equal in authority to, the Written Torah. The Oral Torah was orally transmitted from generation to generation and ultimately compiled as the Talmud. Thus, it is difficult and can be misleading to envision the Jewish legal system based solely on the Written Torah. The law relating to capital punishment is a prime example of the need to consider both the Oral and Written Torahs because the Written Torah provides broad principles, and the Oral Torah provides most of the legal details that determine the practical application of the law.

IV. Capital Punishment in the Oral Torah

As Judge Bright accurately observed in Hayes v. Lockhart, "selective quoting" from the text of the Torah to suggest that the ancient Jewish law supports the use of the death penalty is "misleading." Judge Bright further noted that the failure to refer to the Oral Torah ignores the "multitude of procedural barriers" set forth in the Oral Law which render the imposition of the death penalty a rare event. Such safeguards were implemented throughout the Jewish criminal justice process, including during the apprehension of the individual, the introduction of evidence at trial, the deliberations, the rendering of a verdict, and post-verdict proceedings.

The Talmud describes at considerable length the various safeguards to be carried out. Among the most noteworthy safeguards, and perhaps those which most contribute to the infrequency of actual judicial imposition of the death penalty, are: (1) in the process of the apprehension, there must be at least two witnesses who observe the defendant while observing each other; (2) the defendant must be told in advance of the illegality of the offense; (3) the defendant must immediately declare an intention to commit the offense anyway; and (4) must immediately carry it out. Throughout the introduction of evidence, each of the witnesses is rigorously cross-examined while being repeatedly reminded of the grave nature of the proceeding and the dearness of the human life at stake.During the deliberations, any feasible argument for acquittal must be considered by the court, even if the argument was developed by students, who are not allowed to present arguments for conviction. If a guilty verdict is found to be erroneous, the ruling is reversed, while an erroneous acquittal cannot be reversed. After a guilty verdict is returned, messengers are dispatched to announce the verdict and call on anyone who can provide exculpatory information; the court then reconvenes to consider any exculpatory information, including claims made by the defendant. These and numerous other safeguards produced a criminal justice system in which the death penalty was implemented somewhat infrequently—certainly not with the frequency that might be suggested by reading the Written Torah alone.

Perhaps the most dramatic and famous expression of the reluctance of ancient Jewish legal authorities to implement the death penalty is found in a Talmudic dialogue between several Rabbis that transpired shortly after the destruction of the Temple in Jerusalem, a time when courts no longer had the authority to adjudicate capital cases.

Without attributing the statement to any particular individual, the Talmud first asserts that a court which implements the death penalty once in seven years is a violent court. The Talmudic discussion continues with the opinions of authorities who found even rare use of capital punishment to be far too frequent. One such authority is Rabbi Eleazer ben Azaria, who insists that a court that imposes the death penalty even one time in seventy years is a violent court. The Talmud further documents the views of Rabbi Tarfon and Rabbi Akiva, who declare that, had they been members of a court with the authority to adjudicate capital cases, there would never have been an execution. Neither Rabbi Tarfon nor Rabbi Akiva explains the precise reason for his absolute opposition to capital punishment, however, the approach appears to be abolitionist in spirit. The discussion concludes with a retort by Rabbi Simeon ben Gamliel that a total abolition of the death penalty would increase the number of murderers. This response seemingly argues that the death penalty serves in some way as a deterrent to murder and that the abolitionist approach would impede this deterrent effect; the result would be an increase in murders.

Despite the obvious parallels to the current debate over the death penalty, a meaningful application of the views presented in the Talmud requires further analysis of the rationale underlying the various positions, including careful consideration of their religious bases. The abolitionist views of Rabbi Tarfon and Rabbi Akiva, in particular, demand careful examination, because they are sometimes cited in contemporary American legal scholarship to support the abolitionist approach. Indeed, Judge Bright's reference to the "virtual impossibility" of an execution in ancient Jewish law coincides with the views of Rabbi Tarfon and Rabbi Akiva. It is unlikely that the reluctance of other Rabbis to invoke the death penalty, even one time in seven years or in seventy years, necessarily meant that the practice of execution was nearly extinct.

Scholars have suggested a number of theories to explain the abolitionist positions of Rabbi Tarfon and Rabbi Akiva. One theory is that Rabbi Tarfon and Rabbi Akiva were concerned with the abiding possibility of human error, despite the numerous and elaborate safeguards already observed as standard procedure in capital cases. Such concerns certainly resonate throughout the abolitionist movement in the United States. Other scholars suggest that these Rabbis were opposed to capital punishment not only because of the practical uncertainties involved, but because they were opposed to execution in principle, even when the defendant was unquestionably guilty. According to this theory, the Rabbis felt an overriding concern for the sanctity of human life that outweighed any justification for implementing the death penalty. Again, such an approach has been adopted by modern abolitionists who likewise value human life so highly as to preclude the killing of anyone, even proven murderers. Yet, while the concept of the sanctity of human life certainly has an ethical basis not necessarily rooted in religion, Rabbi Tarfon and Rabbi Akiva likely argued from a decidedly religious perspective, which again raises the question of the propriety of utilizing their opinions to decide legal issues in the United States.

Moreover, the views of Rabbi Tarfon and Rabbi Akiva are not representative of the whole of Jewish law; rather, their opinions are two among many and did not represent the opinions of mainstream Jewish legal authorities. Thus, Judge Bright's statement regarding the "virtual impossibility" of an execution in ancient Jewish law reflects a minority opinion. In fact, Professor Blidstein, on whose article Judge Bright's statement was based, deemed Rabbi Akiva to be "the final expositor of a muted tradition." Blidstein further observed that Rabbi Simeon ben Gamliel, who contested the views of Rabbi Tarfon and Rabbi Akiva, "was probably not alone in protesting this virtual abolition of the death penalty. His is merely the clearest voice." The view of Rabbi Simeon ben Gamliel appears to find support in other rabbinic statements, which dispute the overriding concerns that motivated Rabbi Tarfon and Rabbi Akiva. For example, the Rabbis of the Talmud comment on the Biblical verse which instructs that in executing a murderer, "do not pity him." According to the Rabbis, this verse was a response to those who would oppose the execution of a murderer on the grounds that, because the victim is already dead, the taking of another life serves no purpose. As Blidstein explains, "[h]owever generous the motive, the perversion of justice is evil, its motivation misguided. The Rabbis feared that true love of humanity could only be undermined by indiscriminate recourse to 'mercy,' which, as Rabbi Simeon ben Gamliel pointed out, would deny an innocent society the concern shown the criminal."

Similarly, those opinions which decried the use of the death penalty even one time in seven years or in seventy years do not necessarily support opposition to the death penalty in the United States. It is evident that Rabbis who made such statements, despite registering their disapproval of the common use of the death penalty, were not confessed abolitionists. At best, to incorporate such views into American jurisprudence would be to suggest that the current number of executions in the country as a whole—and in the State of Texas in particular—should decrease considerably to prevent the development of "violent courts" in the United States.

Even this modest hypothesis, however, is an inconclusive inference from the statements of the Rabbis. Although their views appear to be based purely on the number of executions that take place, the Rabbis' primary concerns might instead be with the number of executions relative to the general population. Consider that the Jewish population in the land of Israel at that time was probably no larger than a few million; thus, the Rabbis' statements criticized the execution of one out of a few million individuals every seven or seventy years. A proportionate analysis in the United States, a nation of nearly three hundred million people, would result in the condemnation of the execution of approximately one hundred people every seven or seventy years. Although this analysis still supports a suspension in the current pace of executions, the resulting criticism of the current system is somewhat muted. Another relevant consideration is that the Rabbis issued their opinions in the context of a society that was probably not plagued by the level of violence currently experienced in United States. Had they been theorizing in a more violent society, the Rabbis may have approved of larger number of executions.

Conversely, the intense degree of violence that has permeated the United States may ultimately provide the most convincing argument that Jewish law would not support this nation's implementation of the death penalty. The Talmud indicates that forty years prior to the destruction of the Second Temple in Jerusalem, the Sanhedrin—the High Court—moved from its location near the Temple in order to negate its own authority to adjudicate capital cases. According to the Talmud, upon the proliferation of capital offenses, the Court recognized that it could no longer judge these cases properly and subsequently decided not to render death sentences any longer. Despite the mainstream acceptance of capital punishment, the Rabbis evidently believed—and acted accordingly—that if capital offenses are committed to such an extent that courts lose their ability to properly adjudicate such cases, then the death penalty should be suspended. It follows from this view that the proliferation of murders in the United States mandates at least a temporary cessation of capital punishment.

Finally, two factors remain that could complicate any attempt to oppose the death penalty by reference to Jewish law. Both factors involve fundamental components of the Jewish legal system that do not have parallels in American law. The first factor, as previously stated, concerns the uniquely religious considerations that often underlie principles in the Jewish criminal justice system.

The willingness of Jewish legal authorities to limit the use of the death penalty was based, at least in part, on an abiding trust in G-d as the ultimate arbiter of justice. The Talmud relates the belief that even when the High Court ceased to adjudicate capital cases, the Heavenly Court continued to mete out the death penalty through a variety of apparently natural or accidental events.In contrast to the belief in an ultimately Divine form of justice, the United States criminal justice system is premised on the principle that the nation's courts are the final forums of justice. Hence, the view towards man-made justice in the United States is fundamentally inconsistent with the religiously-based aspects of Jewish law that allow for the limitation or abolishment of capital punishment.

The second factor complicating the use of Jewish law to oppose the death penalty is that Jewish law provides for extrajudicial imposition of capital punishment. For example, the Talmud instructs that if the "needs of the hour" so demand, a court may issue a capital sentence without invoking the ordinary evidentiary and procedural safeguards. The Talmud also permits, under extraordinary circumstances, the imposition of the death penalty for offenses that are not ordinarily considered capital offenses. In addition, if a murderer is not subject to the death penalty through the usual judicial process, then the King has the prerogative to execute the murderer based on "societal need" and "the needs of the hour."

The very fact that Jewish law authorizes multiple means for imposing capital punishment weakens modern attempts to rely on Jewish law to oppose the death penalty. It is clear that the extrajudicial imposition of capital punishment is extraordinary even within the Jewish legal system and has no parallel in American law. The existence of extrajudicial alternatives to the judicial imposition of capital punishment probably provided a measure of assurance to some of those authorities who limited the judicial enforcement of the death penalty. If so, it is perhaps less certain that these authorities provide support for modern opponents of capital punishment in the United States, where there are no extrajudicial means for imposing capital punishment.

V. Conclusion

Any student of the law who studies the Jewish legal system and the American legal system will observe many parallels in both substance and methodology. As a result of these parallels and the apparent similarities in the moral beliefs found in Jewish tradition and American society, some legal scholars look to Jewish law to help resolve complex issues in American law, particularly those with deep moral implications.

Inasmuch as the death penalty persists as one of the most complex and controversial moral questions in American legal thought, it is not surprising that courts and legal scholars have turned to Jewish law for guidance. Unfortunately, however, references to Jewish law in the area of the death penalty are often incomplete and inaccurate. A prudent application of Jewish law to the modern death penalty requires a complete analysis of the Jewish legal system in its proper context. In particular, one must acknowledge, appreciate, and understand the interaction between fundamental legal and religious principles that are central to Jewish law in order to make meaningful and illuminating comparisons and contrasts between the Jewish and American legal systems.

Saint Mary's Law Journal, 1998
Symposium: Thoughts on Death Penalty Issues
25 Years after Furman v. Georgia
Essay

Lesson

3

JUSTICE, JUSTICE SHALL YOU PURSUE

STANDARDS OF EVIDENCE IN THE TALMUD

Interieur van een rechtbank (Interior of a Courtroom),
Anonymous; J. Hermans, engraver; Leeuwarden, 1635.
(Rijksmuseum, Amsterdam)

Justice may be blind, but judges and juries must be clear-sighted. This lesson explores the concept of evidentiary standards as it arises in several overlapping areas of Talmudic and secular law: How can we assess the truth of testimony? Does every criminal confession pass muster, or are some inadmissible? When can informants be considered credible?

❓ QUESTION FOR DISCUSSION

Should Brendan Dassey's confession to the rape and murder of Teresa Halbach be considered a voluntary, valid confession?

The Seventh Circuit Court of Appeals hears arguments about the Brendan Dassey case. Thomas Gianni, 2017.

Figure 3.1

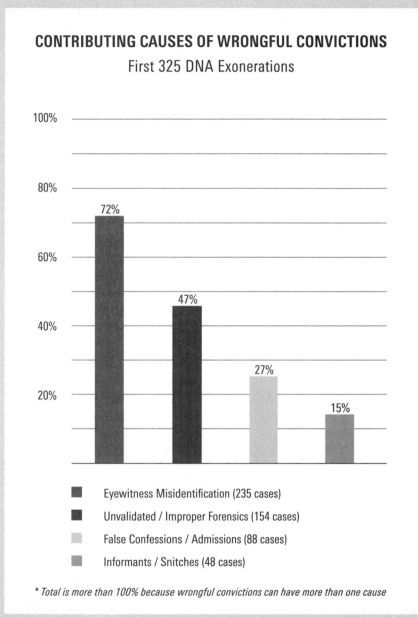

CONTRIBUTING CAUSES OF WRONGFUL CONVICTIONS

First 325 DNA Exonerations

- ■ Eyewitness Misidentification (235 cases)
- ■ Unvalidated / Improper Forensics (154 cases)
- ■ False Confessions / Admissions (88 cases)
- ■ Informants / Snitches (48 cases)

* Total is more than 100% because wrongful convictions can have more than one cause

THE INNOCENCE PROJECT, "CONTRIBUTING CAUSES OF WRONGFUL CONVICTIONS,"
WWW.INNOCENCEPROJECT.ORG

*Watch Brendan Dassey's lawyer, **Professor Steven Drizin**, discuss his client and false confessions:*

MYJLI.COM/CRIME

QUESTION FOR DISCUSSION

If you were on a jury and presented with informant testimony, how would you treat it?

TEXT 1a

DEUTERONOMY 19:15

עַל פִּי שְׁנֵי עֵדִים אוֹ עַל פִּי שְׁלשָׁה עֵדִים יָקוּם דָּבָר.

A matter must be established by the testimony of two or three witnesses.

TEXT **1b**

MAIMONIDES, *MISHNEH TORAH*, LAWS OF THE SANHEDRIN 18:6

גְּזֵרַת הַכָּתוּב הִיא שֶׁאֵין מְמִיתִין בֵּית דִּין וְלֹא מַלְקִין אֶת הָאָדָם בְּהוֹדָיַת פִּיו אֶלָּא עַל פִּי שְׁנַיִם עֵדִים . . .

שֶׁמָּא נִטְרְפָה דַעְתּוֹ בְּדָבָר זֶה. וְשֶׁמָּא מִן הָעֲמֵלִין מָרֵי הַנֶּפֶשׁ הוּא הַמְחַכִּים לָמוּת, שֶׁתּוֹקְעִין הֶחֱרָבוֹת בְּבִטְנָם וּמַשְׁלִיכִין עַצְמָן מֵעַל הַגַּגּוֹת, כָּךְ זֶה יָבֹא וְיֹאמַר דָּבָר שֶׁלֹּא עָשָׂה כְּדֵי שֶׁיֵּהָרֵג. וּכְלָלוֹ שֶׁל דָּבָר גְּזֵרַת מֶלֶךְ הִיא.

RABBI MOSHE BEN MAIMON (MAIMONIDES, RAMBAM) 1135–1204

Halachist, philosopher, author, and physician. Maimonides was born in Córdoba, Spain. After the conquest of Córdoba by the Almohads, he fled Spain and eventually settled in Cairo, Egypt. There, he became the leader of the Jewish community and served as court physician to the vizier of Egypt. He is most noted for authoring the *Mishneh Torah,* an encyclopedic arrangement of Jewish law, and for his philosophical work, *Guide for the Perplexed.* His rulings on Jewish law are integral to the formation of halachic consensus.

It is a scriptural decree that a court cannot execute a person or sentence him to receive corporal punishment on account of a confession, but only based on the testimony of two witnesses. . . .

Perhaps he is mentally disturbed regarding this matter and therefore confessed in error. Or, perhaps he is one of those embittered people who wish for death, who pierce their bellies with swords and throw themselves from the rooftops. We fear that such a person may come and confess to committing an act that he did not perform, so that he will be executed. At any rate, the disqualification of confessions is ultimately a decree of the Divine King.

TEXT **2a**

TALMUD, GITIN 40B

הוֹדָאַת בַּעַל דִין כְּמֵאָה עֵדִים דָמִי.

The confession of a litigant is as strong as the testimony of a hundred witnesses.

BABYLONIAN TALMUD

A literary work of monumental proportions that draws upon the legal, spiritual, intellectual, ethical, and historical traditions of Judaism. The 37 tractates of the Babylonian Talmud contain the teachings of the Jewish sages from the period after the destruction of the Second Temple through the fifth century CE. It has served as the primary vehicle for the transmission of the Oral Law and the education of Jews over the centuries; it is the entry point for all subsequent legal, ethical, and theological Jewish scholarship.

Geketende oude man verschijnt voor de rechter (Chained Old Man Appears in Court), Anonymous, etching; Jan Luyken, printmaker; Amsterdam, 1687. (Rijksmuseum, Amsterdam)

TEXT 2b

RABBI DAVID IBN ZIMRA, *LAWS OF THE SANHEDRIN* 18:6

וְאֶפְשָׁר לָתֵת קְצָת טַעַם, לְפִי שֶׁאֵין נַפְשׁוֹ שֶׁל אָדָם קִנְיָינוֹ אֶלָא קִנְיַן הַקָּדוֹשׁ בָּרוּךְ הוּא. שֶׁנֶּאֱמַר, "הַנְּפָשׁוֹת לִי הֵנָה" (יְחֶזְקֵאל יח, ד) . . . וּמַלְקוֹת פַּלְגוּ דְמִיתָה הוּא. אֲבָל מָמוֹנוֹ הוּא שֶׁלוֹ, וּמִשּׁוּם הָכִי אָמְרִינָן הוֹדָאַת בַּעַל דִין כְּמֵאָה עֵדִים דָמֵי.

וְכִי הֵיכִי דְאֵין אָדָם רַשַּׁאי לַהֲרוֹג אֶת עַצְמוֹ, כֵּן אֵין אָדָם רַשַּׁאי לְהוֹדוֹת עַל עַצְמוֹ שֶׁעָשָׂה עֲבֵירָה שֶׁחַיָּיב עָלֶיהָ מִיתָה.

RABBI DAVID IBN ZIMRA (RADVAZ) 1479–1573

Noted halachist. Radvaz was born in Spain and immigrated to Safed, Israel upon the expulsion of the Jews from Spain in 1492. In 1513, he moved to Egypt and served as rabbi, judge, and head of the yeshiva in Cairo. He also ran many successful business ventures and was independently wealthy. In 1553, he returned to Safed where he would later be buried. He authored what would later become a classic commentary to Maimonides's code of law, and wrote many halachic responsa, of which more than ten thousand are still extant.

It is possible to rationalize this somewhat. Our life does not belong to us; it belongs to G-d. As the verse states, "Behold, life is Mine" (EZEKIEL 18:4). . . . Accordingly, just as we are forbidden to kill ourselves, we are also not allowed to confess to having committed a capital offense. The same applies to any physical punishment.

But our money does belong to us, and therefore the law is that "the admission of a litigant is as strong as the testimony of a hundred witnesses."

RABBI YITSCHAK BEN SHESHET, *RESPONSA* 234

רִאשׁוֹנָה: הִסְתַּפַּקְתֶּם . . . אִם מַעֲלֶה וּמוֹרִיד לְקַבֵּל הוֹדָאָתוֹ אִם לָאו . . .
בְּדִינֵי נְפָשׁוֹת לְפִי שׁוּרַת הַדִּין . . . אֵינוֹ מִתְחַיֵּיב מִיתָה עַל פִּי עַצְמוֹ רַק עַל
פִּי עֵדִים, וְאֵין הוֹדָאָתוֹ מַעֲלֶה וּמוֹרֶדֶת . . .

עַתָּה בִּזְמַנֵּנוּ זֶה מַה שֶּׁדָּנִין בְּדִינֵי נְפָשׁוֹת הוּא לְפִי צוֹרֶךְ הַשָּׁעָה, שֶׁהֲרֵי
בָּטְלוּ דִינֵי נְפָשׁוֹת. אֶלָּא שֶׁבֵּית דִּין מַכִּין וְעוֹנְשִׁין שֶׁלֹּא מִן הַדִּין לְפִי צוֹרֶךְ
הַשָּׁעָה, וְאַף שֶׁלֹּא בְּעֵדוּת גְּמוּרָה, כָּל שֶׁיֵּדְעוּ בַּאֲמַתְלָאוֹת בְּרוּרוֹת שֶׁעָבַר
הָעֲבֵירָה.

לָזֶה נָהֲגוּ לְקַבֵּל הוֹדָאַת פִּי הָעוֹבֵר אַף בְּדִינֵי נְפָשׁוֹת, לְמַעַן יִתְבָּרֵר הַדָּבָר
גַּם מִתּוֹךְ דְּבָרָיו עִם קְצָת אֲמַתְלָאוֹת אִם אֵין עֵדוּת בְּרוּרָה.

**RABBI YITSCHAK BEN SHESHET
(RIVASH) 1326–1408**

Halachist. Rivash studied under Rabbeinu Nisim of Gerona (Ran) in Barcelona, and served as rabbi there and in other important Jewish communities in Spain. Because of the eruption of anti-Jewish riots in 1391, he fled to North Africa and settled in Algiers. He was the first to address the halachic status of Marranos. Rivash's halachic responsa are his most important work; they contain sources no longer extant and served, in part, as a basis for the Code of Jewish Law.

Your first question was . . . whether or not it is advantageous to receive the suspect's confession. . . .

The letter of the law is that in capital cases . . . one can only be sentenced to death based on witness testimony, not one's own confession. A confession would have no impact whatsoever on the case. . . .

But nowadays, when we judge capital cases, it is based on the need of the time. We no longer have the Torah-based authority to judge capital cases, and our authority is premised on the allowance for courts to administer punishment even when strict Torah law would not sanction it. This allows us to rule on cases even without clear eyewitness testimony, so long as we have clear logical proof that the crime was committed.

Our practice is, therefore, to receive the offender's confession even in capital cases. This is done to enable us to discern the facts of the case from his words, together with some supporting evidence, if we do not have clear eyewitness testimony.

The Insult, from the series *Les Gens de Justice* (*Barristers*), Honoré Daumier, lithograph cartoon, 1845. (The Phillips Collection, Washington)

TEXT **4**

RABBI YOSEF CARO, *RESPONSA BEIT YOSEF* 8

גּוּלְמַאי דַּאֲמָרִינָן דְּאִיכָּא לְמֵיחַשׁ שֶׁמָּא מֵאֵימַת הַיִּסּוּרִים הוֹדוּ מַה שֶׁלֹּא עָשׂוּ...

יֵשׁ לוֹמַר, דְּלֹא חַיְישִׁינָן לְהָכִי. דְּהָנֵי מִילֵי כְּשֶׁמְיַיסְּרִים אוֹתוֹ עַד שֶׁיוֹדֶה אִם הָרַג לִפְלוֹנִי, דְּהָתָם כְּשֶׁיוֹדֶה שֶׁהָרְגוּ לֹא יְיַסְּרוּהוּ עוֹד.

אֲבָל כְּשֶׁמְיַיסְּרִים אוֹתוֹ שֶׁיוֹדֶה מַה שֶׁעָשָׂה, אֵין דֶּרֶךְ לִבְדוֹת מִלִּבּוֹ מַה שֶׁלֹּא עָשָׂה וְלַעֲמוֹד בְּדִיבּוּרוֹ. שֶׁאֵינוֹ נִפְטָר בְּכָךְ מִן הַיִּסּוּרִין, דְּאַדְרַבָּה, הוֹדָאָתוֹ זֹאת סִבָּה שֶׁיְיַסְּרוּהוּ עוֹד לוֹמַר תּוֹדֶה יוֹתֵר. אֲבָל כְּשֶׁלֹּא יוֹדֶה... יִהְיֶה יוֹתֵר קָרוֹב שֶׁלֹּא יְיַסְּרוּהוּ עוֹד.

וּכְבָר הוֹכַחְתִּי דְּבִנְדוֹן דִּידָן לֹא הָיוּ שׁוֹאֲלִין לָרַצְחָנִים שֶׁיוֹדוּ אִם הָרְגוּ לַיְהוּדִי הַזֶּה וְלַהוֹלְכִים בְּחֶבְרָתוֹ, אֶלָּא שֶׁיוֹדוּ מַה שֶׁעָשׂוּ. וְאִם כֵּן אֲפִילוּ יְיַסְּרוּ אוֹתָם עַד שֶׁיוֹדוּ, נֶאֱמָנִים. דְּאִי לָאו דְּקוּשְׁטָא קָאָמְרֵי, לֹא הָיוּ מוֹדִים...

וְעוֹד יֵשׁ לוֹמַר, שֶׁמֵּאַחַר שֶׁהֶחָקֹר לֹא הִזְכִּיר שֶׁיְיַסְּרָם אֵין לָנוּ לְהוֹסִיף עַל דְּבָרָיו. וְאֶפְשָׁר דְּבְלֹא יִסּוּרִים הוֹדוּ לוֹ כֵּן, עַל יְדֵי שֶׁהֶחְלִיקָן בִּדְבָרִים שֶׁיוֹדוּ כָּל מַה שֶׁעָשׂוּ וְיִפְטְרֵם, שֶׁכֵּן דֶּרֶךְ הַחוֹקְרִים לְדַבֵּר לָרַצְחָנִים. הִילְכָּךְ שַׁפִּיר אִיכָּא לְמִיסְמָךְ אַדִּבְרֵי רַצְחָנִים הַלָּלוּ.

**RABBI YOSEF CARO
(MARAN, *BEIT YOSEF*) 1488–1575**
Halachic authority and author. Rabbi Caro was born in Spain but was forced to flee during the expulsion in 1492 and eventually settled in Safed, Israel. He authored many works including the *Beit Yosef, Kesef Mishneh,* and a mystical work, *Magid Meisharim*. Rabbi Caro's magnum opus, the Shulchan Aruch (Code of Jewish Law), has been universally accepted as the basis for modern Jewish law.

You argued that we should be concerned about the possibility that the murderers confessed to something they did not do because of the fear of torture. . . .

I believe that this is not a concern in our case. People are prone to falsely confess if they are tortured and asked to confess to killing so and so. In this case, their confession will spare them from more torture.

But when a person is tortured and asked to confess to everything he has done, he will not falsely confess to crimes he did not commit and continue to stand by his confession later. Such a confession will not spare him from torture; on the contrary, it will invite more torture in order to extract further confessions from him. Refusal to confess . . . would be more likely to save him from torture.

It has already been established that in our case the murderers were not specifically asked to confess to killing this Jew and his companions. Rather, they were asked to confess to all crimes they have committed. Therefore, even if the confession was obtained through torture, it can be believed. For had they not actually committed the crime they would not have confessed to it. . . .

In addition, since their interrogator did not mention that they had been tortured, we should not automatically assume this was the case. He may have sweet-talked them into confessing by telling them they would be pardoned if they confessed all of their crimes. Interrogators often do this with suspects. Therefore, we can accept the testimony of these murderers.

Exercise 1

Fill in the following chart with Rabbi Caro's opinion about the reliability of different types of confessions.

	GENERAL	SPECIFIC TO A CRIME
Torture	Reliable / Unreliable	Reliable / Unreliable
Sweet-talk	Reliable / Unreliable	Reliable / Unreliable

QUESTION FOR DISCUSSION

Based on this text, would Rabbi Caro accept Brendan Dassey's confession as reliable?

Luke Berg, assistant Wisconsin Attorney General, argues against overturning the conviction of Brendan Dassey, before the U.S. Seventh Circuit Court of Appeals. Cheryl Cook, 2017.

Figure 3.2

Criminal Confessions in Jewish Law

1 Under strict Torah law, no criminal confessions are accepted.

2 Under emergency law, a completely voluntary confession can be considered credible if there is some corroborating evidence.

3 Giving an incentive to make a confession concerning any crimes in general that may have been committed—without specifically mentioning a particular crime—does not taint a specific confession given in response. If the suspect was incentivized to confess a specific crime, the confession is not considered reliable.

*Watch **Professor Steven Drizin**, cofounder of the **Center on Wrongful Convictions of Youth**, and noted lawyer and author **Scott Turow** discuss deceptive interrogation tactics, self-incrimination, guilty pleas, and other due process issues:*

MYJLI.COM/CRIME

TEXT **5**

TALMUD, BAVA BATRA 29A

> רָבָא אָמַר, כְּגוֹן דְּאָתוּ בֵּי תְּרֵי וְאָמְרִי: אֲנַן אַגְרִינָן מִינֵּיה, וְדָרִינָן בֵּיה תְּלַת שְׁנִין בִּימָמָא וּבְלֵילְיָא.
>
> אָמַר לֵיה רַב יֵימַר לְרַב אַשִׁי: הַנֵּי נוֹגְעִין בְּעֵדוּתָן הֵן. דְּאִי לֹא אָמְרִי הָכִי, אַמְרִינָן לְהוּ: זִילוּ הָבוּ לֵיה אַגַּר בֵּיתָא לְהַאי.
>
> אָמַר לֵיה דַּיָּינֵי דְּשָׁפִילֵי הָכִי דָּאִינֵי. מִי לֹא עַסְקִינָן כְּגוֹן דְּנָקְיטִי אַגַּר בֵּיתָא וְאַמְרִי, לְמַאן לֵיתְבֵי?

Rava said: A possessor can establish presumptive ownership of a house if two witnesses come and testify, "We rented the house from him and lived in it for three years, day and night."

Rabbi Yeimar said to Rabbi Ashi: These tenants should be disqualified as witnesses because they have an interest in their testimony. If they do not testify so, and the current possessor loses ownership, they will be told, "Go and pay rent for the past three years to the legal owner."

Rabbi Ashi replied to Rabbi Yeimar: Indeed, in such a scenario only an ignorant judge would accept the testimony. The testimony of the tenants can only be considered reliable if they are still holding the unpaid rent for their three years of residence and are asking, "Whom should we give it to?"

TEXT  **6**

MAIMONIDES, *MISHNEH TORAH*, LAWS OF TESTIMONY 16:4

וּדְבָרִים אֵלּוּ אֵינָן תְּלוּיִין אֶלָּא בְּדַעַת הַדַּיָּין וְעוֹצֶם בִּינָתוֹ שֶׁיָּבִין עִיקַר
הַמִּשְׁפָּטִים וְיֵדַע דָּבָר הַגּוֹרֵם לְדָבָר אַחֵר וְיַעֲמִיק לִרְאוֹת. אִם יִמְצָא שֶׁיֵּשׁ
לָזֶה הָעֵד צַד הֲנָאָה בְּעֵדוּת זוֹ אֲפִילּוּ בְּדֶרֶךְ רְחוֹקָה וְנִפְלָאָה הֲרֵי זֶה לֹא
יָעִיד בָּהּ.

These matters depend on the assessment of the judges and the depth of their perception. They must understand the legal principles, know how one thing leads to another, and carefully consider whether the witness will derive benefit from the testimony. Even if the benefit will come about in a distant and uncommon manner, they should not allow that person to testify.

Duyfken en Willemynken voor de magistraat (*Duyfken and Willemynken for the Magistrate*), anonymous; Boetius Adamsz Bolswert, engraver; c. 1590–1627. (Rijksmuseum, Amsterdam)

TEXT 7

RABBI BINYAMIN SOLNIK, *MASAT BINYAMIN* 98 🔯

לְפִי מַעֲמָד . . . שֶׁעָשָׂה הָעֵד כְּמַר בָּרוּךְ עִם הָאִשָּׁה שֶׁאִם יוֹעִיל עֵדוּתוֹ
שֶׁתִּהְיֶה מוּתֶּרֶת לְהִנָּשֵׂא שֶׁתִּתֵּן לוֹ הָאִשָּׁה שָׂכָר כַּךְ וְכַךְ, וְאִם לֹא יוֹעִיל
עֵדוּתוֹ תִּתֵּן לוֹ פָּחוֹת מִסַּךְ זֶה.

שֶׁזֶּה וַדַּאי נוֹגֵעַ בְּעֵדוּת הוּא וְעֵדוּתוֹ בָּטֵל וּפָסוּל מִדְּאוֹרַיְיתָא.

The agreement . . . that Mr. Baruch made with the woman was that if his testimony successfully results in her being allowed to remarry, he will receive a certain sum of money. But if his testimony is not successful, they agreed that he will receive a smaller amount of money.

Mr. Baruch is certainly a biased witness and his testimony is disqualified by Torah law.

RABBI BINYAMIN SOLNIK
1550–1619

Polish Talmudist. Rabbi Solnik served as rabbi in the cities of Silesia and Podhajce and was a leading member of the "Council of Four Lands" that governed Jewish communal affairs in Eastern Europe. Rabbi Solnik is best known for his work of halachic responsa, *Masat Binyamin*.

TEXT **8**

RABBI AVRAHAM SHAPIRA, *TECHUMIN*, VOL. 3, PP. 238–239

מַה שֶּׁאַתָּה שׁוֹאֵל שְׁאֵלָה אַקְטוּאֵלִית - הַיַּחַס לְ"עֵד מְדִינָה", הַמְקוּבָּל כְּהֶסְדֵּר תָּקֵף בַּמְּדִינָה.

הַהֲלָכָה מִתְיַחֶסֶת לְכָךְ בִּשְׁלִילָה. הָעֵד נוֹגֵעַ בַּדָּבָר, וְאֵיךְ נַאֲמִין לוֹ? אָמְנָם עֶקְרוֹנִית יֵשׁ לַמְּדִינָה סַמְכֻיּוֹת מְסֻיָּמוֹת מִדִּין הַמַּלְכוּת בְּעִנְיְנֵי פְּלִילִים, אַךְ גְּבוּל יֵשׁ לַדָּבָר . . .

אָמְנָם יֵשׁ לְעַיֵּן אִם יֵשׁ לִפְסוֹל טוֹטָלִית אֶת הַשִּׁמּוּשׁ בְּעֵד מְדִינָה. יִתָּכֵן וְיֵשׁ לְהַבְחִין בֵּין פְּשָׁעִים שׁוֹנִים; כַּאֲשֶׁר מְדוּבָּר בְּמוּעָדִים לִפְשָׁעִים הַחֲשׁוּדִים בְּרֶצַח, יֵשׁ סַכָּנָה לַצִּיבּוּר, וַהֲרֵי זֶה גּוֹבֵל בְּפִיקוּחַ נֶפֶשׁ מַמָּשׁ, וְיֵשׁ מָקוֹם לְהָקֵל. אַךְ כְּלָלִית יֵשׁ לְהִתְרַחֵק מִדֶּרֶךְ זוּ . . .

אָמְנָם יֵשׁ לְהֵיעָזֵר בְּעֵד כָּזֶה לְשֵׁם גִּילּוּי מִסְמָכִים וְהוֹכָחוֹת יְדוּעוֹת רַק לוֹ וְכוּ', אַךְ לֹא לְקַבֵּל דְּבָרָיו כִּפְשׁוּטָם.

RABBI AVRAHAM ELKANA KAHANA SHAPIRA 1914–2007

Chief Rabbi of Israel. Raised in Jerusalem, Rabbi Shapira studied at the Chevron Yeshiva, and went on to teach at and head Yeshivat Merkaz Harav for more than 60 years. A leading rabbinic figure in Israel's Religious Zionist movement, Rabbi Shapira served as a judge in Israel's rabbinic court system, and in 1983 was elected as the fifth Ashkenazi Chief Rabbi of Israel. His Talmudic lectures have been published as *Shiurei Maran HaGra Shapira*, and his halachic writings were collected in *Minchat Avraham*.

Regarding your practical question about state witnesses, which is accepted in this country as a valid arrangement:

Halachah negates this. The witness is biased: How can he be believed? It is true that the state has the power to make new regulations regarding criminal law, but this too has its limits. . . .

However, we need to consider whether the use of state witnesses should be completely banned. Perhaps we can distinguish between different crimes. Known criminals who are suspected of murder are a danger to the public, bordering on actual endangerment of life. Regarding such people, there is room to be lenient and accept the testimony of cooperating witnesses against them. But as a general rule we should distance ourselves from this path. . . .

It is, however, possible to make use of such a witness in order to uncover documents and evidence that only he knows about. But we cannot accept the words of these witnesses at face value.

*Robert Meeropol acknowledges that his father **Julius Rosenberg** spied for the Soviets, but argues that his mother **Ethel Rosenberg** was framed by a cooperating witness. Hear his side of the story:*

MYJLI.COM/CRIME

The Jury, George Bellows, planographic prints, 1916. (Amon Carter Museum of American Art, Fort Worth, Texas)

KEY POINTS

1 Jewish law does not accept confessions as evidence in criminal cases, considering it possible that mental illness or a self-harming intent can cause false confessions.

2 In civil cases, Jewish law does accept confessions. In monetary matters the prospect of false confession isn't considered of such concern, because people have the right to do as they wish with their money.

3 Under the relaxed evidentiary standards of Jewish "emergency law," freely offered confessions can be accepted in criminal cases if they are supported by corroborating evidence.

4 If a suspect was incentivized to confess to a specific crime, their confession is considered unreliable, even under "emergency law." However, a general incentive to confess to any crimes committed does not taint a specific confession received as a result.

5 Jewish law does not accept testimony from biased witnesses, even in civil cases. Consequently, testimony offered by an incentivized informant would be disqualified as unreliable.

6 Even under the standards of "emergency law," incentivized testimony is inadmissible in court, unless the incentive was offered in general terms, not for

Should the use of criminal confessions be more—or less—restricted?
***Take a poll** at:*

MYJLI.COM/CRIME

information related to a specific case. Nevertheless, incentivized testimony can be valuable as an investigative tool to help uncover new evidence that can be evaluated independently.

7 The standard of evidence required by Jewish law would make the job of prosecutors significantly more difficult. But it would also reduce the number of wrongful convictions and build greater public confidence in the justice system.

Appendix

TEXT 9

JOSHUA 6:16–19, 7:1–12, 18–25

וַיֹּאמֶר יְהוֹשֻׁעַ אֶל הָעָם . . . וְהָיְתָה הָעִיר חֵרֶם, הִיא וְכָל אֲשֶׁר בָּהּ . . . וְרַק אַתֶּם שִׁמְרוּ מִן הַחֵרֶם, פֶּן תַּחֲרִימוּ וּלְקַחְתֶּם מִן הַחֵרֶם, וְשַׂמְתֶּם אֶת מַחֲנֵה יִשְׂרָאֵל לְחֵרֶם וַעֲכַרְתֶּם אוֹתוֹ. וְכֹל כֶּסֶף וְזָהָב וּכְלֵי נְחֹשֶׁת וּבַרְזֶל קֹדֶשׁ הוּא לַה' אוֹצַר ה' יָבוֹא . . .

וַיִּמְעֲלוּ בְנֵי יִשְׂרָאֵל מַעַל בַּחֵרֶם, וַיִּקַּח עָכָן בֶּן כַּרְמִי בֶן זַבְדִּי בֶן זֶרַח לְמַטֵּה יְהוּדָה מִן הַחֵרֶם, וַיִּחַר אַף ה' בִּבְנֵי יִשְׂרָאֵל.

וַיִּשְׁלַח יְהוֹשֻׁעַ אֲנָשִׁים מִירִיחוֹ הָעַי אֲשֶׁר עִם בֵּית אָוֶן מִקֶּדֶם לְבֵית אֵ-ל, וַיֹּאמֶר אֲלֵיהֶם לֵאמֹר, עֲלוּ וְרַגְּלוּ אֶת הָאָרֶץ, וַיַּעֲלוּ הָאֲנָשִׁים וַיְרַגְּלוּ אֶת הָעָי.

וַיָּשֻׁבוּ אֶל יְהוֹשֻׁעַ וַיֹּאמְרוּ אֵלָיו, אַל יַעַל כָּל הָעָם כְּאַלְפַּיִם אִישׁ אוֹ כִּשְׁלֹשֶׁת אֲלָפִים אִישׁ יַעֲלוּ וְיַכּוּ אֶת הָעָי, אַל תְּיַגַּע שָׁמָּה אֶת כָּל הָעָם כִּי מְעַט הֵמָּה.

וַיַּעֲלוּ מִן הָעָם שָׁמָּה כִּשְׁלֹשֶׁת אֲלָפִים אִישׁ, וַיָּנֻסוּ לִפְנֵי אַנְשֵׁי הָעָי. וַיַּכּוּ מֵהֶם אַנְשֵׁי הָעַי כִּשְׁלֹשִׁים וְשִׁשָּׁה אִישׁ וַיִּרְדְּפוּם לִפְנֵי הַשַּׁעַר עַד הַשְּׁבָרִים וַיַּכּוּם בַּמּוֹרָד, וַיִּמַּס לְבַב הָעָם וַיְהִי לְמָיִם. וַיִּקְרַע יְהוֹשֻׁעַ שִׂמְלֹתָיו וַיִּפֹּל עַל פָּנָיו אַרְצָה לִפְנֵי אֲרוֹן ה' עַד הָעֶרֶב, הוּא וְזִקְנֵי יִשְׂרָאֵל, וַיַּעֲלוּ עָפָר עַל רֹאשָׁם.

וַיֹּאמֶר יְהוֹשֻׁעַ, אֲהָהּ ה' אֱלֹקִים, לָמָה הֵעֲבַרְתָּ הַעֲבִיר אֶת הָעָם הַזֶּה אֶת הַיַּרְדֵּן לָתֵת אֹתָנוּ בְּיַד הָאֱמֹרִי לְהַאֲבִידֵנוּ, וְלוּ הוֹאַלְנוּ וַנֵּשֶׁב בְּעֵבֶר הַיַּרְדֵּן. בִּי ה', מָה אֹמַר אַחֲרֵי אֲשֶׁר הָפַךְ יִשְׂרָאֵל עֹרֶף לִפְנֵי אֹיְבָיו. וְיִשְׁמְעוּ הַכְּנַעֲנִי וְכֹל יֹשְׁבֵי הָאָרֶץ וְנָסַבּוּ עָלֵינוּ וְהִכְרִיתוּ אֶת שְׁמֵנוּ מִן הָאָרֶץ, וּמַה תַּעֲשֵׂה לְשִׁמְךָ הַגָּדוֹל.

וַיֹּאמֶר ה' אֶל יְהוֹשֻׁעַ, קֻם לָךְ לָמָּה זֶּה אַתָּה נֹפֵל עַל פָּנֶיךָ. חָטָא יִשְׂרָאֵל וְגַם עָבְרוּ אֶת בְּרִיתִי אֲשֶׁר צִוִּיתִי אוֹתָם וְגַם לָקְחוּ מִן הַחֵרֶם וְגַם גָּנְבוּ וְגַם כִּחֲשׁוּ וְגַם שָׂמוּ בִכְלֵיהֶם. וְלֹא יֻכְלוּ בְּנֵי יִשְׂרָאֵל לָקוּם לִפְנֵי אֹיְבֵיהֶם, עֹרֶף יִפְנוּ לִפְנֵי אֹיְבֵיהֶם כִּי הָיוּ לְחֵרֶם. לֹא אוֹסִיף לִהְיוֹת עִמָּכֶם אִם לֹא תַשְׁמִידוּ הַחֵרֶם מִקִּרְבְּכֶם . . .

וַיִּלָּכֵד עָכָן בֶּן כַּרְמִי בֶן זַבְדִּי בֶן זֶרַח לְמַטֵּה יְהוּדָה. וַיֹּאמֶר יְהוֹשֻׁעַ אֶל עָכָן, בְּנִי שִׂים נָא כָבוֹד לַה' אֱלֹקֵי יִשְׂרָאֵל וְתֶן לוֹ תוֹדָה, וְהַגֶּד נָא לִי מֶה עָשִׂיתָ אַל תְּכַחֵד מִמֶּנִּי.

וַיַּעַן עָכָן אֶת יְהוֹשֻׁעַ וַיֹּאמַר, אָמְנָה אָנֹכִי חָטָאתִי לַה' אֱלֹקֵי יִשְׂרָאֵל וְכָזֹאת וְכָזֹאת עָשִׂיתִי. וָאֶרְאֶה בַשָּׁלָל אַדֶּרֶת שִׁנְעָר אַחַת טוֹבָה וּמָאתַיִם שְׁקָלִים כֶּסֶף וּלְשׁוֹן זָהָב אֶחָד חֲמִשִּׁים שְׁקָלִים מִשְׁקָלוֹ וָאֶחְמְדֵם וָאֶקָּחֵם, וְהִנָּם טְמוּנִים בָּאָרֶץ בְּתוֹךְ הָאָהֳלִי וְהַכֶּסֶף תַּחְתֶּיהָ.

וַיִּשְׁלַח יְהוֹשֻׁעַ מַלְאָכִים וַיָּרֻצוּ הָאֹהֱלָה, וְהִנֵּה טְמוּנָה בְּאָהֳלוֹ וְהַכֶּסֶף תַּחְתֶּיהָ. וַיִּקָּחוּם מִתּוֹךְ הָאֹהֶל וַיְבִאוּם אֶל יְהוֹשֻׁעַ וְאֶל כָּל בְּנֵי יִשְׂרָאֵל וַיַּצִּקֻם לִפְנֵי ה'.

וַיִּקַּח יְהוֹשֻׁעַ אֶת עָכָן בֶּן זֶרַח וְאֶת הַכֶּסֶף וְאֶת הָאַדֶּרֶת וְאֶת לְשׁוֹן הַזָּהָב וְאֶת בָּנָיו וְאֶת בְּנֹתָיו וְאֶת שׁוֹרוֹ וְאֶת חֲמֹרוֹ וְאֶת צֹאנוֹ וְאֶת אָהֳלוֹ וְאֶת כָּל אֲשֶׁר לוֹ וְכָל יִשְׂרָאֵל עִמּוֹ, וַיַּעֲלוּ אֹתָם עֵמֶק עָכוֹר.

וַיֹּאמֶר יְהוֹשֻׁעַ מֶה עֲכַרְתָּנוּ, יַעְכָּרְךָ ה' בַּיּוֹם הַזֶּה.

[When the Israelites laid siege to Jericho,] Joshua commanded the army . . . "the city and all that is in it are to be consecrated to G-d. . . . Keep away from the consecrated things, so that you will not bring about your own destruction by taking any of them. Otherwise you will make the camp of Israel liable to destruction and bring trouble on it. All the silver and gold and the vessels of bronze and iron are sacred to G-d and must go into His treasury. . . ."

But the Israelites were unfaithful and trespassed against the consecrated property: Achan son of Carmi, the son of Zavdi, the son of Zerach, of the tribe of Judah, took some of them. G-d's anger flared against the Israelites.

Joshua sent men from Jericho to Ai, which is near Beth-aven, east of Beth-el, and told them, "Go up and spy out the land." The men went up and spied out Ai.

They returned to Joshua and said to him, "Not all the people will have to go up against Ai. Send two or three thousand men to take it and do not weary the whole people, for only a few people live there."

About three thousand men went up, but they were routed by the men of Ai, who killed about thirty-six of them. They chased the Israelites from the city gate until Shebarim and struck them down on the downward slope. At this the hearts of the people melted and became like water. Joshua tore his clothes and fell facedown to the ground before the Ark of G-d, remaining there until evening. The elders of Israel did the same, and sprinkled dust on their heads.

Joshua said, "Alas, O G-d, why did you bring this people across the Jordan to deliver us into the hands of the Amorites to make us perish? If only we had been content to dwell on the other side of the Jordan! Please, my G-d, what should I say now that Israel has turned their back fleeing from its enemies? The Canaanites and all the other inhabitants of the land will hear about this and they will surround us and wipe out our name from the earth. What will You do for Your great name?"

G-d said to Joshua, "Stand up! What are you doing down on your face? Israel has sinned—they have violated My covenant that I commanded them to keep; they have taken from the consecrated property; they have stolen; they have lied; and they have placed it among their own possessions. The Israelites will not be able to stand against their enemies; they will turn their backs to their enemies and run because they have become worthy of destruction. I will not continue to be with you until you destroy the consecrated property from your midst. . . ."

Achan son of Karmi, the son of Zavdi, the son of Zerach, of the tribe of Judah was singled out by a lottery. Joshua said to Achan, "My son, please give honor to the G-d of Israel, and give a confession to Him. Tell me please what you have done; do not hide it from me."

Achan answered Joshua and said, "Indeed I have sinned against the G-d of Israel, and thus have I done. I saw among the spoils a beautiful robe from Babylonia, two hundred shekels of silver, and a bar of gold weighing fifty shekels. I coveted them and took them. They are hidden in the ground inside my tent, with the silver underneath."

Joshua sent messengers. They ran to the tent, and there it was, hidden in his tent, with the silver underneath. They took the things from the tent, brought them to Joshua and all the Israelites and spread them out before G-d.

Joshua, together with all of Israel, took Achan son of Zerach, the silver, the robe, the gold bar, his sons and daughters, his ox, his donkey and sheep, his tent, and all that he had, to the Valley of Achor.

Joshua said, "Why have you ruined us? G-d will ruin you on this day."

Additional Readings

MAIMONIDES, MIRANDA, AND THE CONUNDRUM OF CONFESSION:
SELF-INCRIMINATION IN JEWISH AND AMERICAN LEGAL TRADITIONS

BECKY ABRAMS GREENWALD

All footnotes have been removed to conserve space. To read the complete article, visit www.myjli.com/crime.

Introduction

Reliability and ethical concerns surrounding self-incriminating statements have plagued legal systems for centuries. In the United States, self-incriminating statements may not be involuntarily coerced or compelled. In the words of the Fifth Amendment, "[n]o person . . . shall be compelled in any criminal case to be a witness against himself." What are the roots of the privilege against self-incrimination? In Miranda v. Arizona, Chief Justice Warren noted that the roots of the privilege go back to ancient times. Citing the Jewish philosopher Maimonides, the Court wrote, "[t]hirteenth century commentators found an analogue to the privilege grounded in the Bible. 'To sum up the matter, the principle that no man is to be declared guilty on his own admission is a divine decree.'"

Given the different historical contexts in which ancient Jewish law and modern American law emerged and functioned, it is unsurprising that concerns surrounding self-incrimination are articulated differently in the two traditions. In Jewish criminal law, there is a seemingly complete ban on self-incriminating statements. In contrast, the American privilege against self-incrimination bars only involuntary or compelled self-incrimination, implying that most confessions, freely given, would be accepted.

Scholarship has focused on the distinctions between the Jewish and American iterations of the principle

BECKY ABRAMS GREENWALD

Lawyer and historian. She holds degrees from Columbia and the Cardozo School of Law.

against self-incrimination. Scholars, for example, characterize Jewish law's approach as an absolute ban on confessions, contrasting it with the "timid and ineffectual" American Miranda protections. They argue that, while the Jewish rule against self-incrimination was "unique and all encompassing," Miranda has been "Tuckered to death," its progressive protection "all but snuff[ed] out" by later decisions and exceptions. They juxtapose the Jewish rule, in which "[n]o blurring of the bright line was permitted," with American protections "lacking . . . a coherent approach."

This Note questions whether a comparison of Jewish and American law on self-incrimination can properly be described in such reductionist and dichotomous terms. Instead, the Note argues that the two legal systems are similar in a certain sense. Both systems express concerns about self-incriminating statements but also accept such statements in particularly demanding situations. Part I traces three long-standing rationales for the privilege against self-incrimination in both Jewish and America law: reliability; respect for the autonomy, self-determination, and privacy of the individual; and the religious belief that criminal confessions can be offered only to G-d. After Part I's explanation of why self-incriminating statements are not judicially accepted, Part II describes circumstances in Jewish and American law when self-incriminating statements are accepted.

Part III uses the comparison of the two traditions to unearth a deeper understanding of the tensions within self-incrimination and confession. It suggests that both Jewish and American law reflect similar conflicting desires —to encourage and also to reject self-incriminating statements. On the one hand, confessions appear to be powerful evidence of guilt and a helpful part of the process of solving crimes and rehabilitating criminal offenders. On the other hand, confessions uncomfortably turn the accused into his own accuser, raising concerns about whether the confession was the result of unreliable internal self-destructive instincts or external coercion. This tension is also evident in the persistent cultural belief in the righteousness of confession alongside increased interest in the DNA-based exoneration of defendants who had falsely confessed.

I. THE IDEAL: REJECTING SELF-INCRIMINATING STATEMENTS
A. Jewish Law
First, a word of background on Jewish law. According to Jewish tradition, the divine revelation at Mount Sinai produced a written law (the Torah) and an oral law (summarized in the Talmud). The Talmud is comprised of the Mishnah and the Gemara. The oral law was handed down from generation to generation and memorized in order to explain the precepts of the written law. However, as time went on, oral transmission became more difficult. The majority view is that at the end of the second century CE, Rabbi Judah Ha-Nasi redacted the Mishnah, reducing to writing the halakhic ("legal") parts of the oral law. The Babylonian Talmud, believed to have been compiled at the end of the fifth century CE, reflects the discussion that occurred in the Babylonian academies regarding the Mishnah, "a kind of précis of the typical debates of the talmudic sages." In the post- Talmudic period, legal authorities around the world continued to debate, interpret, and codify Biblical and Talmudic precepts. For example, Maimonides' Mishneh Torah, written in the twelfth century CE, is one of the most authoritative works published in this post-Talmudic period.

In this Part, I explain the sources and rationales behind the privilege against self-incrimination in Jewish law. Maimonides described the rejection of self-incriminating statements based on the assumption that they may be false and unreliable. However, an examination of the Talmudic sources that predated Maimonides reveals a concern not only with reliability, but also with the privacy and autonomy of the individual who, even if reliably guilty of some forbidden act, should not be made to testify against himself. Finally, I present the explanation of Radbaz, a commentator on Maimonides, who explained the privilege based on the spiritual conception that humans cannot—even reliably or voluntarily —surrender their bodies and souls for punishment since both belong to G-d.

1. The Unreliability of Confessions and the Psychological Impulses of Confessors

Moshe ben Maimon, known in Hebrew as Rambam and in English as Maimonides (1138-1204), is one of the most important Jewish thinkers. He codified the privilege against self-incrimination in the criminal context in his treatise on Jewish courts. "It is a scriptural decree that the court shall not put a man to death or flog him on his own admission (of guilt). . . . To sum up the matter, the principle that no man is to be declared guilty on his own admission is a divine decree." Thus, confessions in the criminal context appear to be wholly rejected.

The principle applies not only to self-incriminating statements made by defendants, but also to self-incriminating statements made by witnesses. According to Jewish law, a witness is disqualified if he is found to be a *rasha*, a transgressor. In his treatise on evidence, Maimonides writes, "No man becomes ineligible [to be a witness] on his own admission of religious delinquency. . . . [N]o man can incriminate himself."

Maimonides, in addition to codifying the rule against self-incrimination, does not just explain the rule as a divine decree that cannot be understood. Rather, Maimonides offers a rationale for the rule — at least in the context of confessions by defendants. He writes:

> The Sanhedrin [court] . . . is not empowered to inflict the penalty of death or of flagellation on the admission of the accused. For it is possible that he was confused in mind when he made the confession. Perhaps he was one of those who are in misery, bitter in soul, who long for death, thrust the sword into their bellies or cast themselves down from the roofs. Perhaps this was the reason that prompted him to confess to a crime he had not committed, in order that he might be put to death.

Here Maimonides paints a vivid picture of the type of person who would confess to a capital crime: someone who is unstable, depressed, and suicidal —and not necessarily guilty. According to Maimonides, the reason behind the law against self-incrimination is that we fear the admission may not be reliable. Maimonides believed some people suffering from intense depression might confess to crimes they did not commit in order to bring physical harm, including death, upon themselves.

Norman Lamm, a contemporary rabbi and past president of Yeshiva University, has expounded on this rationale and supplemented it with insight from modern psychoanalytic theory. As Lamm explains, Maimonides recognized what Freud, some seven hundred years later, described as the Death Wish or Death Instinct, "an inherent tendency of life to revert to its lifeless origin, which is the inorganic state, or death." Sometimes the Death Wish results in homicide; however, if frustrated, it may be "redirected towards the self" and result in suicide. Similarly, Lamm cites Freud's disciple, Karl Menninger, who explained that even if a person is not driven to actually take his own life, he may display other forms of self-destruction. Often the internal impulses may cause a person to relegate the destruction to a third party, in this case the court, which would explain why one would confess to a crime instead of simply taking one's own life. "Thus," Lamm concludes, "modern psychoanalytic theory supports Maimonides' explanation of the Halakhic view on self-incrimination, an explanation which relies on the universality of the instinct of self-destruction."

2. Critiques Based on Moral Considerations and Respect for the Individual

In addition to Maimonides' psychological rationale, other sources suggest additional rationales questioning the use of confessions. The principle against self-incrimination appears in the Talmud in the context of a debate about whether witnesses are disqualified on the basis of self-incriminating statements. Sanhedrin 9b deals with the testimony of a potential witness who has engaged in an illicit sexual act with the person on trial for committing the act. One school

of thought, attributed to Rabbi Joseph, is that if the witness testifies that the accused committed the act with him forcibly, the witness' testimony is accepted. However, if the witness admits that he acceded to the act, the witness is a *rasha*, a transgressor, according to his own testimony, and is disqualified from acting as a witness. In other words, according to Rabbi Joseph, a witness can be disqualified based on self-incriminating statements.

A second school of thought, articulated by Rava, is that a person cannot disqualify himself by establishing himself as a *rasha*. Since self-incriminating statements are rejected, the witness' testimony against himself (that he participated in an illicit act) is not accepted, the witness is not rendered a *rasha*, and his testimony regarding the defendant is accepted. Thus, he can join with another witness in testifying against the accused. This is accomplished through the legal concept that testimony is divisible. According to Rabbi Joseph, testimony is not divisible; the court accepts all of the testimony or none of it. Rava, however, holds that testimony is divisible, and therefore he accepts the part of the witness' testimony that is not self-incriminating. Interestingly, here the rejection of the self-incriminating statement by the witness leads to the inclusion of testimony that is incriminating with regard to the defendant.

Similarly, the Talmud in Yevamot 25a and 25b addresses the concept of splitting self-incriminating testimony of witnesses. Here, the Talmud deals with the issue of a woman whose marital status is ambiguous due to the undetermined fate of her husband. If her husband is found to be dead, she is deemed a widow and may remarry. However, if her husband is alive but missing, she is still married and cannot remarry. The Talmud deals with the case of a witness who claims he knows the husband is dead because he (the witness) killed him. The majority view is that in such a case, the testimony of the witness is accepted and the woman may remarry, though she may not marry the witness. However, Rabbi Judah says that if the witness testifies that he (the witness) killed the husband, the witness' testimony is rejected, and the woman may not remarry.

The Talmud questions the majority approach: How can we accept the testimony of a witness who is an admitted murderer? The Talmud reconciles the majority approach as one in line with the position of Rava from Sanhedrin, namely the position of divided testimony. The majority holds that the court rejects the part of the testimony that is self-incriminating — that the witness murdered the husband —but accepts the part that is not self-incriminating —that the husband is dead.

Both views expressed in the Talmud suggest a more complex understanding of self-incriminating testimony than Maimonides offered. On the one hand, Rava and the majority view in Yevamot advocate splitting testimony, accepting the part of a witness' statement that is incriminating of others, but rejecting the part that is self-incriminating. However if, as Maimonides suggests, the testimony of one who confesses to committing a crime is unreliable, why do we accept any part of the testimony? On the other hand, according to Rabbi Joseph and Rabbi Judah, if the witness makes statements incriminating both himself and others, all of the witness' testimony is rejected because the testimony of a transgressor is invalid. However, by labeling the witness a transgressor, Rabbi Joseph and Rabbi Judah show that they believe the witness' statement that he has transgressed. In other words, Rabbi Joseph and Rabbi Judah reject the testimony of a confessing witness because they view the witness' statement as reliable. Both of these schools of thought, then, are in contrast to Maimonides' view, which, as we have seen, viewed confessions as inherently unreliable.

The positions in the Talmud point to an additional reason behind the rule against self-incrimination: that a person cannot disqualify himself from testifying by establishing himself a transgressor because "a person is considered related to himself." Testimony by relatives is not accepted. Just like a person cannot testify regarding a relative, so too a person cannot testify regarding himself, because one's closest relative is oneself. One could argue that here again is an argument about reliability. Just as we cannot trust the biased account of a person's relative, we cannot rely on a person's own testimony because a person is not an objective or reliable source of information regarding himself. However, one could also argue that the rationale here is a deeper one: that a person cannot testify against a relative because the court should not turn family members against one another. The law creates a separation between a person's private family and the public forum in which those family members must testify against the accused.

Similarly, a person cannot testify against himself because "a person is considered related to himself" and it would be a gross encroachment on a person's dignity to allow him to make the case for his own physical punishment or death. As Professor Moshe Halbertal writes, "The rejection of self-incrimination is based on the argument that the legal system should not allow someone to harm himself through its own laws. It is about immunity from self-harm and preserving the autonomy of the person in relationship to the legal stature." According to this view, a Jewish court does not reject confessions because they are unreliable, as Maimonides suggested, but because of the infringement on autonomy that comes from hinging an individual's punishment on his own statements.

3. The Spiritual Approach: One Cannot Give What One Does Not Own

Rabbi David ben Zimra (sixteenth century CE), also known as Radbaz, offers a more spiritual approach to the privilege against self-incrimination. According to Radbaz, criminal confessions are problematic because they involve the surrendering of one's life or body for punishment. In Radbaz's view, a person may confess to a civil offense and render himself liable for a monetary punishment because a person's money is his to give. However, a person may not confess to a crime that would require giving up his body for punishment because his body and soul do not belong to him. According to Radbaz, a person's body and soul belong to G-d. Just as it is prohibited for a person to take his own life, so too, a court may not kill or flog an offender based on his own statements.

In sum, while Maimonides was concerned about the truthfulness or accuracy of confessions, and the Talmud appears concerned with the moral consequences of convicting a man based on his own self-destructive testimony, Radbaz harbors a religious or spiritual concern that man cannot decide to destroy a life that G-d has created.

B. American Law

The U.S. Supreme Court has relied on the Fifth, Sixth, and Fourteenth Amendments to delineate the boundaries of American confession law. Based on these constitutional principles, the Court has excluded certain self-incriminating statements made by defendants from their criminal trials. Unlike the Jewish rule that on its face appears to exclude all confessions ("no man is to be declared guilty on his own admission"), American law excludes only those self-incriminating statements that are involuntary, coerced, or compelled. This Part examines the same three rationales from Part I.A in the American law context.

1. The Unreliability of Coerced Confessions: Explaining Voluntariness

As in Jewish law, one of the concerns that underlie the privilege against self-incrimination in American law is reliability. However, in the American tradition, only involuntary confessions are seen as unreliable. In 1884, the Supreme Court recognized the common law rule prohibiting the use of confessions obtained by inducements, promises, or threats, and explained its reliability rationale. "A confession, if freely and voluntarily made, is evidence of the most satisfactory character." However, "the presumption upon which weight is given to such evidence, namely, that one who is innocent will not imperil his safety or prejudice his interests by an untrue statement, ceases when the confession appears to have been made either in consequence of inducements . . . or because of a threat or promise . . . ." In other words, whereas voluntary self-incriminating statements are reliable because they are statements against a person's interest that have been confessed only out of sheer and overbearing guilt about the truth of crimes committed, involuntary confessions are the product of fear or hope and are not reliable recitations of the truth.

Eventually, the voluntariness standard received constitutional support from the Due Process Clause of the Fourteenth Amendment. In Brown v. Mississippi, a sheriff and "a number of white men" rounded up the defendants, described as "ignorant negroes," and declared them guilty of murder. In order to secure confessions, the "defendants were made to strip and they were laid over chairs and their backs were cut to pieces with a leather strap with buckles on it." The Court found the defendants' confessions involuntary and therefore inadmissible because they were secured only after brutal whipping and torture. Referring to the defendants' "so-called confessions" as "spurious" and "extorted," the Court held that the defendants' rights to due process were violated because "[i]t would be difficult to conceive of methods more revolting to the sense of justice than those taken to procure the confessions of these petitioners." While the Court was troubled by the race-based brutality and blatant due process violations that the defendants suffered, it was also concerned that the spurious and extorted nature of the confessions rendered them completely unreliable.

The Court has rejected confessions produced from violence based upon reliability concerns in other cases as well. In Stein v. New York, for example, the Court wrote that the tendency "to risk remote results of a false confession rather than suffer immediate pain is so strong that judges long ago found it necessary to . . . treat[ ] any confession made concurrently with torture or threat of brutality as too untrustworthy to be received as evidence of guilt." The Court described the Fourteenth Amendment as a "guarantee against conviction on inherently untrustworthy evidence," and explained that a coerced confession "vitiates a conviction because such a confession combines the persuasiveness of apparent conclusiveness with what judicial experience shows to be illusory and deceptive evidence." Involuntary confessions are rejected, in other words, because they may simply be false.

2. Beyond Reliability: Banning Coercive Confessions Because of Fundamental Values and Respect for Individual Rights

In addition to the reliability thread that runs through the case law, the Supreme Court has also offered other rationales for rejecting self-incriminating statements. Characterizing the privilege against self-incrimination as "one of the great landmarks in man's struggle to make himself civilized," the Court has described some of these other rationales as reflecting: "many of our fundamental values and most noble aspirations"; "our sense of fair play which dictates a fair state-individual balance . . . by requiring the government in its contest with the individual to shoulder the entire load"; and "our respect for the inviolability of the human personality and of the right of each individual to a private enclave where he may lead a private life." These rationales share an emphasis not on the questionable accuracy of confession evidence, but on the moral responsibility of the state to respect the autonomy, self-determination, and privacy of the individual.

For example, in determining whether confessions satisfy the Due Process voluntariness standard, the Court has focused both on the reliability of the statement and on whether it was the product of the defendant's "free will." The Court relied upon various fact-specific factors, such as personal characteristics of the accused (his age, educational background, mental abilities) and the level of deprivation or mistreatment by the police (including physical and psychological pressure) to decide whether the confession was voluntarily and freely offered by the defendant. Here, the emphasis is less on reliability and more on the moral belief that "men are not to be exploited for the information necessary to condemn them." It is the state, not the defendant citizen, who must "produce the evidence against him by the independent labor of its officers, not by the simple, cruel expedient of forcing it from his own lips." This is similar to the argument we extrapolated from the Talmud in Part I.A.2, namely, that the privilege against self-incrimination preserves the autonomy of the person in relation to the legal system.

In 1966, in the watershed decision of Miranda v. Arizona, the Supreme Court "declared that the Fifth Amendment is the touchstone for determining the admissibility of any statements obtained through custodial interrogation by government officials." The Fifth Amendment states, "[n]o person . . . shall be compelled in any criminal case to be a witness against himself." The Miranda Court held that when a person is taken into custody and interrogated by the police, any self-incriminating statements are inherently compelled unless the suspect is given certain warnings. The warnings that the Court required are the now-famous right to remain silent, right to know that statements made can be used in a court of law, and right to an attorney, either retained or appointed. Thus, instead of having to dissect a suspect's state of mind under a Due Process Clause voluntariness analysis, the Court set a bright line rule —the need for police to articulate specific warnings —that would be easier to apply.

A cursory look at Miranda and the Fifth Amendment reveals a strikingly different general principle than the one articulated in Jewish law. Although the Fifth Amendment only prohibits compelled self-incrimination (no one may be compelled to testify against himself), Jewish law is articulated as a blanket rejection of all self-incrimination (no one is to be declared guilty on his own admission). However, a closer look at Miranda reveals a more similar schema. Specifically, the Miranda Court assumed that all custodial interrogations were coercive environments, and therefore that all incriminating statements made by suspects in the course of custodial interrogations (in the absence of warnings) were coerced and inadmissible. A ban on all self-incriminating statements made during custodial interrogation sounds quite similar to a ban on confessions generally.

Moreover, it is possible that the Miranda Court assumed that by requiring police to warn every suspect in clear and unequivocal terms of his right to silence and to counsel, suspects would, on the whole, cease making self-incriminating statements altogether. Indeed, in Justice Harlan's dissent in Miranda, he argued that, "the new rules are not designed to guard against police brutality or other unmistakably banned forms of coercion . . . . Rather, the thrust of the new rules is to negate all pressures, to reinforce the nervous or ignorant suspect, and ultimately to discourage any confession at all." Similarly, Justice White wrote in dissent:

> *The obvious underpinning of the Court's decision is a deep-seated distrust of all confessions. As the Court declares that the accused may not be interrogated without counsel present, absent a waiver*

of the right to counsel, and as the Court all but admonishes the lawyer to advise the accused to remain silent, the result adds up to a judicial judgment that evidence from the accused should not be used against him in any way, whether compelled or not . . . that it is inherently wrong for the police to gather evidence from the accused himself.

Of course, the dissenters' vision of Miranda is not universally accepted. The Miranda majority itself wrote explicitly, "[W]e do not purport to find all confessions inadmissible. Confessions remain a proper element in law enforcement." Nevertheless, it would be plausible and logical to assume that by rendering all custodial interrogations coercive and ordering police to clearly warn defendants of their right to silence and counsel, Miranda would drastically reduce the number of confessions obtained in criminal prosecutions.

Upon closer inspection, it appears the Jewish and American rules on self-incrimination are similar in that they both reflect a strong hesitance toward using confessions as evidence against the accused. Underlying the Court's resistance to confession is a restatement of the self-determination rationale. Its focus is on the right of the individual against the state. The privilege is a "substantive right," and reflects the "respect a government —state or federal —must accord to the dignity and integrity of its citizens." Thus, while the language of the Fifth Amendment prohibits only compelled self-incrimination, in Miranda, the Court revealed its discomfort with accepting self-incriminating statements more generally.

3. The Religious or Spiritual Approach

The privilege against self-incrimination in American law has been explained in spiritual and religious terms as well. Abe Fortas, before becoming a Supreme Court Justice, described the privilege as recognition that every person is "entitled to treatment as an individual in G-d's image, and not merely as a vessel of the state." Just as Radbaz felt that a person's body and soul were not his to give, Fortas writes that a person's life is his "inviolable temple." He describes the privilege as intangible, just like "man's immortal soul." For Fortas, confession is so deeply private and powerful

that it belongs only in a private exchange with G-d. "A man may be punished, even put to death, by the state; but . . . he should not be made to prostrate himself before its majesty. Mea culpa belongs to a man and his G-d. It is a plea that cannot be exacted from free men by human authority."

Similarly, scholars have also described the rationale behind the privilege in religious or spiritual terms. For example, Robert Gerstein has described the substance of confessions as "a special sort of information," including "the admission of wrongdoing, the self-condemnation, the revelation of remorse." According to Gerstein, these revelations should be regarded as "a matter between a man and his conscience or his G-d," just as a person's religious opinions are regarded as between himself and his G-d. Gerstein analogizes self-condemnation in criminal law to self-condemnation in religious experience, where he identifies a similar emphasis on the privacy of confessions. In this context, he cites Puritan leaders in the late sixteenth century who decried the practice of public confession: "Much more is it equall that a mans owne private faults should remayne private to G-d and him selfe till the L-rd discover them . . . the magistrate should [[not]] seeke into the offenses of his subjects and not by oathe to rifle the secretts of theare hearts."

II. CONFRONTING REALITY: EXCEPTIONS WHEN SELF-INCRIMINATING STATEMENTS ARE ACCEPTED

A. Jewish Law

Although the Jewish rule on self-incrimination appears to be a blanket ban on confessions, this Part will explore various exceptions to the rule that have been utilized throughout history, namely the royal prerogative, the emergency exception, and the existence of corroborating evidence.

1. Royal Prerogative

Although some commentators locate biblical support for the privilege against self-incrimination, the Bible also contains examples of individuals who are punished based on self-incriminating statements. For example, in 2 Samuel chapter one, the story is told about an Amalekite who recounts to David a narrative of

King Saul's death. After battle, the Amalekite appears before David and says that Saul and Saul's son Jonathan are dead:

> I happened to be at Mount Gilboa, and I saw Saul leaning on his spear, and the chariots and horsemen closing in on him. He looked around and saw me, and he called to me. When I responded, 'At your service,' he asked me, 'Who are you?' And I told him that I was an Amalekite. Then he said to me, 'Stand over me, and finish me off, for I am in agony and am barely alive.' So I stood over him and finished him off . . . . Then I took the crown from his head and the armlet from his arm, and I have brought them here to my lord.

Immediately upon hearing the news, David weeps, mourns, and rebukes the young man for daring to kill King Saul. Thereupon, David orders his attendant to kill the Amalekite, and says, "Your blood be on your own head! Your own mouth testified against you when you said, 'I put the L-rd's anointed to death.'"

While David seems to have been convinced of the reliability of the confessing bearer of bad news, the reader of the story will know that in the previous chapter, the death of Saul was recounted differently:

> Saul said to his arms-bearer, 'Draw your sword and run me through, so that the uncircumcised may not run me through and make sport of me.' But his arms-bearer, in his great awe, refused; whereupon Saul grasped the sword and fell upon it. When his arms-bearer saw that Saul was dead, he too fell on his sword and died with him.

Here we may see, as Maimonides feared, that one of the fundamental problems with confessions is their unreliability.

The story of King David and the Amalekite allows us to explore several situations in which Jewish law allows acceptance of self-incriminating statements. Many commentators are quick to point out that there are various exceptions to the general rule against self-incrimination that could justify David's actions. One explanation is that David was not bound by the ordinary rules of criminal procedure because he was a king. Some rabbis relied upon this royal prerogative exception in the context of medieval Spain where the Spanish king gave Jewish communities the authority to adjudicate disputes between Jewish litigants. In that time, the problem of Jewish informers, individual Jews who would submit allegations about other Jews to the secular authorities, posed a most serious danger to the Jewish community. A report by a Jewish informer could bring fines and even expulsion upon an entire Jewish community. It was in the case of one such informer that Shlomo ben Aderet (1235-1310), known as Rashba, used the "law of the king" reasoning to allow a loosening of the laws regarding acceptable evidence in a Jewish court. He writes: "[P]unishment is meted out by royal prerogative even on the basis of the testimony of relatives and even on the basis of the confession of the accused himself . . . for royal justice seeks the truth only (regardless of procedure)." "For if you do not grant this," Rashba continues, "but insist strictly upon Torah law as fulfilled by the Sanhedrin [the chief Jewish court], the world would be destroyed."

Rashba was able to use the exception of royal justice to suspend some of the traditional requirements of criminal procedure required by Jewish law. His language, though, also hints that the strict traditional rules were intended to be circumvented in certain situations. The rules, in other words, reflected an ideal: a judicial system in which no one ever had to be put to death. As Rashba notes, the Rabbinic sages had said that, "Every Sanhedrin that executes two times is called a murderous [court]." And yet, a reality also existed in which dangerous crimes took place, and Jewish leaders needed to be able to respond. David did not have to stand by when a man confessed to murdering an Israelite king, and Rashba did not have his hands tied when the Jewish community of medieval Spain needed a way to deal effectively with informers who would bring destruction upon the community. While as a general rule self-incriminating statements were rejected, in circumstances such as these, they were allowed.

2. Emergency Exception
A second explanation of David's actions and second exception to the rule against self-incrimination is that

David was acting in the case of an emergency. The Talmud says that as a rule, a court has the authority to impose extralegal penalties when the times demand it. This exception was also relied upon in medieval Spain. For example, Rabbi Isaac ben Shesheth Barfat [Perfet] (1326-1408), known as Ribash, expounded on the emergency doctrine in a letter to the officials of the Jewish community of Teurel, a city in the province of Aragon. The communal leaders wrote to Ribash regarding a Jewish informer who had confessed to reporting to the secular authorities. Ribash recognized that in capital cases, "according to the strict letter of the law no heed is paid to a confession . . . and his confession makes no difference." However, he writes, in light of the "emergency needs of the times," and since "the times demand it," the Jewish court may impose flagellation and pronounce capital sentences "even without full [Talmudically required] evidence."

As Ribash also notes in his letter, the very fact that the Jewish court was meting out punishments of flagellation and the death penalty at that time was because of the emergency doctrine. "[T]he fact that we do judge capital cases in these times, although capital jurisdiction has been suspended [Talmudically] is due to the emergency needs of the times." Thus, the emergency exception was one that "permeated the judicial procedure of the authorities combatting crimes which were regarded as serious breaches of morality and public order" when the times demanded it. As with the royal prerogative exception, the emergency exception seems a realistic acknowledgment that no rule is ever appropriate at all times and places.

3. Corroborating Evidence
A third explanation of David's actions in the Bible and an exception to the general rule against self-incrimination is that the case of the confessing Amalekite contained corroborating evidence—Saul's crown and armlet. A similar case is found in 2 Samuel, chapter four, where David condemns two men to death on the basis of their admission to killing Ish-bosheth. When the two men, Rechab and Baanah, bring the head of Ish-bosheth to David, David responds by putting them to death. Here too we have a case of punishment based on self-incriminating statements,

but with the added indicia of reliability of corroborating evidence—in this case the decapitated head of the victim.

Indeed, in modern day Israel (which, although a secular system, is informed by Jewish tradition) the rule is that a confession must be supplemented by an additional element of corroboration in order to convict a defendant. In Al Bahiri v. State of Israel, Chief Justice Menachem Elon explained that the reason for the requirement that to suffice for a conviction there be "something in addition" to a defendant's confession is to counteract Maimonides' fear that "there may have been 'internal pressure' on the defendant, who may blame himself for a crime that someone else has committed." Elon explained the modern rule as an outgrowth of the traditional Jewish rule. He wrote that while Jewish law originally "maintained that a defendant's self-incriminating confession was absolutely inadmissible," over the course of time, "with the changing needs of the times and of society, various changes were made towards easing the methods of proof in criminal law." One of these major changes was the ability to convict a defendant based upon his confession, but only if there was "some measure of corroboration to support the veracity of the confession."

As with the other exceptions, the acceptance of confessions when accompanied by corroborating evidence seems to be a compromise approach that was meant to admit confessions when the court could be satisfied as to the reliability of the confession. According to Elon, "This approach seems most appropriate both in terms of justice to the defendant, who should not be convicted if innocent, and in terms of finding the truly guilty parties, who should not be allowed to escape the legally prescribed punishment." While the existence of corroboration might satisfy Maimonides' accuracy concerns, it would not rebut the other rationales underlying the privilege against self-incrimination, namely, a person's inalienable right to privacy and autonomy, and the religious problems with allowing a person to take his own life via the criminal system.

To sum up, the basic Jewish law is that no one may be convicted on the basis of his confession. However, over time, the rule has been interpreted malleably in certain instances. Confessions were accepted based on royal authority, in times of emergency, and when enough other corroborating evidence was available. Interestingly, the exceptions were treated less like deviations and more like a reflection that Jewish law itself seems to expect and authorize the exceptions when necessary to meet overriding goals.

B. American Law

Although many viewed Miranda as a radical decision, and it created a bright line rule of exclusion for statements made by suspects in custodial interrogation not preceded by warnings and waiver, many further exceptions to the rule against self-incrimination beyond those enumerated in Miranda have developed. Some even argue that the exceptions have swallowed the rule. Empirical studies have also shown that Miranda has had little effect on the overall ability of the police to obtain confessions. This section will explore three exceptions to the Miranda exclusionary rule: impeachment, emergency, and the Miranda-endorsed exception of waiver. These exceptions describe situations in which self-incriminating statements made by a suspect during custodial interrogation without sufficient warnings can be used in court.

1. Impeachment

In Harris v. New York the Court limited Miranda by holding that while a defendant's Miranda-defective self-incriminating statements may not be used in the government's case-in-chief, those statements may be used to impeach the credibility of a defendant who chooses to testify. In Harris, for example, the police had failed to warn the defendant of his right to counsel before interrogating him. Therefore, while the defendant's subsequent incriminating statement could not be used as substantive proof of the offense of selling drugs, his statement was lawfully raised by the prosecution in its cross-examination of Harris. The Court justified the decision by stating that, "[t]he shield provided by Miranda cannot be perverted into a license to use perjury by way of a defense, free from the risk of confrontation with prior inconsistent utterances."

Harris' impeachment exception to Miranda is significant because impeachment evidence can be misconstrued as substantive evidence by juries. Thus, a defendant who has made a Miranda-defective confession is faced with a dilemma. Either the defendant may choose to testify on his own behalf, knowing that his confession may be read in court —even though it was offered without the proper Miranda warnings —or he may choose not to testify and face a greater chance of conviction.

2. Emergency

The emergency exception allows officers to question a suspect without Miranda warnings in the case of an emergency. Any incriminating statements that a defendant makes can then be used against him in court, even though Miranda warnings were not given. For example, in New York v. Quarles, two officers were approached by a woman who said she had been raped by a man carrying a gun. With the victim's assistance, the police were able to locate a suspect in a nearby supermarket. While apprehending the suspect, the officer noticed the suspect's shoulder holster was empty and asked him where the gun was. The suspect gestured toward some empty cartons and said, "the gun is over there." The police uncovered the gun from one of the cartons. The defendant's response to the officer's question was later used at his trial. The Court, citing "overriding considerations of public safety," held that the officer was allowed to ask Quarles about the gun without warnings because the officer "needed an answer to his question not simply to make his case against Quarles but to insure that further danger to the public did not result from the concealment of the gun in a public area."

3. Waiver

Perhaps the biggest limitation to Miranda protection of criminal defendants — found in the Miranda decision itself —is that Miranda rights are waivable. Once a defendant waives his rights, any of his subsequent self-incriminating statements can be used in court, as long as the government can show that the waiver was voluntary, knowing, and intelligent. In determining the boundaries of voluntary, knowing, and intelligent waivers, the Court has held that a defendant does not have to know the subject of the interrogation in order to waive. Additionally, the Court has held that a defendant can validly waive his right to counsel, and his confession can be admitted, even though he was not told that an attorney hired by a family member was trying to contact him.

The Court has found that a defendant waives his right to silence or to an attorney just by talking to the police. If a defendant wishes to invoke, rather than waive, his right to silence or counsel, the invocation must be "unambiguous" and "unequivocal." This means, as Justice Sotomayor pointed out in a stinging dissent in Berghuis v. Thompkins, that a suspect who wishes to invoke his right to remain silent must "counterintuitively, speak —and must do so with sufficient precision to satisfy a clear-statement rule that construes ambiguity in favor of the police."

Finally, according to the language of Miranda, once a defendant invokes his right to silence or counsel, interrogation must cease. However, subsequent case law has established that after a defendant invokes his right to silence, the police can continue to interrogate him after waiting two hours.

III. DUELING INTERESTS: EXPLAINING THE COMPARISON

While scholars have focused on the differences between the Jewish and American perspectives on self-incrimination, and some have pointed out ways in which the lessons of one tradition should be extended to the other, this Note has highlighted certain similarities. Part I illustrated the parallels between the rationales offered for the privilege against self-incrimination in both systems. Both traditions express concerns about the reliability of confessions, as well as the human dignity and privacy concerns that arise when a person's word is used to convict him. Both traditions also contain strains of an argument that confession is so inherently private that it belongs in the realm of thoughts shared only with G-d. This Note has also argued that a broad reading of the Miranda decision, as envisioned by the dissents and perhaps even by the majority, looks similar to the Jewish ban on confession.

Part II described how, in both Jewish and American law, some jurists have relaxed the rules rejecting or limiting self-incriminating evidence, allowing more expansive forms of self-incriminating testimony to be considered in certain instances. Exceptions were made to the Jewish ban on confessions in cases of exigency, royal prerogative, and where corroborating evidence was available. So too, in American law, the Supreme Court created a number of exceptions to Miranda's supposedly bright line rule of exclusion by allowing incriminating statements to be used in the cases of impeachment, exigency, and waiver.

While the similarities between Jewish and American law are intriguing and previously under-explored, I am careful not to overstate them. To start, the heritages of the two traditions are quite different. Jewish law has a three-thousand-year history during which Jews have lived in varying degrees of autonomy and political subservience, and in geographic areas across the globe. The American Constitution, by contrast, is less than three hundred years old, and is operational in U.S. courtrooms every day. Moreover, the two rules are not identical. The Jewish approach derives from the principle that no one may render himself guilty on his own admission, which is certainly distinct from the American principle, that focuses on ensuring that confessions are voluntary and uncompelled. The exceptions to the Jewish and American rules are also distinct. While the Jewish exceptions from the Middle Ages related to Jewish informers, a limited problem that posed extreme danger to the Jewish community, the American exceptions to the privilege against self-incrimination have more sweeping consequences. Most basically, for example, the waivability of Miranda rights, recognized by the Miranda Court itself, is a profound limitation on the rights to silence and to counsel.

This Note argues that both Jewish and American law —operating in markedly different times, places, and contexts —reflect a simultaneous attraction toward and repulsion from self-incriminating statements, revealing a tension inherent in the subject of confession. Underlying the complex history of the right against self-incrimination is "the law's semiconscious struggle to come to terms with the difficult, layered, perplexing notion of the speech-act that follows from the statement 'I confess.'"

The tension within confession law represents two different ways of looking at confessions. On the one hand, some view confession as an act that should be encouraged. They believe that through confession comes self-recognition, reflection, and hopefully reformation and rehabilitation. On the other hand, some view confessions as extremely intimate and private, as well as suspicious and vulnerable to elicitation through coercion. These two visions of confession are ever-present and always in tension, and this struggle is reflected in the law.

For some, confessions are virtuous. Justice Scalia, for example, in a scathing dissent in Minnick v. Mississippi, felt that "even if I were to concede that an honest confession is a foolish mistake, I would welcome rather than reject it." "More fundamentally," he writes, "it is wrong, and subtly corrosive of our criminal justice system, to regard an honest confession as a 'mistake.' While every person is entitled to stand silent, it is more virtuous for the wrongdoer to admit his offense and accept the punishment he deserves." For Justice Scalia, confessions are desirable because they show that a person takes responsibility for his actions and recognizes his shortcomings in an effort to "do what is right." According to Justice Scalia, we should "rejoice at an honest confession, rather than pity the 'poor fool' who has made it; and we should regret the attempted retraction of that good act, rather than seek to facilitate and encourage it."

Justice Scalia's view of confession is apparent in other aspects of American law and culture as well. As his dissent notes, the U.S. Sentencing Guidelines allow for a reduction in sentence if a defendant accepts responsibility for his actions and aids the government in its investigation. Similarly, it is a common belief that if one makes a mistake or commits a bad act, the best course of action is to come clean and tell the truth. "Confession of misdeeds has become part of the everyday pedagogy of Western societies, normally with the understanding that recalcitrance in confession will aggravate punishment, while full confession will both cleanse the soul and provide possible mitigation of sanctions." One need only turn on any

television channel to view someone —either fictional or not —confessing to a misdeed.

This redemptive view of confession is apparent in Jewish tradition as well. At the beginning of the Book of Genesis, a number of people commit sins. First, Adam eats from the tree of knowledge, the only tree that was forbidden to him in the Garden of Eden. Later, Adam's son, Cain, kills his brother Abel. Adam's reaction when confronted about his sin is to shift blame to Eve: "The woman You put at my side —she gave me of the tree, and I ate." However, according to some traditions, unlike Adam's passing the buck, Cain's response to his crime and punishment is confession and repentance. A fascinating midrash, a rabbinic text, recounts an interaction between Adam and Cain, father-and-son criminals as it were. According to the story, Cain appeared happy. His father asked him, "What happened with your judgment?" Cain responded, "I repented and am reconciled." Suddenly Adam begins beating his head and exclaims, "How awesome is the power of repentance, and I did not know!" The midrash underscores the power and importance of repentance, and highlights the cathartic and rehabilitative effect that confession and repentance can provide.

However, despite the possibly cathartic effect of confessions, both American and Jewish traditions contain other viewpoints heavy with the awareness that confessions can also be both undesirable and lethally misleading. In Escobedo v. Illinois, the Court noted that "a system of criminal law enforcement which comes to depend on the 'confession' will, in the long run, be less reliable and more subject to abuses than a system which depends on extrinsic evidence independently secured through skillful investigation." First, reliance on confessions —which are such powerful pieces of evidence —can lead to insufficient investigation of the crime and inadequate exploration of other evidence and suspects. Second, reliance on confessions can encourage police misconduct. "The simple and peaceful process of questioning breeds a readiness to resort to bullying and to physical force and torture. If there is a right to an answer, there soon seems to be a right to the expected answer —that is, to a confession of guilt." A well-intentioned use of the seemingly incontrovertible evidence of confession, the reasoning goes, can grow into a system of abuse. Therefore, according to the Court, "[A]ny system of administration which permits the prosecution to trust habitually to compulsory self-disclosure as a source of proof must itself suffer morally thereby." The Court's conclusions echo the centuries of both American and Jewish concern that systems founded on self-incriminating statements may prove fatally, fundamentally unsound.

Such concerns have been bolstered in recent years by advancements in the fields of scientific DNA analysis and psychology. According to the Innocence Project, there have been 316 convictions overturned in the United States based on DNA evidence. In approximately 25% of those cases, "innocent defendants made incriminating statements, delivered outright confessions or pled guilty." In addition to the irrational self-destructive tendencies of the human psyche, scholars have attributed false confessions to psychological techniques used by police officers, which can cause even innocent people to confess. According to Professors Richard Ofshe and Richard Leo, psychological interrogation techniques limit and control the alternatives available to suspects, and then rely on the natural human tendency to make "optimizing choices" given the available alternatives. In addition, the literature highlights that vulnerable populations — such as children and the mentally ill —are especially likely to falsely confess because they have undeveloped judgment, cannot fully appreciate and evaluate risks in decision-making, are easily persuaded, and are eager to please authority figures.

In sum, we are left with two ways of viewing confessions: as statements that provide important details about the commission of a crime and reflect a positive acceptance of responsibility by a defendant; and as unreliable statements that are too often attained by manipulation. Our sense of what confession is and does "hovers in a zone of uncertainty that has much to do with the multiform nature of confession and its uses for cleansing, amelioration, conversion, counseling, as well as conviction." As legal understanding moves ever forward, jurists must grapple with self-incriminating statements while keeping sight of this tension. Future decisions involving self-incriminating statements must be made with an awareness of the benefits of utilizing self-incriminating statements but also of the hesitations that have animated both traditions regarding such statements.

Conclusion

This Note has shown how two disparate legal systems struggle to strike a fair balance in applying the privilege against self-incrimination. On the one hand, there are many reasons to reject self-incriminating evidence —suspicions of unreliability, respect for personal integrity, the need for boundaries between state and individual, and the exceedingly private and self-destructive nature of confessions. On the other hand, self-incriminating evidence may be the missing piece in solving the puzzle of a crime. Weighed against the values of protecting the innocent and respecting the dignity of defendants are the values of reaching justice on behalf of victims and protecting society from perpetrators of violence. In addition, confessions can enable guilty defendants to admit their crimes and begin the process of rehabilitation. An examination of the American and Jewish legal systems reveals that, whichever values take precedence in a particular case, the decision whether to admit or reject a confession will always involve a conundrum: Do we believe the confessor that he has raped, murdered, or stolen but assert that he is now telling the truth? Or, do we refuse to accept that he is a rapist, murderer, or thief but find him to be liar?

New York University Law Review, November, 2014

Lesson

CLEAN SLATE

HOW DO CRIMINALS MAKE AMENDS?

Unattributed illustration posted on *Prison Culture* blogsite, June 7, 2011.

What is the ultimate aim of the criminal justice system? If society seeks restitution for crimes and rehabilitation for criminals, it needs a better plan. It must consider what rehabilitation looks like, for which offenders and offenses it is applicable, and how to ensure sentencing contributes to this end. This class examines the extensive, systematic program of repentance laid out in the Talmud and considers what insights this process holds for the above questions and present-day criminal rehabilitation.

TEXT 1

BASED ON: "NOTTINGHAM TEEN JAILED FOR MANSLAUGHTER
AFTER CRICKET FAN'S DEATH," BBC.COM, NOVEMBER 2011

James Hodgkinson, a twenty-eight-year-old trainee paramedic, went out with friends to a local pub after attending a cricket match in Nottingham, England, in July 2011.

At the pub, an argument broke out between Hodgkinson and the heavily drunk Jacob Dunne, 19. Dunne struck Hodgkinson with a single punch, causing him to fall back and hit his head on the pavement.

Hodgkinson suffered a fractured skull and brain hemorrhage, and died of his injury nine days later.

TEXT

BASED ON: PATRICK RILEY, "NORTH NAPLES WOMAN EMBEZZLED $140,000 FROM FORMER EMPLOYER," *NAPLES DAILY NEWS*, MARCH 16, 2018, WWW.NAPLESNEWS.COM

Stacie R., of North Naples, Florida, has been arrested on suspicion of embezzling more than $140,000 from her former employer between 2011 and 2014.

The accused was an office manager responsible for managing all the business accounts at a North Naples air conditioning company. She is suspected of writing checks to herself, under the guise of reimbursement for office expenses she had paid for from her personal account. Police charge that the office manager was not authorized to pay for business expenses from her private funds and then reimburse herself, and the company did not receive the services supposedly paid for.

Exercise 1

In addition to the cases described in Texts 1–2, briefly describe a criminal case you are familiar with in the space provided for Case Study 3.

Can people who have committed crimes such as those described in these cases studies rehabilitate themselves? If yes, what would that entail?

CASE	REHABILITATION PROCESS
Case Study 1: Manslaughter	
Case Study 2: Theft	
Case Study 3	

TEXT 3

MAIMONIDES, *MISHNEH TORAH*, LAWS OF *TESHUVAH* 1:3

הַתְּשׁוּבָה מְכַפֶּרֶת עַל כָּל הָעֲבֵירוֹת. אֲפִילוּ רָשָׁע כָּל יָמָיו וְעָשָׂה תְּשׁוּבָה בָּאַחֲרוֹנָה, אֵין מַזְכִּירִין לוֹ שׁוּם דָּבָר מֵרִשְׁעוֹ. שֶׁנֶּאֱמַר, "וְרִשְׁעַת הָרָשָׁע לֹא יִכָּשֶׁל בָּהּ בְּיוֹם שׁוּבוֹ מֵרִשְׁעוֹ" (יְחֶזְקֵאל לג, יב).

RABBI MOSHE BEN MAIMON (MAIMONIDES, RAMBAM) 1135–1204

Teshuvah atones for all sins. Even for people that were wicked their entire life, and did *teshuvah* at the last moment—their wickedness is no longer held against them. This is the meaning of the verse, "The wicked person will not stumble due to his wickedness on the day he does *teshuvah* for it" (EZEKIEL 33:12).

Halachist, philosopher, author, and physician. Maimonides was born in Córdoba, Spain. After the conquest of Córdoba by the Almohads, he fled Spain and eventually settled in Cairo, Egypt. There, he became the leader of the Jewish community and served as court physician to the vizier of Egypt. He is most noted for authoring the *Mishneh Torah,* an encyclopedic arrangement of Jewish law, and for his philosophical work, *Guide for the Perplexed.* His rulings on Jewish law are integral to the formation of halachic consensus.

Lawyers, Igor Pose, watercolor, Paris, 2004.

TEXT 4

MIDRASH, *PIRKEI RABBI ELIEZER* 43

תֵּדַע לְךָ כֹּחַ הַתְּשׁוּבָה. בֹּא וּרְאֵה מֵרַ' שִׁמְעוֹן בֶּן לָקִישׁ שֶׁהָיָה הוּא וּשְׁנֵי רֵעָיו בֶּהָרִים, גַּזְלִין וְחוֹמְסִין כָּל אֲשֶׁר יַעֲבוֹר עֲלֵיהֶם בַּדֶּרֶךְ.

מַה עָשָׂה רַ' שִׁמְעוֹן, הִנִּיחַ לִשְׁנֵי רֵעָיו שׁוֹדְדִין בֶּהָרִים וְשָׁב לֵאלֹקֵי אֲבוֹתָיו בְּכָל לִבּוֹ בְּצוֹם וּבִתְפִילָה, וְהָיָה מַשְׁכִּים וּמַעֲרִיב לְבֵית הַכְּנֶסֶת לִפְנֵי הַקָּדוֹשׁ בָּרוּךְ הוּא, וְהָיָה עוֹסֵק בַּתּוֹרָה כָּל יָמָיו וּבְמַתְּנוֹת עֲנִיִּים וְלֹא שָׁב עַל מַעֲשָׂיו הָרָעִים עוֹד, וְנִתְרַצֵּית תְּשׁוּבָתוֹ.

The power of *teshuvah* can be learned from the story of Rabbi Shimon ben Lakish. He and two comrades would wander in the mountains and rob everyone who would cross their path.

What did Rabbi Shimon do eventually? He left his two outlaw friends and returned to G-d wholeheartedly, fasting and praying earnestly. He would go to the synagogue every morning and evening, and spent all of his days studying Torah and giving charity to the poor. He never returned to his negative ways, and G-d accepted his repentance.

PIRKEI RABBI ELIEZER

A Midrash bearing the name of Rabbi Eliezer ben Hyrcanus, a prominent rabbinic sage living during the first and second centuries. *Pirkei Rabbi Eliezer* commences with the story of the early days of Rabbi Eliezer's life and then chronologically narrates and expounds upon events from the Creation until the middle of the journeys of the Children of Israel in the wilderness.

TEXT 5

MAIMONIDES, *MISHNEH TORAH*, LAWS OF *TESHUVAH* 2:2

וּמַה הִיא הַתְּשׁוּבָה? הוּא שֶׁיַּעֲזוֹב הַחוֹטֵא חֶטְאוֹ, וְיָסִירוֹ מִמַּחְשַׁבְתּוֹ, וְיִגְמוֹר בְּלִבּוֹ שֶׁלֹּא יַעֲשֵׂהוּ עוֹד, שֶׁנֶּאֱמַר, "יַעֲזֹב רָשָׁע דַּרְכּוֹ וְאִישׁ אָוֶן מַחְשְׁבֹתָיו" (יְשַׁעְיָהוּ נה, ז).

וְכֵן יִתְנַחֵם עַל שֶׁעָבַר, שֶׁנֶּאֱמַר, "כִּי אַחֲרֵי שׁוּבִי נִחַמְתִּי" (יִרְמְיָהוּ לא, יח), וְיָעִיד עָלָיו יוֹדֵעַ תַּעֲלוּמוֹת שֶׁלֹּא יָשׁוּב לְזֶה הַחֵטְא לְעוֹלָם, שֶׁנֶּאֱמַר, "וְלֹא נֹאמַר עוֹד אֱלֹקֵינוּ לְמַעֲשֵׂה יָדֵינוּ" (הוֹשֵׁעַ יד, ד).

וְצָרִיךְ לְהִתְוַדּוֹת בִּשְׂפָתָיו וְלוֹמַר עִנְיָנוֹת אֵלּוּ שֶׁגָּמַר בְּלִבּוֹ.

Watch a text-based lecture about repentance through the lens of Jewish mysticism:

MYJLI.COM/CRIME

What constitutes *teshuvah*? *Teshuvah* is when transgressors abandon their transgressions, remove them from their thoughts, and resolve in their heart never to commit them again. This is what the verse says, "Let the wicked forsake their ways, and the unrighteous their thoughts" (ISAIAH 55:7).

Returnees must also regret the past, as the verse states, "After I returned, I regretted" (JEREMIAH 31:18).

Returnees must reach the level where G-d, Who knows the hidden, will testify about them that they will never return to this sin again, as the verse states, "We will no longer say to the work of our hands, 'You are our gods'" (HOSEA 14:4).

They must also verbally confess their sins and state these matters which they resolved in their heart.

TEXT 6

RABBI SHALOM DOVBER SCHNEERSOHN, *KUNTRES UMAAYAN*
MIBEIT HASHEM 13:1

עוֹד זֹאת הִיא רָעָה חוֹלָה, מַה שֶׁהָאָדָם מַצְדִּיק אֶת עַצְמוֹ עַל מַעֲשֵׂה הַחֵטְא שֶׁעָשָׂה. כִּי הִנֵּה הָאָדָם בְּטִבְעוֹ . . . אִם הַדָּבָר הוּא טוֹב הִנֵּה הוּא תוֹלֶה וּמְיַיחֲסוֹ לְעַצְמוֹ, וְאִם הַדָּבָר הוּא רַע הִנֵּה הוּא תוֹלֶה וּמְיַיחֲסוֹ לְזוּלָתוֹ.

וְטַעַם הַדָּבָר הוּא מִפְּנֵי אַהֲבַת עַצְמוֹ. דִּלְהְיוֹת הָאָדָם בְּטִבְעוֹ אוֹהֵב אֶת עַצְמוֹ, הִנֵּה אַהֲבָתוֹ זֹאת לֹא זוּ בִּלְבַד שֶׁמְכַסָּה עַל פִּשְׁעֵי עַצְמוֹ שֶׁאֵינוֹ מַרְגִּישׁ כְּלָל אֲשֶׁר הוּא בְּעַצְמוֹ הָאָשֵׁם בָּזֶה, אֶלָּא עוֹד זֹאת שֶׁהוּא מַצְדִּיק אֶת עַצְמוֹ.

וְהִנֵּה אַף כִּי אֱמֶת הַדָּבָר אֲשֶׁר הַרְבֵּה יַלְדוּת עוֹשֶׂה וְהַרְבֵּה חֲבֵרִים רָעִים עוֹשִׂים וּבִפְרָט שֶׁנֵיהֶם יַחְדָּו, אֲבָל בֶּאֱמֶת הוּא בְּעַצְמוֹ אָשֵׁם בָּזֶה שֶׁבָּחַר לוֹ חֲבֵרִים רָעִים וּסְבִיבָה רָעָה. וְעַל כָּל פָּנִים אֵינוֹ צָרִיךְ לְהָאֲשִׁים רַק אֶת זוּלָתוֹ וּבִפְרָט לְהַצְדִּיק אֶת עַצְמוֹ, וְאֵין זֶה אֶלָּא מִפְּנֵי טֶבַע הָאָדָם בְּאַהֲבַת עַצְמוֹ גּוֹרֵם לוֹ חִסָּרוֹן זֶה . . .

לִפְעָמִים הוּא תוֹלֶה שֶׁכָּל זֶה בָּא לוֹ לְסִבַּת תִּגְבֹּרֶת הַחוֹם הַטִּבְעִי, דִּלְהְיוֹתוֹ מְרוּתָּח בְּטִבְעוֹ לָכֵן בְּהִתְגַּבְּרוּת חוֹם הַטִּבְעִי יֵחַם לְבָבוֹ וְאֵינוֹ יָכוֹל לַעֲצוֹר בַּעֲדוֹ מִן הַכַּעַס וְהַדִּבּוּר אוֹ מַחֲשָׁבָה בְּדִבּוּרִים וְהִרְהוּרִים אֲסוּרִים וְכֵן בְּמַעֲשֶׂה בְּפוֹעַל . . .

דְּבֶאֱמֶת הִנֵּה כָּל עִיקָר הִתְנַצְּלוּתוֹ אֵינוֹ אֶלָּא הַטָּעָה שֶׁמַטְעֶה עַצְמוֹ מִפְּנֵי אַהֲבָתוֹ לְעַצְמוֹ, וְרַק זוֹ הִיא הַסִּבָּה מַה שֶׁמַּצְדִּיק עַצְמוֹ. דְּהִנֵּה הַטַּעֲנָה דְּהִתְגַּבְּרוּת חוֹם הַטִּבְעִי אֵינָהּ טַעֲנָה בֶּאֱמֶת, שֶׁהֲרֵי הַחוֹם הַטִּבְעִי הוּא מֵהַנֶּפֶשׁ הַטִּבְעִית הַבַּהֲמִית, וְעַל זֶה נִיתְּנָה לוֹ הַנֶּפֶשׁ הָאֱלֹקִית שֶׁיִּתְגַּבֵּר עַל הַנֶּפֶשׁ הַטִּבְעִית.

וְזֶה תַּכְלִית בְּרִיאָתוֹ בָּעוֹלָם, לְהַגְבִּיר הַכֹּחוֹת דְּנֶפֶשׁ הָאֱלֹקִית וּלְהַכְנִיעַ הַכֹּחוֹת דְּנֶפֶשׁ הַטִּבְעִית . . . וְאִם הַנֶּפֶשׁ הַטִּבְעִית שֶׁלּוֹ שֶׁהוּא חוּמְרִי יוֹתֵר וְהַחוֹם הַטִּבְעִי הוּא בְּהִתְגַּבְּרוּת יְתֵרָה, בְּוַדַּאי גַּם בְּהַנֶּפֶשׁ הָאֱלֹקִית שֶׁלּוֹ יֵשׁ כֹּחוֹת חֲזָקִים יוֹתֵר, וְיֵשׁ בְּכֹחוֹ לְהִתְגַּבֵּר עַל הַחוֹם הַטִּבְעִי שֶׁלּוֹ, כִּי אֵין נוֹתְנִים לָאָדָם יוֹתֵר מֵעֶרֶךְ כֹּחוֹתָיו.

RABBI SHALOM DOVBER SCHNEERSOHN (RASHAB) 1860–1920

Chasidic rebbe. Rabbi Shalom Dovber became the fifth leader of the Chabad movement upon the passing of his father, Rabbi Shmuel Schneersohn. He established the Lubavitch network of *yeshivot* called Tomchei Temimim. He authored many volumes of Chasidic discourses and is renowned for his lucid and thorough explanations of kabbalistic concepts.

The fact that people make excuses for their transgressions is a major problem. Our nature is such that . . . when we do something good we credit ourselves, and when we do something wrong we blame others for it.

This is because of our self-love. By nature we love ourselves, and this causes us to be in denial about our own transgressions and to fail to recognize that we are at fault for them. Even worse, this also causes us to make justifications for our negative actions.

Although it is true that a negative environment and the wrong friends influence us greatly, the truth is that we are to blame for this, because we chose to associate ourselves with the wrong people and environment. We definitely can't *only* blame others for this and justify ourselves. . . .

Sometimes we blame our negative actions on our excitable temperament. We reason that because we get excited easily, we are impulsive and can't control ourselves from getting angry, speaking and thinking negative things, and committing negative actions. . . .

The excuse of an excitable temperament is not a real excuse. Our temperament comes from our animalistic soul, but we were also given a G-dly soul that has the ability to overpower our animalistic soul.

This is the very purpose of our creation, to use the power of our G-dly soul to overcome and subdue the inclinations of our animalistic soul. . . . If our animalistic soul is coarse and easily excitable, our G-dly soul surely has even stronger powers that give us the ability to overcome our natural inclinations. G-d does not make demands of us that are beyond our abilities.

TEXT 7

MAIMONIDES, *MISHNEH TORAH*, LAWS OF *TESHUVAH* 2:9

עֲבֵירוֹת שֶׁבֵּין אָדָם לַחֲבֵירוֹ, כְּגוֹן הַחוֹבֵל אֶת חֲבֵירוֹ אוֹ הַמְקַלֵּל חֲבֵירוֹ אוֹ גוֹזְלוֹ וְכַיּוֹצֵא בָּהֶן, אֵינוֹ נִמְחָל לוֹ לְעוֹלָם, עַד שֶׁיִּתֵּן לַחֲבֵירוֹ מַה שֶׁהוּא חַיָּיב לוֹ וִירַצֶּהוּ.

אַף עַל פִּי שֶׁהֶחֱזִיר לוֹ מָמוֹן שֶׁהוּא חַיָּיב לוֹ, צָרִיךְ לְרַצּוֹתוֹ וְלִשְׁאוֹל מִמֶּנּוּ שֶׁיִּמְחוֹל לוֹ. אֲפִילוּ לֹא הִקְנִיט אֶת חֲבֵירוֹ אֶלָּא בִּדְבָרִים, צָרִיךְ לְפַיְּיסוֹ וְלִפְגֹּעַ בּוֹ עַד שֶׁיִּמְחוֹל לוֹ.

Learn more about forgiveness in Jewish thought:

MYJLI.COM/CRIME

Interpersonal sins, such as causing physical injury, cursing, or stealing, are never forgiven until the offender pays the necessary restitution and appeases the victim.

Even after repaying restitution to the victim, the offender must appease the victim and ask for forgiveness. Even for verbal abuse that did not cause any tangible loss, the offender must appease the victim and seek forgiveness until it is granted.

Figure 4.1

Five Steps of *Teshuvah*

1 Resolution not to reoffend

2 Remorse for the offense

3 Restitution for financial damages

4 Appeasement of the victim

5 Verbal confession, statement of remorse
and resolution for the future

TEXT 8

TALMUD, BERACHOT 34B

> אָמַר רַבִּי אַבָּהוּ, מָקוֹם שֶׁבַּעֲלֵי תְשׁוּבָה עוֹמְדִין צַדִּיקִים גְּמוּרִים אֵינָם עוֹמְדִין.

Rabbi Avahu said: In the place where returnees stand, even completely righteous people cannot stand.

TEXT 9

MAIMONIDES, *MISHNEH TORAH*, LAWS OF *TESHUVAH* 2:4

> מִדַּרְכֵי הַתְּשׁוּבָה לִהְיוֹת הַשָּׁב צוֹעֵק תָּמִיד לִפְנֵי הַשֵּׁם בִּבְכִי וּבְתַחֲנוּנִים, וְעוֹשֶׂה צְדָקָה כְּפִי כֹּחוֹ, וּמִתְרַחֵק הַרְבֵּה מִן הַדָּבָר שֶׁחָטָא בּוֹ. וּמְשַׁנֶּה שְׁמוֹ, כְּלוֹמַר: אֲנִי אַחֵר וְאֵינִי אוֹתוֹ הָאִישׁ שֶׁעָשָׂה אוֹתָן הַמַּעֲשִׂים. וּמְשַׁנֶּה מַעֲשָׂיו כֻּלָּן לְטוֹבָה וּלְדֶרֶךְ יְשָׁרָה, וְגוֹלֶה מִמְּקוֹמוֹ, שֶׁגָּלוּת מְכַפֶּרֶת עָוֹן מִפְּנֵי שֶׁגּוֹרֶמֶת לוֹ לְהִכָּנַע וְלִהְיוֹת עָנָיו וּשְׁפַל רוּחַ.

Among the paths of repentance is for returnees to constantly call out before G-d, crying and entreating; to perform charity to the best of their ability; to greatly distance themselves from the object of their sin; to change their name, as if to say, "I am a different person and not the same one who sinned"; to positively change all of their behavior to the path of righteousness; and to travel in exile from their home. Exile atones for sin because it causes people to humble themselves and be meek of spirit.

BABYLONIAN TALMUD

A literary work of monumental proportions that draws upon the legal, spiritual, intellectual, ethical, and historical traditions of Judaism. The 37 tractates of the Babylonian Talmud contain the teachings of the Jewish sages from the period after the destruction of the Second Temple through the fifth century CE. It has served as the primary vehicle for the transmission of the Oral Law and the education of Jews over the centuries; it is the entry point for all subsequent legal, ethical, and theological Jewish scholarship.

TEXT 10

RABBI ELAZAR OF WORMS, *YOREH CHATAIM* 58

הַדֶּרֶךְ הָאַחֲרוֹן שֶׁל כָּל בַּעַל תְּשׁוּבָה צָרִיךְ שֶׁיָּשִׁיב רַבִּים וִילַמֵּד וְיַדְרִיךְ בְּנֵי אָדָם בְּדֶרֶךְ יְשָׁרָה. וְיַזְהִירָן וְיוֹכִיחָן וְיוֹדִיעָן וִיחַטְּאֵן עֹנְשָׁן וּמַתַּן שְׂכָרָן אֵיךְ שֶׁהַקָּבָּ"ה מְקַבֵּל בַּעֲלֵי תְּשׁוּבָה. כְּמוֹ שֶׁאָמַר דָּוִד בְּהִתְפַּלְלוֹ עַל עֲוֹנוֹ "אֲלַמְּדָה פֹשְׁעִים דְּרָכֶיךָ וְחַטָּאִים אֵלֶיךָ יָשׁוּבוּ" (תְּהִלִּים נא, טו).

The final thing every returnee should do is to inspire others to do *teshuvah* by teaching and instructing them to follow the correct path. The returnee should caution people and inform them of the negative consequences of transgression, the reward for following the correct path, and how G-d accepts returnees. This is what King David said when he prayed to G-d about his sin, "I will teach transgressors Your ways, so that they will return to You" (PSALMS 51:15).

RABBI ELAZAR BEN YEHUDAH OF WORMS C. 1160–1230

Kabbalist and liturgical poet. Student of Rabbi Elazar of Metz and Rabbi Yehudah Hachasid. Rabbi Elazar wrote on halachah, kabbalah, and the siddur, but is best known for his halachic work titled *Rokeach*. His wife and son were killed during one of the massacres committed during the Crusades.

Divine Inspiration: Father and Son, (Painting inspired by Rabbi Simon Jacobson studying with his son), LN M, watercolor, Canada, undated.

TEXT 11

RABBI YISRAEL OF BRUNA, *RESPONSA* 265–266

וְעַתָּה אֲסַדֵּר לְאוֹתוֹ שִׂמְחָה תְּשׁוּבָתוֹ לְפִי הַנִּרְאֶה עַל פִּי הַכְּתָבִים. אֲבָל אֵינִי מַכִּיר אֶת הָאִישׁ וְאֶת שִׂיחוֹ וְאֶת טִבְעוֹ לָכֵן אִם נִרְאֶה לְלוֹמְדֵי פּוֹזְנַאנ"ה יצ"ו לְהוֹסִיף אוֹ לִגְרוֹעַ הָרְשׁוּת בְּיָדָם. וְזֶהוּ סֵדֶר תְּשׁוּבָתוֹ:

יָמִים תִּהְיֶה גְאוּלָתוֹ. פֵּירוּשׁ, שָׁנָה תְּמִימָה יֵלֵךְ בְּגָלוּת וְיֵלֵךְ לְמַסָּעָיו, שֶׁבְּכָל יוֹם יָבוֹא לְבֵית הַכְּנֶסֶת אוֹ לְפָחוֹת שֵׁנִי וַחֲמִישִׁי וְיַעֲשֶׂה לוֹ שָׁלֹשׁ חֲשׁוּקֵי בַּרְזֶל, ב' עַל ב' יָדָיו שֶׁעָשָׂה בָּהֶן הָעֲבֵרָה וְא' עַל גוּפוֹ, וּבִכְנִיסָתוֹ לְבֵית הַכְּנֶסֶת יְקַשְּׁרֵם וְיִתְפַּלֵּל בָּהֶם.

וּבָעֶרֶב יֵלֵךְ יָחֵף לְבֵית הַכְּנֶסֶת וְיוֹשִׁיב הַחַזָּן קוֹדֶם וְהוּא רַחוּם וְיִלְקֶה בָּרְבִים וְיַכְרִיז וְיֹאמַר, דְּעוּ רַבּוֹתַי שֶׁרוֹצֵחַ אֲנִי כִּי הָרַגְתִּי אֶת נִיסָן בְּמֵזִיד וְזֶה כַּפָּרָתִי, וּבְקָשׁוּ עָלַי רַחֲמִים . . .

וְיִתְעַנֶּה בְּכָל יוֹם שָׁנָה תְּמִימָה חוּץ מִבְּיוֹם שֶׁאֵין אוֹמְרִים תַּחֲנָה. וְלֹא יֹאכַל בָּשָׂר וְלֹא יִשְׁתֶּה יַיִן וְלֹא יִשְׁתַּכֵּר. וְרָאוּי לְזָהֵר מֵאוֹתוֹ מִין שֶׁנִּשְׁתַּכֵּר, שֶׁאֵרַע עַל יָדוֹ הַמַּעֲשֶׂה הָרַע עַל יְדֵי שִׁכְרוּת.

וְלֹא יִשְׁכַּב עַל כַּר וְכֶסֶת כִּי אִם בְּשַׁבָּתוֹת וְיָמִים טוֹבִים חֲנוּכָּה וּפוּרִים. וְכָל יְמֵי גָלוּתוֹ לֹא יְגַלַּח שְׂעַר רֹאשׁוֹ וּזְקָנוֹ כִּי זֶה דַּרְכֵי הַתְּשׁוּבָה כִּדְאָמְרִינָן בְּפֶרֶק זֶה בּוֹרֵר בְּסַנְהֶדְרִין (כה, א). וְלֹא יִרְחַץ בְּחַמִּין כִּי אִם בְּעֶרֶב יוֹם טוֹב וְלֹא בְּעֶרֶב שַׁבָּת. וְלֹא יָחוֹף רֹאשׁוֹ כִּי אִם פַּעַם אַחַת בְּחֹדֶשׁ וְלֹא יְכַבֵּס בְּגָדִים כִּי אִם פַּעַם אַחַת בַּתְּקוּפָה.

וְלֹא יְטַיֵּיל בְּבָתֵּי מִשְׁתָּאוֹת כִּי בָּהֶם אֵירַע לוֹ תְּחִלָּה הַקִּלְקָלָה. וְלֹא יִשְׂחוֹק בְּשׁוּם שְׂחוֹק כִּי מֵחֲמַת הַשְּׂחוֹק אֵירַע לוֹ הַהֲרִיגָה.

וְאִם יְחָרְפוּהוּ וְיֹאמְרוּ לוֹ רוֹצֵחַ אַתָּה, יִשְׁתּוֹק וִיקַבֵּל מֵאַהֲבָה מַה שֶׁיַּלְבִּינוּ פָּנָיו וְיֹאמַר זֶה כַּפָּרָתִי.

וְיִזָּהֵר בִּקְרִיאַת שְׁמַע וּבִתְפִלָּה וְיִתְוַודֶּה בְּכָל יוֹם ג' פְּעָמִים וִידוּי הַיָּדוּעַ. וְאַחַר הַוִּידוּי יֹאמַר, אָנָּא הַשֵּׁם קַבֵּל אֶת תְּשׁוּבָתִי כִּי פִשַּׁעְתִּי וְשָׁפַכְתִּי דַם נָקִי וְעֵינִי נַפְשִׁי וּכְלִימָתִי תְּהֵא כַפָּרָתִי.

וְאַחַר הַשָּׁנָה יִתְעַנֶּה עוֹד שָׁנָה כָּל שֵׁנִי וְחֲמִישִׁי. וְכָל יָמָיו יִזָּהֵר כְּשֶׁיַּגִּיעַ אוֹתוֹ חֹדֶשׁ וְאוֹתוֹ יוֹם שֶׁעָשָׂה יוֹם הָרְצִיחָה, בְּאוֹתוֹ זְמַן יִתְעַנֶּה ג' יָמִים רְצוּפִים אִם הוּא בָּרִיא, וְאִם חַלָּשׁ הוּא דַּי לוֹ בְּב' יָמִים, יוֹם הַהַכָּאָה וְיוֹם שֶׁמֵּת בּוֹ נִיסָן.

RABBI YISRAEL OF BRUNA
1400–1480

Talmudic and halachic authority. He served as rabbi and head of a yeshiva in Ratisbon (today Regensburg, Germany). Rabbis and scholars from various countries sent him their halachic queries. His collection of halachic responsa served as a primary source for Rabbi Moshe Isserles's glosses on the Shulchan Aruch (Code of Jewish Law).

וְיִתְעַסֵּק כָּל יָמָיו בְּפִדְיוֹן שְׁבוּיִים וּבִגְמִילוּת חֲסָדִים וְהַצָּלַת נְפָשׁוֹת תַּחַת הַנֶּפֶשׁ. וְיִפַּשֵּׁר עִם יוֹרְשָׁיו לְהַחֲיוֹתָם בְּדָבָר נָכוֹן, וִיבַקֵּשׁ מֵהֶם מְחִילָה וּמִן הָאַלְמָנָה.

וְיָשׁוּב אֶל ה' וִירַחֲמֵהוּ,
נְאָם יִשְׂרָאֵל מִבְּרוּנָא

I will now detail the *teshuvah* process for Simcha based on what I have understood from earlier sources. However, I do not know this man and his character, so if the scholars of Poznan see fit to make changes to the process they may do so. This is the process of *teshuvah* for him:

He should go out into exile and travel for a full year. He should attend the local synagogue every day—or at least on Mondays and Thursdays—and pray wearing three iron shackles, one on each of his hands with which he committed the crime, and one on his body.

In the evening he should come to the synagogue barefoot, and the leader of the services should give him lashes in public before the prayers. He should announce to the assembled, "Know, my masters, that I am a murderer because I intentionally killed Nissan. This is my process of atonement, please pray for divine mercy for me." . . .

He should fast every day for an entire year, except on festive days. He should not eat meat, drink wine, or become intoxicated. He should abstain completely from the particular alcoholic beverage that he was intoxicated from when he committed the terrible act.

He should not sleep with a pillow or cushion except on Shabbat and Jewish holidays. During the entire period of exile, he should not cut his hair or beard, because refraining from this is a practice associated with *teshuvah*. He should not bathe with hot water during the week and before Shabbat, except for the day preceding a festival. He should only wash his head once a month and only wash his clothes once in a while.

He should not visit taverns, because this is where he started to act wrongly. He should not play any gambling games at all, because this led to the murder.

If people malign him and call him a murderer, he should remain silent, lovingly accept the embarrassment, and say, "This is an atonement for me."

He should be particular about reciting the Shema and the daily prayers and recite a special confessional prayer three times a day. After the confession, he should say, "Please G-d, accept my *teshuvah* because I have transgressed and spilled innocent blood. May my suffering and embarrassment atone for me."

After the end of this year, he should fast every Monday and Thursday for another entire year. For the rest of his life he should be particular to commemorate the month and day on which he committed the murder. During this period of time, he should fast for three consecutive days if he is healthy enough. If he is weak, he can suffice with fasting for two days: the day on which the attack occurred and the day on which Nissan died.

For the rest of his life he should occupy himself with redeeming captives, acts of charity, and saving lives, as a substitute for the life he took. He should reach a financial settlement with Nissan's heirs that will take care of their needs properly, and ask forgiveness from the orphans and widow.

He should return to G-d and He will have mercy on him, Yisrael of Bruna

QUESTIONS FOR DISCUSSION

1 What do you find to be noteworthy about this text?

2 What purpose/s does this sentence serve?

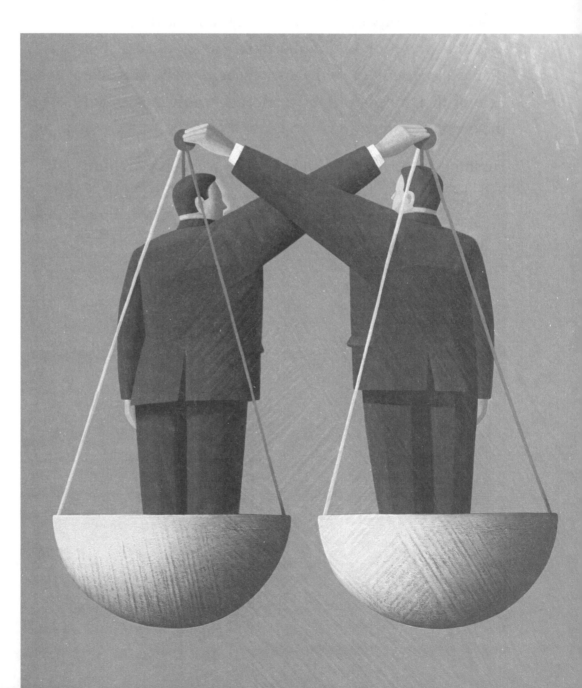

Lawyering, Nik Ad, acrylic and paper on paper, undated.

Exercise 2

Return to the case study in Text 1 and, based on the sources we have studied, devise a *teshuvah*-focused process Jacob Dunne should follow.

CASE	*TESHUVAH* PROCESS
Case Study 1: Manslaughter	

TEXT 12

RABBI ELAZAR OF WORMS, *SEFER HAROKE'ACH*, LAWS OF *TESHUVAH* 16

גָּנַב אוֹ גָזַל... הֲרֵי עָבַר עַל לָאו. יֵשׁ לוֹ לְהָשִׁיב הַגְּזֵילָה כּוּלָּהּ אוֹ הַגְּנֵיבָה...
וִיבַקֵּשׁ מִמֶּנּוּ מְחִילָה וְיִלְקֶה עַל לָאו וְיִתְעַנֶּה וְיִתְוַדֶּה.

וְיִשְׁמוֹר שֶׁלֹּא יְקַבֵּל פִּקְדוֹנוֹת וְלֹא יֵלַךְ עַל מָמוֹן חֲבֵירוֹ כִּי גֶזֶל נַפְשׁוֹ שֶׁל
אָדָם חוּמְדָתוֹ (חֲגִיגָה יא, ב) עַל כֵּן יִתְרַחֵק מֵהֶן. וְיַעֲשֶׂה גְּמִילוּת חֲסָדִים
בֵּין בְּגוּפוֹ בֵּין בְּמָמוֹנוֹ וְיוֹתֵר מִמַּה שֶׁיֵּשׁ לוֹ.

To atone for the transgression of theft, thieves must return what they stole in full, ask forgiveness from the victim, receive punishment for the transgression, fast, and confess to G-d.

Returnees from theft should also be careful not to hold monetary deposits for others, or deal with a fellow's money. "Theft is tempting by nature" (TALMUD, CHAGIGAH 11B), so they should distance themselves from other people's money. They should perform charitable acts with their person, as well as with their money, beyond their means.

Exercise 3

Return to the case study in Text 2 and the third case study you added in Exercise 1, and devise a *teshuvah*-focused process that a person guilty of such a crime should follow, based on the sources we have studied.

CASE	*TESHUVAH* PROCESS
Case Study 2: Theft	
Case Study 3	

Exercise 4

Propose an alternative sentencing plan for the three case studies in Exercise 1.

CASE	ALTERNATIVE SENTENCING PLAN
Case Study 1: Manslaughter	
Case Study 2: Theft	
Case Study 3	

*Find out how the **Aleph Institute** helps offenders and judges with alternative sentencing:*

MYJLI.COM/CRIME

TEXT 13

THE REBBE, RABBI MENACHEM MENDEL SCHNEERSON, *IGROT KODESH* 31:186

תַּכְלִית בֵּית הָאֲסוּרִים אֵינוֹ לְצַעֵר וּלְהַעֲנִישׁ לְשֵׁם עוֹנֶשׁ, כִּי אִם לְהָבִיא אֶת הָעֲבַרְיָין לְהִתְבּוֹנֵן בְּמַצָּבוֹ, לַחֲרָטָה עַל הֶעָבַר וּלְהַחְלָטָה טוֹבָה עַל לְהַבָּא.

כְּלוֹמַר, לְהִשְׁתַּחְרֵר עוֹד בְּשִׁבְתּוֹ בַּכֶּלֶא מֵהַתְּכוּנוֹת וְהַסִּבּוֹת שֶׁגָּרְמוּ לְמַצָּבוֹ בִּכְדֵי שֶׁיּוּכַל כְּכַלּוֹת מוֹעֵד מַאֲסָרוֹ לָשׁוּב לְמַסְלוּל חַיִּים תַּקִּינִים וּלְחַיּוֹת הַחַיִּים שֶׁל חֵרוּת אֲמִתִּית, חֵרוּת נַפְשִׁית.

The purpose of a prison isn't to punish for the sake of punishment. The purpose should be to bring prisoners to reflect upon their situation, achieve remorse for the past, and make positive resolutions for the future.

Meaning, while prisoners are still in jail they should free themselves from the character traits and causes that got them into this situation. This will enable them to follow the proper path when they are released, and live a life of true freedom—freedom of the soul.

RABBI MENACHEM MENDEL SCHNEERSON
1902–1994

The towering Jewish leader of the 20th century, known as "the Lubavitcher Rebbe," or simply as "the Rebbe." Born in southern Ukraine, the Rebbe escaped Nazi-occupied Europe, arriving in the U.S. in June 1941. The Rebbe inspired and guided the revival of traditional Judaism after the European devastation, impacting virtually every Jewish community the world over. The Rebbe often emphasized that the performance of just one additional good deed could usher in the era of Mashiach. The Rebbe's scholarly talks and writings have been printed in more than 200 volumes.

*Watch **Rabbi Manis Friedman** discuss his innovative program for helping prisoners rehabilitate themselves:*

MYJLI.COM/CRIME

KEY POINTS

1 Jewish rehabilitation is known as "*teshuvah*." *Teshuvah* can be done (a) for *everything*, (b) by *everyone*, (c) *anytime*. *Teshuvah* focuses on the individual—the criminal must be reformed for his own sake, because he is a human being created in G-d's image.

2 *Teshuvah* entails completely restoring the world to the state it was in before the transgression was committed. For crimes that affected other people, this entails five steps: (a) a resolution to never re-offend, (b) remorse for the crime, (c) a verbal confession to G-d, (d) paying full restitution to the victim, and (e) appeasing the victim emotionally.

3 In addition to *teshuvah* for the transgression, offenders must work to change their character and lifestyle to ensure they don't relapse.

4 Historically, rabbis fashioned personalized rehabilitative sentences for those offenders that genuinely wished to do *teshuvah* for their actions.

5 In the modern criminal justice system, "alternative sentencing" allows for rehabilitative sentences that fit the offender and the crime. Rehabilitative programs can also be incorporated into the prison system. Jewish law and values call upon us to increase the availability of these programs.

Additional Readings

TESHUVA

A LOOK AT REPENTANCE, FORGIVENESS AND ATONEMENT IN JEWISH LAW AND PHILOSOPHY AND AMERICAN LEGAL THOUGHT

SAMUEL J. LEVINE

All footnotes have been removed to conserve space. To read the complete article, visit www.myjli.com/crime.

Introduction

In his contribution to a recent UCLA Law Review symposium, Professor Stephen Garvey introduces and develops the possibility of viewing "punishment as atonement." Garvey describes an "ideal community" in which punishment serves as "a form of secular penance aimed at the expiation of the wrongdoer's guilt and his reconciliation with the victim and the community." Recognizing that the concept of atonement "sounds religious," Garvey insists and sets out to demonstrate that "atonement makes perfectly good sense independent of religion." Nevertheless, Garvey acknowledges that "religion is one place where you'll find atonement's roots" and identifies St. Anselm's eleventh century work as an early example of a theological discussion of atonement. In further discussions of "theological atonement," Garvey cites not only Christian sources but also, briefly, Jewish sources, which he traces to the biblical book of Leviticus.

Garvey posits that his analysis of theological atonement "shed[s] some light on the problem of punishment in our secular world." According to Garvey, parallel to theological accounts of atonement, which "depend critically on treating G-d as the object of the sinner's identification," a secular account of

atonement "take[s] the object of identification not to be G-d, but one's community and its members." Thus, having largely dispensed with the need to distinguish, for analytical purposes, between theological and secular approaches, Garvey relies on sources based in various forms of moral philosophy to develop an extensive description of the "process of atonement."

The aim of this Essay is to carry forward Professor Garvey's project through a more detailed exploration of the concept of *teshuva* in Jewish law and philosophy. The principle of teshuva is fundamental to Jewish law and philosophy. Jewish law views it as apparent that human beings are, by their very nature, fallible and incapable of avoiding all sin, and thus through the possibility—indeed the obligation—of teshuva, G-d provides humans a means of achieving atonement for wrongdoings.

Though the verses in Leviticus cited by Garvey represent an early depiction of the mechanics and purposes of atonement in Jewish law, teshuva has occupied a central place in Jewish thought, from the Bible and the Talmud to the legal and philosophical writings of medieval and modern scholars. These sources portray a complex process consisting of several steps required of the penitent individual, a process strikingly similar to that which Garvey describes. This Essay looks to further develop some of Garvey's ideas by closely analyzing teshuva, which stands as an illuminating conceptual analog to Garvey's depiction of secular atonement.

The Process of Atonement: A Comparative Analysis

The process of atonement that Garvey proposes places separate obligations on the wrongdoer and

SAMUEL J. LEVINE

Samuel Levine is a professor of law at Touro Law Center and the director of the Jewish Law Institute. He has published more than 40 law review articles in the areas of legal ethics, criminal law, law and religion, Jewish law, and constitutional law.

the victim. The initial burden, understandably, falls on the wrongdoer, who must engage in "expiation," a moral journey consisting of the four steps of "repentance, apology, reparation and penance." After the wrongdoer has completed this journey, the victim is then obligated to forgive the wrongdoer, thus completing the process of atonement through a "reconciliation of the wrongdoer and the wronged." This Essay likens Garvey's system of atonement to the process of teshuva, comparing the obligations placed on both parties and the requisite methodology for achieving true atonement.

I. THE OBLIGATIONS OF THE WRONGDOER

In Jewish thought, the process of teshuva is often described broadly in four stages, similar to Garvey's process. Although the precise enumeration and identification of these stages varies among scholars, the general formulation of the process of teshuva contains essentially the same elements listed by Garvey: remorse, resolution not to repeat the wrongdoing, confession and changing one's ways. The similarity in the general conceptual frameworks of Garvey's process of secular atonement and the process of teshuva may allow for meaningful comparisons and contrasts of the two systems.

A. Repentance

Garvey relies on a definition of "repentance" as

the remorseful acceptance of responsibility for one's wrongful and harmful actions, the repudiation of the aspects of one's character that generated the actions, the resolve to do one's best to extirpate those aspects of one's character, and the resolve to atone or make amends for the [wrong and] harm that one has done.

Garvey thus sees repentance as a crucial first step in removing the taint of wrongdoing because it is "active," leading "[t]he repentant self [to] focus [[ ] on the wrongdoing that produced the stain in the first place and on what the self can now do about it."

In Jewish law and philosophy, remorse for a wrong, coupled with the resolution not to repeat the wrongdoing, is likewise essential to any possibility of

atonement. In particular, as Maimonides writes in his Code of Law, these elements of repentance are prerequisites to effective confession. Words of apology that are not accompanied by sincere feelings of regret and resolve to change remain empty, bereft of the crucial element that lends them meaning.

Citing a powerful analogy from the Talmud, Maimonides emphasizes the futility of an attempted confession that lacks the proper intent. The analogy compares such a confession to an immersion for ritual purity undertaken while the impure individual continues to grasp onto the very object that rendered the individual ritually impure. Just as it is impossible for ritual purification to take effect until the individual casts away the impure object, it is inconceivable that the purifying effects of confession will set in before the improper acts have been cast aside through regret and resolve for the future.

In addition to its value as an illustration of some of the underlying principles of teshuva, the analogy to the laws of ritual purity underlines the legal nature of teshuva in Jewish thought. Indeed, since the times of Maimonides, scholars of Jewish law have used Maimonides' Laws of Teshuva, incorporated as a section in his Code of Law, as a springboard for extensive legal discussions of the concept of teshuva. Among the works of contemporary scholars, Rabbi Joseph B. Soloveitchik's discourses are perhaps the most notable example of careful and technical legal analysis of teshuva through an exposition on Maimonides' Code of Law.

Rabbi Soloveitchik posits that according to Maimonides, the role of resolve for the future in the process of teshuva depends on the specific nature of the individual's teshuva. Rabbi Soloveitchik observes that, in Chapter 1 of Laws of Teshuva, Maimonides lists remorse prior to resolution for the future, while in Chapter 2, the order of these two elements is reversed.

Asserting that there is no contradiction between the two descriptions, Rabbi Soloveitchik instead suggests that in Chapter 1, Maimonides refers to teshuva that is motivated by emotion, resulting from the wrongdoer's spontaneous inner feelings of shame, which instinctively lead to remorse. In such a scenario, he explains, it is the individual's sense of utter remorse that automatically brings about the resolve never to commit the same wrongs. Chapter 2, according to Rabbi Soloveitchik, describes an individual who has arrived at teshuva on an intellectual level, who understands the impropriety and negative effects of sinful behavior and therefore resolves not to engage in such behavior in the future. In such a case, the individual does not immediately experience passionate feelings of remorse; rather, remorse will grow out of the individual's continued determination not to repeat the wrongful actions in the future.

Thus, the first step in both Garvey's process of atonement—repentance—and in the path of teshuva—remorse and resolution not to repeat the wrongdoing— incorporate elements of emotional commitment and future resolve, which must be met before continuing on the road to atonement.

B. Apology

The next stage Garvey sees in the process of atonement, "confession," serves as "the wrongdoer's public expression of his repentance, whereby he openly acknowledges his wrongdoing and simultaneously disowns it." Alluding again to the theological roots of the concept of atonement, Garvey refers to an apology as a "secular ritual of expiation." Such expiation is achieved through the profound willingness of the self to "accept [ ] responsibility for its wrongdoing but at the same time disavow[ ] the wrong." In short, an apology "embraces" guilt and then "expels" it. Vidui—confession, or apology—likewise serves an indispensable function in the process of teshuva. Through vidui, the individual unequivocally accepts responsibility for wrongdoing, at the same time displaying an outward expression of remorse and a willingness to make amends for the wrong. Maimonides delineates the essential elements of vidui, which include: language demonstrating a clear admission of having committed a wrong against another; precise articulation of the wrong; a statement of strong remorse; and a declaration of a desire not to repeat the wrong.

In his more detailed description of vidui, Maimonides, who is known for precision and economy of language, repeatedly emphasizes the importance of verbalizing the feelings of remorse and resolve. In addition, Maimonides cites Talmudic sources that praise an individual who recites an extended form of vidui by expanding on the more basic elements of confession and apology.

Building on Maimonides' discussions, Rabbi Soloveitchik offers an important psychological insight to explain the power and significance of verbal vidui. Rabbi Soloveitchik notes that human nature sometimes leads a person, consciously or otherwise, to refuse to accept the reality of certain unfavorable facts. Among the mechanisms a person may employ in the attempt to deny an unfortunate reality, he observes, is to avoid verbally expressing the unpleasant truth. Perhaps one of the most difficult truths that a person must face involves the acknowledgment of having committed a wrongful act. Through the verbal expression of vidui, then, rather than continuing to evade responsibility by deluding others and possibly one's self as well, the individual admits to the truth of the wrongdoing, thereby facilitating the process of teshuva.

Thus the second stages of both Garvey's process and of teshuva require a public expression and acceptance of the wrongdoer's responsibility for the bad act, and an overt articulation of regret and repudiation of the wrong.

C. Reparation and penance

In Garvey's depiction of the process of atonement, it is incumbent upon the wrongdoer, after feeling remorse and, through apology, verbally expressing such feelings, to "make amends." Garvey suggests that most crimes result in both harm and a moral wrong; therefore, according to Garvey, the remedy for a wrongdoing consists of two corresponding actions, reparation and penance. Because reparation, in the form of restitution or compensation, "makes amends for the harm the wrongdoer does, but not for the wrong he has done," Garvey explains, in addition to making reparations, "the wrongdoer must submit to penance." Thus, Garvey refers to penance as "the final, critical piece of the expiation half of the atonement process."

Garvey defines penance as "a self-imposed punishment, i.e., self-imposed hardship or suffering, which completes the process of expiation and finally rids the wrongdoer of his guilt." Penance plays a unique role in Garvey's view of atonement, which "insists that punishment should do more: It should restore the offender to full standing in the community." To explore the potent question of "[h]ow suffering manage[s] to effect this restoration," Garvey mandates the need "to shift perspectives." Specifically, Garvey's approach requires us "to look at punishment not from the victim's perspective, but from the wrongdoer's." This simple yet profound suggestion recognizes that often a wrongdoer "will feel smaller than before" and "will experience anger and resentment toward himself." Significantly, Garvey explains, "the wrongdoer cannot restore his own moral standing unless he submits to punishment."

Regarding penance, Rabbi Soloveitchik's discourses on teshuva again provide a helpful complement to Garvey's thoughts. Like Garvey, Rabbi Soloveitchik establishes a framework for analyzing the concept of penance based on the premise that the commission of a wrong results in two interrelated but distinct consequences. He explains that, on one level, in relation to the victim, a wrongful act produces liability on the part of the offender. Similar to Garvey, Rabbi Soloveitchik posits that to counteract this culpability, the individual must engage in reparation, through the payment of restitution or compensation. Thus, one kind of teshuva effects *kappara*, a form of forgiveness or acquittal from wrongdoing. An individual who undertakes this kind of teshuva both literally and metaphorically pays a debt owed to another and is thereby released from further liability. Indeed, Rabbi Soloveitchik notes an etymological link that underscores the corresponding conceptual similarity between reparation and this form of forgiveness: *kappara* derives from the same root as *kofer*, the Hebrew term for payment of an obligation.

Yet, this form of *teshuva* does not adequately amend for the second result that Rabbi Soloveitchik attributes to the commission of a wrongful act. Employing an approach that anticipates Garvey's, and relying on various sources of Jewish thought, Rabbi Soloveitchik examines the effect of wrongdoing on the individual who has committed the improper act.

Specifically, he acknowledges the spiritual defilement caused by the impurity of sin. To return from such spiritual defilement, Rabbi Soloveitchik explains, the individual must do more than merely pay the victim any obligation arising out of the wrongdoing. As in Garvey's system, in the final stages of *teshuva*, Jewish law demands not only reparation, but, more importantly, penance, in the form of fundamental change in the individual's mode of behavior.

To erase fully the taint of the wrongdoing and thus to obtain a restored place in the community, an individual must engage in what Rabbi Soloveitchik terms *teshuva* of *tahara* (repentance of purification), a more extensive form of spiritual purification or expiation. Like penance, *teshuva* of *tahara* requires that a person undertake self-imposed forms of hardship, ones that relate to and address directly the particular nature of the act committed. Through *teshuva* of *tahara*, then, an individual truly regains and returns to the state of undefiled spirituality lost as a consequence of the wrongdoing.

II. THE OBLIGATIONS OF THE WRONGED: RECONCILIATION

Once the wrongdoer has successfully completed expiation and the guilt has thereby been removed, Garvey writes, it is then time for the victim to complete the process of atonement through forgiveness. According to Garvey, forgiveness "achieves the reconciliation of wrongdoer and wronged." Specifically, Garvey suggests, just as expiation "enables an offender to purge the taint of guilt," expiation coupled with forgiveness "enables the victim to overcome his resentment." Discussing the mechanics of forgiveness, Garvey argues that although

[a] victim may permissibly extend forgiveness to a wrongdoer who has done nothing but repent . . . a victim may also legitimately withhold forgiveness until the wrongdoer has paid his debt in full, i.e., until the wrongdoer has not only repented but also apologized, made reparations, and endured his penance. Indeed, forgiveness may take some time in coming.

Ultimately, however, Garvey considers forgiveness "one of th[e victim's] responsibilities." Indeed, Garvey finds that "[i]t reflects a moral failure . . . for victims to withhold forgiveness unreasonably from offenders who have done all they can do to expiate their guilt."

A similar approach to the dynamics of forgiveness is found in Jewish thought. Discussing the obligations owed to the victim, Maimonides explains that *teshuva* in the form of reparations is not sufficient, but that the wrongdoer must repeatedly appease the victim and ask for forgiveness. The responsibility on the wrongdoer is such that, if the victim initially refuses the request, the wrongdoer must continue to make a number of attempts to obtain forgiveness.

Nevertheless, once the wrongdoer has repeatedly demonstrated a sincere hope for reconciliation, parallel to Garvey's approach, Jewish law places the burden on the victim to grant forgiveness. In the powerful formulation of Maimonides, if the victim continuously denies forgiveness, the wrongdoer is released from further action, as the victim is then deemed to be the sinner. Indeed, Maimonides emphasizes the responsibility incumbent on the victim, writing that it is improper for a person to withhold forgiveness; instead, a victim should be receptive to the wrongdoer's genuine attempts at reconciliation and atonement.

Conclusion

Despite the prominent position it has held for millennia in religious and moral thinking, the atonement model is relatively new to American legal theory. Professor Garvey's attempt to offer a systematic depiction and analysis of the process of atonement and its possible relevance to American law appears to represent the most extensive such effort to date.

As Garvey himself concedes, any application of a theory of atonement to the American legal system will encounter a number of problems and objections. For example, he acknowledges that "[i]f in the end you remain convinced that the ideal of community on which I base my account of atonement is indeed dangerous or irretrievable, then you will . . . be forced to turn elsewhere for your understanding of punishment." These difficulties only increase when the analysis relates the concept of *teshuva* from Jewish law and philosophy to American law. Nevertheless, Garvey's attempt is successful, for reasons that would appear to apply to theories of *teshuva* as well.

First, Garvey emphasizes that his "immediate aim is normative, not practical," and, therefore, "the discussion proceeds at a high level of abstraction" rather than "develop[ing] any concrete proposals for institutional or doctrinal reform." Second, Garvey explains that a new model is necessary based on his conclusion that "the prevailing models of punishment . . . deterrence[,] retributivism[,] restorativism and libertarianism . . . fall short." Finally, as Professor David Dolinko noted in introducing the symposium in which Garvey participated, Garvey's proposal offers a fresh perspective at a time when "[c]riminal punishment is an institution that is large, growing, and quite possibly mutating into new and surprising forms." Ultimately, it is perhaps ironic that, in providing a new theory of punishment for American legal thought to consider in a future millennium, Garvey has in fact looked back to theories of atonement and *teshuva* that have spanned millennia of the past. The path to *teshuva* may indeed provide insight in formulating a new perspective on the notions of punishment underlying American law.

27 Fordham Urb. L.J. 1677
Fordham Urban Law Journal, June, 2000
Essay
Copyright © 2000 Fordham University School of Law; Samuel J. Levine

Lesson

5

MOVING FORWARD

REACCEPTANCE AND THE CRIMINAL BACKGROUND CHECK

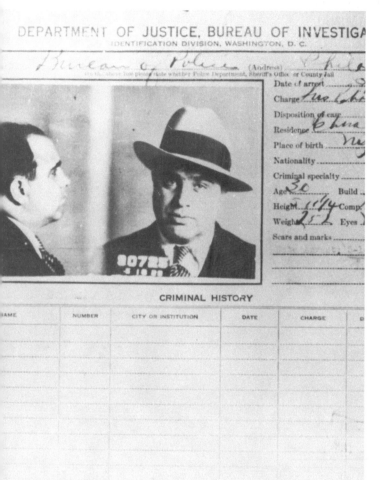

Al Capone's U.S. Department of Justice, Bureau of Investigation, arrest and criminal history record card, 1920. (Alcatraz Island, U.S. National Park Service, San Francisco)

All of your deeds are recorded in a book: so declares the Rosh Hashanah liturgy, and so it is within the contemporary criminal justice system. Every year, hundreds of thousands of Americans are released from prison and seek to rejoin society, but many are stymied by the public availability of their criminal records. Is it possible to find a balance between the needs of society, prospective employers, and ex-offenders? After surveying the contemporary situation, this class looks for answers in the paradigms of Jewish law.

Figure 5.1

The Use of Criminal Background Checks in Hiring Decisions in the U.S.

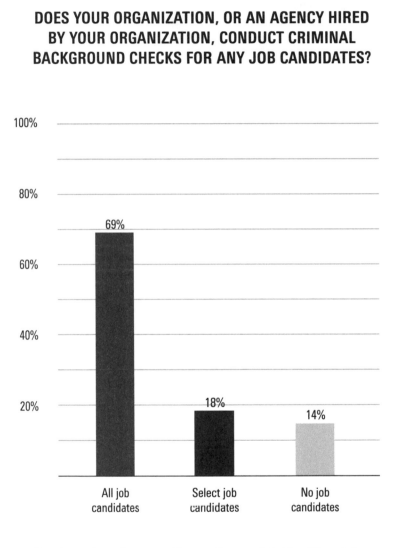

DOES YOUR ORGANIZATION, OR AN AGENCY HIRED BY YOUR ORGANIZATION, CONDUCT CRIMINAL BACKGROUND CHECKS FOR ANY JOB CANDIDATES?

- All job candidates: 69%
- Select job candidates: 18%
- No job candidates: 14%

Note: Respondents who answered "not sure" were excluded from this analysis. Percentages may not equal 100% due to rounding.

SOCIETY FOR HUMAN RESOURCE MANAGEMENT, "THE USE OF CRIMINAL BACKGROUND CHECKS IN HIRING DECISIONS," 2012

TEXT 1

ADAM CHANDLER, "PAYING (AND PAYING AND PAYING) A DEBT TO SOCIETY," *THE ATLANTIC*, MAY 2016

Neil Cardoso . . . applied for a job as a chauffeur shortly after a conviction and a brief incarceration in New York City for a white-collar financial crime. Cardoso was offered a position only to have it rescinded after a criminal background check was done.

"They wanted me, they loved me, the people who did the hiring wanted me to start right away," he says. "And then the HR department did the background check that was the last part of the hiring process." The company saw his conviction and declined to hire him. Cardoso takes umbrage at the fact that the job had nothing to do with the offense for which he was convicted. "I had no fiduciary responsibilities as a chauffeur, I would just be driving people around."

*The **Delancey Street Foundation** provides convicted criminals with rehabilitation services and vocational training, with the aim of reintegrating them into society. Watch a former criminal describe the difference this program made in his life:*

MYJLI.COM/CRIME

Exercise 5.1

Would you give Neil Cardoso a job as a chauffeur?

Yes / No

List some jobs you would give Neil Cardoso despite his criminal conviction.

1	
2	
3	
4	
5	

List some jobs you would not give Neil Cardoso due to his criminal conviction.

1	
2	
3	
4	
5	

TEXT 2

MARINA DUANE, ET AL., "CRIMINAL BACKGROUND CHECKS: IMPACT ON EMPLOYMENT AND RECIDIVISM," URBAN INSTITUTE REPORT, 2017

Involvement in the criminal justice system and unemployment form a vicious cycle. Research indicates that employment after incarceration is a key factor in reducing an individual's risk of recidivism. At the most basic level, employment provides secure income and allows people to become self-reliant, enabling them to provide for themselves and their families. Job stability provides informal social control and creates new and positive social networks that can protect against re-engaging in criminal activity.

Importantly, these findings are echoed by people returning from incarceration themselves; many studies show that people feel that employment would help them stay out of the justice system. . . .

A body of evidence is also emerging on the impact of criminal background checks on recidivism. In a recently published empirical study, researchers analyzed recidivism among "provisionally cleared" health care workers in New York State, who had been cleared to work despite their criminal records.

The study found that the likelihood of provisionally cleared employees being rearrested within three years fell 4.2 percent, with significant and differentiated impact by gender: men's risk fell 8.4 percent while women's risk dropped only 2.2 percent.

Test your knowledge about criminal background checks and the employment of ex-offenders in the U.S.:

MYJLI.COM/CRIME

TEXT **3a**

LEVITICUS 19:16

לֹא תֵלֵךְ רָכִיל בְּעַמֶּיךָ.

You shall not go around as a gossipmonger amongst your people.

TEXT **3b**

MAIMONIDES, *MISHNEH TORAH*, LAWS OF CHARACTER DEVELOPMENT 7:2, 5

אֵי זֶהוּ רָכִיל, זֶה שֶׁטּוֹעֵן דְּבָרִים וְהוֹלֵךְ מִזֶּה לָזֶה וְאוֹמֵר, כָּךְ אָמַר פְּלוֹנִי כָּךְ וְכָךְ שָׁמַעְתִּי עַל פְּלוֹנִי. אַף עַל פִּי שֶׁהוּא אֱמֶת, הֲרֵי זֶה מַחֲרִיב אֶת הָעוֹלָם.

יֵשׁ עָוֹן גָּדוֹל מִזֶּה עַד מְאוֹד וְהוּא בִּכְלַל לָאו זֶה, וְהוּא לְשׁוֹן הָרַע; וְהוּא הַמְסַפֵּר בִּגְנוּת חֲבֵרוֹ, אַף עַל פִּי שֶׁאוֹמֵר אֱמֶת.

אֲבָל הָאוֹמֵר שֶׁקֶר נִקְרָא מוֹצִיא שֵׁם רַע עַל חֲבֵרוֹ. אֲבָל בַּעַל לְשׁוֹן הָרַע זֶה שֶׁיּוֹשֵׁב וְאוֹמֵר, כָּךְ וְכָךְ עָשָׂה פְּלוֹנִי, וְכָךְ וְכָךְ הָיוּ אֲבוֹתָיו, וְכָךְ וְכָךְ שָׁמַעְתִּי עָלָיו, וְאוֹמֵר דְּבָרִים שֶׁל גְּנַאי . . .

אֶחָד הַמְסַפֵּר בִּלְשׁוֹן הָרַע בִּפְנֵי חֲבֵרוֹ, אוֹ שֶׁלֹּא בְּפָנָיו. וְהַמְסַפֵּר דְּבָרִים שֶׁגּוֹרְמִין אִם נִשְׁמְעוּ אִישׁ מִפִּי אִישׁ לְהַזִּיק חֲבֵרוֹ בְּגוּפוֹ אוֹ בְּמָמוֹנוֹ, אֲפִלּוּ לְהָצֵר לוֹ אוֹ לְהַפְחִידוֹ, הֲרֵי זֶה לְשׁוֹן הָרַע.

A gossiper is one who collects information and then goes from person to person, saying, "So said this one; I heard so and so regarding this one." Even if the information is true, it destroys the world.

RABBI MOSHE BEN MAIMON (MAIMONIDES, RAMBAM) 1135–1204

Halachist, philosopher, author, and physician. Maimonides was born in Córdoba, Spain. After the conquest of Córdoba by the Almohads, he fled Spain and eventually settled in Cairo, Egypt. There, he became the leader of the Jewish community and served as court physician to the vizier of Egypt. He is most noted for authoring the *Mishneh Torah,* an encyclopedic arrangement of Jewish law, and for his philosophical work, *Guide for the Perplexed*. His rulings on Jewish law are integral to the formation of halachic consensus.

Included in this prohibition is a transgression that is much more severe: *lashon hara*—speaking disparagingly about others, even if speaking the truth.

Lashon hara does not refer to the invention of lies—that is referred to as defamation of character. Rather, one who speaks *lashon hara* is someone who sits and relates, "This is what so and so has done," "This person's parents were such and such," or "This is what I have heard about so and so," telling uncomplimentary things. . . .

There is no difference whether one speaks *lashon hara* about a person in his presence or behind his back. Any statement which, when passed from one person to another, will cause harm to someone's person or property—or even merely upset or frighten another—is considered *lashon hara*.

Village Gossip, Gerard Sekoto, oil painting, undated. (Johannesburg Art Gallery, Johannesburg)

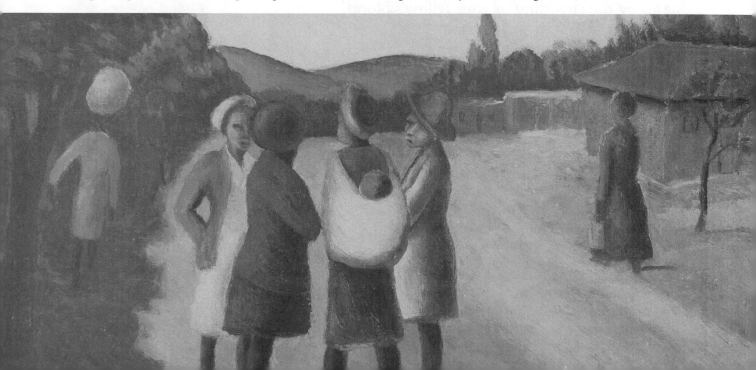

TEXT 4a

LEVITICUS 19:16

לֹא תַעֲמֹד עַל דַּם רֵעֶךָ.

You shall not stand by the shedding of your fellow's blood.

TEXT 4b

MAIMONIDES, *MISHNEH TORAH*, LAWS OF MURDERERS AND THE PROTECTION OF LIFE 1:14

שֶׁשָּׁמַע גּוֹיִם אוֹ מוֹסְרִים מְחַשְּׁבִים עָלָיו רָעָה אוֹ טוֹמְנִים לוֹ פַּח וְלֹא גִלָּה אֹזֶן חֲבֵירוֹ וְהוֹדִיעוֹ . . . עוֹבֵר עַל לֹא תַעֲמֹד עַל דַּם רֵעֶךָ.

If one hears of evildoers plotting to cause harm or intending to set a trap for his friend and does not inform him . . . he violates the prohibition of "You shall not stand by the shedding of your fellow's blood."

TEXT **5**

RABBI ELIEZER MELAMED, *PENINEI HALACHAH, LIKUTIM II, BEIN ADAM LECHAVEIRO* 13 ⊕

הַכְּלָל הַבְּסִיסִי הוּא, שֶׁכְּדֵי לְהַצִּיל חָבֵר מִלִּיפּוֹל בְּפַח, מוּתָּר לְהַזְהִירוֹ עַל כָּךְ.

לְמָשָׁל, כַּאֲשֶׁר רְאוּבֵן רוֹצֶה לַעֲשׂוֹת שׁוּתָּפוּת עִם שִׁמְעוֹן, וְלֵוִי - חֲבֵירוֹ שֶׁל רְאוּבֵן - יוֹדֵעַ כִּי יֵשׁ חֲשָׁשׁ שֶׁשִּׁמְעוֹן יְרַמֶּה אוֹתוֹ, מִפְּנֵי שֶׁשִּׁמְעוֹן נוֹטֶה לְעִיתִּים לְרַמּוֹת. אִם יִשְׁאַל אוֹתוֹ רְאוּבֵן עַל שִׁמְעוֹן, עָלָיו לוֹמַר לוֹ אֶת הָאֱמֶת, וּבִלְבַד שֶׁיִּיזָּהֵר מְאוֹד שֶׁלֹּא לְהַגְזִים בִּדְבָרָיו.

וְאִם מִסְתַּבֵּר לוֹ שֶׁשִּׁמְעוֹן עוֹמֵד לְרַמּוֹת אֶת רְאוּבֵן, גַּם אִם רְאוּבֵן לֹא בָּא לִשְׁאוֹל בַּעֲצָתוֹ, צָרִיךְ לֵוִי לָבוֹא אֵצֶל רְאוּבֵן וּלְהַזְהִירוֹ.

וְזֹאת בִּתְנַאי שֶׁכַּוָּונָתוֹ תִּהְיֶה טְהוֹרָה, כְּדֵי לְהַצִּיל אֶת רְאוּבֵן מִלִּיפּוֹל בְּפַח, וְיִיזָּהֵר מְאוֹד שֶׁלֹּא לְהַגְזִים בִּדְבָרָיו.

RABBI ELIEZER MELAMED
1961–

Israeli rabbi and *rosh yeshiva*. Rabbi Melamed is the author of *Peninei Halachah*, a series of books on various halachic subjects discussing practical laws as well as their spiritual foundations.

The basic rule is that, in order to save people from harm, it is permissible to warn them.

For example: Reuben intends to enter into a business partnership with Simon, and Reuben's friend Levi knows that there are reasonable grounds to suspect that Simon will defraud him, because Simon has been known to do so in the past. In this case, if Reuben asks Levi about Simon, Levi must tell him the truth, while taking great care not to exaggerate in any way.

If Levi believes it is probable that Simon will swindle Reuben, then he must go to Reuben on his own in order to warn him, even if Reuben did not approach him and inquire about Simon.

All this is on the condition that his intentions are pure—to save Reuben from harm—and that he is extremely careful not to exaggerate anything he says.

Learn more about the laws and ethics of gossip (lashon hara):

MYJLI.COM/CRIME

QUESTION FOR DISCUSSION

Based on the laws of *lashon hara,* how would criminal background information be regulated?

TEXT 6

TOSEFTA, DEMAI 2:8

וְכוּלָן שֶׁחָזְרוּ בָּהֶן . . . מְקַבְּלִין אוֹתָן שֶׁנֶּאֱמַר, "שׁוּבוּ בָּנִים שׁוֹבָבִים
וגו'"(יִרְמְיָהוּ ג, כב).

Thieves and those who weren't particular about separating tithes in the past that have done *teshuvah . . .* are accepted as reliable. As the verse states, "Turn back, rebellious children, and I will heal your rebellion."

TOSEFTA

A compendium of laws similar in format to that of the Mishnah; it consists of teachings of the sages of the Mishnah. At times, the material in both works is similar; at other times, there are significant differences between the two. The Talmud often compares these texts in its analysis. According to tradition, the *Tosefta* was redacted by Rabbis Chiyah and Oshiyah in the beginning of the third century in the Land of Israel.

TEXT 7

RABBI GERSHOM ME'OR HAGOLAH, *RESPONSA* 4

עַל עֵסֶק כֹּהֵן שֶׁנִּשְׁתַּמֵּד וְעָשָׂה תְּשׁוּבָה, אִם רָאוּי לִישָׂא כַּפָּיו וְלִקְרוֹת בַּתּוֹרָה תְּחִלָּה אוֹ לֹא.

כָּךְ דַּעְתִּי נוֹטָה, שֶׁאַף עַל פִּי שֶׁנִּשְׁתַּמֵּד, כֵּיוָן שֶׁעָשָׂה תְּשׁוּבָה רָאוּי לַעֲלוֹת לַדּוּכָן וְלִישָׂא אֶת כַּפָּיו . . . כְּבָר כָּתַב עַל יְדֵי נְבִיאָיו, "שׁוּבוּ אֵלַי וְאָשׁוּבָה אֲלֵיכֶם" (מַלְאָכִי ג, ז), וְכֵיוָן שֶׁשָּׁב קִבְּלוֹ הַמָּקוֹם וּמַסְכִּים עַל יָדוֹ בְּבִרְכָתוֹ.

הִלְכָּךְ אֵין לָנוּ רְאָיָה לֹא מִן הַמִּקְרָא וְלֹא מִן הַמִּשְׁנָה לְפוֹסְלוֹ. אֶלָּא יֵשׁ לְסַיֵּעַ מִן הַמִּקְרָא וּמִמִּשְׁנָה שֶׁלֹּא לְפוֹסְלוֹ, דִּכְתִיב, "וְלֹא תוֹנוּ אִישׁ אֶת עֲמִיתוֹ" (וַיִּקְרָא כה, יז) בְּאוֹנָאַת דְּבָרִים הַכָּתוּב מְדַבֵּר. כֵּיצַד, אִם הָיָה בַּעַל תְּשׁוּבָה לֹא יֹאמַר לוֹ זְכֹר מַעֲשֶׂיךָ הָרִאשׁוֹנִים. וְאִם תֹּאמַר לֹא יַעֲלֶה לַדּוּכָן וְלֹא יִקְרָא בַּתּוֹרָה תְּחִלָּה, אֵין לְךָ אוֹנָאָה גְּדוֹלָה מִזּוֹ.

וְעוֹד נִמְצֵאתָ אַתָּה מְרַפֶּה יְדֵיהֶם שֶׁל בַּעֲלֵי תְּשׁוּבָה, וְלֹא נָכוֹן לַעֲשׂוֹת כֵּן. דְּאָמַר רַבִּי יוֹחָנָן, "כָּל הָאוֹמֵר מְנַשֶּׁה חָטָא אֵין לוֹ חֵלֶק לָעוֹלָם הַבָּא לְפִי שֶׁמְּרַפֶּה יְדֵיהֶם שֶׁל בַּעֲלֵי תְּשׁוּבָה" (סַנְהֶדְרִין קג, א). וְאִם תֹּאמַר לֹא יַעֲלֶה לַדּוּכָן וְלֹא יִקְרָא בַּתּוֹרָה תְּחִלָּה, מְהַרְהֵר בְּלִבּוֹ לְשִׁמְדָתוֹ וְאוֹמֵר, אוֹי לָהּ לְאוֹתָהּ בּוּשָׁה אוֹי לָהּ לְאוֹתָהּ כְּלִימָה . . .

הִלְכָּךְ מִכָּל טְעָמִים אֵלּוּ, אַף עַל פִּי שֶׁנִּשְׁתַּמֵּד, כֵּיוָן שֶׁעָשָׂה תְּשׁוּבָה הֲרֵי הוּא כִּשְׁאָר אֶחָיו הַכֹּהֲנִים וְעוֹלֶה לַדּוּכָן וְקוֹרֵא רִאשׁוֹן בַּתּוֹרָה.

RABBI GERSHOM ME'OR HAGOLAH
960–1040

Halachic authority and commentator on the Bible and Talmud. Rabbi Gershom is known for his rulings, accepted by all European Jews, regarding social and family life. Among these laws are prohibitions of polygamy and of opening others' mail.

Regarding the case of a *kohen* who converted to Christianity and the question of whether it is appropriate for him to give the priestly blessing and be called to the Torah as a *kohen*:

My opinion is that although he converted to Christianity, because he has done *teshuvah* he may receive the priestly honors. G-d told us through His prophet Malachi,

"Return to Me, and I will return to you" (MALACHI 3:7). Because this person has returned, G-d has accepted him and endorses his blessings.

There is no support from Scripture or the Mishnah to disqualify him from these honors. On the contrary, there is proof from Scripture and the Mishnah that he is to be accepted. The verse states, "You shall not wrong each other" (LEVITICUS 25:17), referring to verbal mistreatment. As an example of this, the Mishnah states, "One may not say to a returnee, 'Remember your former deeds'" (MISHNAH, BAVA METSI'A 4:10). There can be no greater verbal mistreatment than telling this person that he is not allowed to receive the priestly honors.

In addition, if you do this, you will weaken the resolve of returnees, and it is wrong to do so. Rabbi Yochanan taught that anyone that says that King Manasseh has no portion in the World to Come has weakened the resolve of returnees (TALMUD, SANHEDRIN 103A). If you bar this man from the priestly honors, he will have thoughts of regret for returning, because of his embarrassment and shame.

For all of these reasons, even though he converted to Christianity, because he has returned he should be afforded all of the priestly honors.

TEXT **8**

TALMUD, SANHEDRIN 25B

> וְאֵימָתַי חֲזָרָתָן, מִשֶּׁיְשַׁבְּרוּ אֶת פִּיסְפָּסֵיהֶן וְיַחְזְרוּ בָּהֶן חֲזָרָה גְמוּרָה,
> דַּאֲפִילוּ בְּחִנָּם לֹא עָבְדֵי.

Professional gamblers can be accepted as reliable witnesses after they break their gambling pieces and abandon this practice completely, not even playing without money.

BABYLONIAN TALMUD

A literary work of monumental proportions that draws upon the legal, spiritual, intellectual, ethical, and historical traditions of Judaism. The 37 tractates of the Babylonian Talmud contain the teachings of the Jewish sages from the period after the destruction of the Second Temple through the fifth century CE. It has served as the primary vehicle for the transmission of the Oral Law and the education of Jews over the centuries; it is the entry point for all subsequent legal, ethical, and theological Jewish scholarship.

Gaming piece and die found in Battle Abbey; Battle, East Sussex, England, c. late 15th to 16th century. (English Heritage Collection)

TEXT 9

TALMUD, SANHEDRIN 25A

הַהוּא טַבָּחָא דְּאִישְׁתַּכַּח דְּנַפְקָא טְרֵיפְתָּא מִתּוּתֵי יָדֵיה, פְּסָלֵיה רַב נַחְמָן וְעַבְּרֵיה.

אֲזַל רַבֵּי מַזְיֵה וְטוּפְרֵיה, סָבַר רַב נַחְמָן לְאַכְשׁוּרֵיה. אָמַר לֵיה רָבָא, דִּילְמָא אִיעֲרוּמֵי קָא מַעֲרִים.

אֶלָּא מַאי תַּקַּנְתֵּיה, כִּדְרַב אִידִי בַּר אָבִין. דְּאָמַר רַב אִידִי בַּר אָבִין, הֶחָשׁוּד עַל הַטְּרֵיפוֹת אֵין לוֹ תַּקָּנָה עַד שֶׁיֵּלֵךְ לְמָקוֹם שֶׁאֵין מַכִּירִין אוֹתוֹ וְיַחֲזִיר אֲבֵידָה בְּדָבָר חָשׁוּב אוֹ שֶׁיּוֹצִיא טְרֵיפָה מִתַּחַת יָדוֹ בְּדָבָר חָשׁוּב מִשֶּׁלּוֹ.

A certain slaughterer was caught selling nonkosher meat to his unwitting customers. Rabbi Nachman disqualified him from testifying as a witness and removed him from his position as a slaughterer.

The slaughterer let his fingernails and his hair grow as a sign of remorse, and Rabbi Nachman thought that he could now be reinstated. But Rava said to him, "Perhaps he is only pretending to have done *teshuvah*."

What then is the slaughterer's remedy? Rabbi Idi bar Avin says, "One who is suspected of passing nonkosher meat as kosher can only restore his status when he goes to a locale where they do not recognize him and returns a lost item of substantial value that he finds, or declares a very valuable piece of meat nonkosher at personal financial loss.

QUESTION FOR DISCUSSION

Why does the Talmud require extra steps to demonstrate *teshuvah* in the cases of Texts 8 and 9?

TEXT 10

RABBI MOSHE SOFER, *RESPONSA CHATAM SOFER, ORACH CHAYIM* 175

וְהִנֵּה, עִיקַר הַתְּשׁוּבָה אֵינָהּ אֶלָּא עֲזִיבַת הַחֵטְא וַחֲרָטָה בְּלֵב וּוִידּוּי פֶּה, וּמִיַּד הוּא צַדִּיק וְנֶאֱמָן.

אֶלָּא לִפְעָמִים אָדָם עוֹשֶׂה כַּנַּ"ל לְהַטְעוֹת הַבְּרִיּוֹת וְהוּא עוֹשֶׂה בְּלִי לֵב וָלֵב. עַל כֵּן אֵין אָנוּ מַאֲמִינִים עַד שֶׁנִּרְאֶה בּוֹ סִימָן תְּשׁוּבָה, כְּגוֹן שֶׁיֵּלֵךְ לְמָקוֹם שֶׁאֵין מַכִּירִין וְיַחֲזִיר אֲבֵידָה בְּדָבָר חָשׁוּב (סַנְהֶדְרִין כ"ה ע"א) לְעִנְיָן חֲשָׁד הֲנָאַת מָמוֹן כְּגוֹן שׁוֹחֵט, וְהוּא הַדִּין בִּשְׁאָרֵי עִנְיָנִים כַּיּוֹצֵא בָּזֶה.

RABBI MOSHE SOFER
(CHATAM SOFER) 1762–1839

A leading rabbinical authority of the 19th century. Born in Frankfurt am Main, *Chatam Sofer* ultimately accepted the rabbinate of Pressburg (now Bratislava), Slovakia. Serving as rabbi and head of the yeshiva that he established, Rabbi Sofer maintained a strong traditionalist perspective, opposing deviation from Jewish tradition. *Chatam Sofer* is the title of his collection of halachic responsa and his commentary to the Talmud.

The primary requirements of *teshuvah* are abandonment of sin, remorse, and verbal confession. People who have completed these steps are immediately considered righteous and faithful.

Sometimes, however, people may do these actions outwardly and insincerely, in order to deceive the public. Therefore, we cannot trust them until we see a demonstrable sign of *teshuvah*, such as going to a place where they are not recognized and returning a valuable lost object there. This is what the Talmud (SANHEDRIN 25A) taught regarding financial dishonesty, as in the case of the slaughterer, and the same applies to similar cases.

TEXT **11**

RABBI HAI GA'ON, PUBLISHED IN *KOL BO* 147

שׁוּרַת הַדִּין שֶׁאֵין לְךָ דָּבָר שֶׁעוֹמֵד בִּפְנֵי תְּשׁוּבָה. אֶלָּא כָּל הַשָּׁבִים שֶׁהַקָּדוֹשׁ בָּרוּךְ הוּא יוֹדֵעַ כִּי נִתְחָרְטוּ עַל מַה שֶּׁעָבְרוּ מִן הַכִּעוּר וְכִי שָׂמוּ אֶל לִבָּם שֶׁלֹּא יָשׁוּבוּ עוֹד לִכְמוֹהוּ, הוּא מוֹחֵל לָהֶם.

וּבְנֵי אָדָם, אַף עַל פִּי שֶׁאֵינָן יוֹדְעִין הַנִּסְתָּרוֹת וְאֵין לָהֶם אֶלָּא הַנִּגְלוֹת, כְּשֶׁעָבַר זְמַן הַרְבֵּה וְאֵין נִרְאֶה עָלָיו לֹא בְגָלוּי וְלֹא בְּסֵתֶר דָּבָר שֶׁלֹּא כַּהוֹגֶן, וְהַלֵּב מַאֲמִין בּוֹ כִּי חָזַר, מְקַבְּלִין אוֹתוֹ.

The basic law is that nothing stands in the way of *teshuvah*. G-d forgives all those returnees that He knows have regretted their reprehensible misdeeds and resolved never to commit them again.

As for mortals, even though we can't see into people's hearts, but can only judge based on observation—once a long time has passed, and the returnee shows no sign of public or private impropriety, and our heart believes that true *teshuvah* has been done, he or she should be accepted.

RAV HAI GA'ON
939–1038

Rabbi, author and poet. Born to a distinguished family that included amongst its ancestors exilarchs and heads of yeshiva, Rav Hai succeeded his aged father, Sherira, as ga'on of Pumpedita (in modern-day Iraq). As head of the Rabbinical Court and later as head of the yeshiva, Rav Hai was seen as the leader of world Jewry, which is evident in his correspondence with Jewish communities worldwide, some of which is still extant. He authored works on Jewish law, Talmud, the Hebrew language, poetry, and Tanach, most of which has not been preserved. With his passing at the ripe age of 99, the epoch of the *ge'onim* came to a close.

TEXT 12a

LEVITICUS 19:15

בְּצֶדֶק תִּשְׁפֹּט עֲמִיתֶךָ.

You shall judge your fellow with righteousness.

TEXT 12b

SEFER HACHINUCH, MITZVAH 235

וְעוֹד יֵשׁ בִּכְלָל מִצְוָה זוּ, שֶׁרָאוּי לְכָל אָדָם לָדוּן אֶת חֲבֵרוֹ לְכַף זְכוּת, וְלֹא
יְפָרֵשׁ מַעֲשָׂיו וּדְבָרָיו אֶלָּא לְטוֹב . . .
בַּמֶּה שֶׁאָמַרְנוּ שֶׁכָּל אָדָם חַיָּב לָדוּן חֲבֵרוֹ לְכַף זְכוּת, שֶׁהוּא בִּכְלָל הַמִּצְוָה,
יִהְיֶה סִיבָּה לִהְיוֹת בֵּין אֲנָשִׁים שָׁלוֹם וְרֵעוּת . . . עִם סִילוּק הַחֲשָׁד
אִישׁ בְּאִישׁ.

This commandment also instructs us that we should all judge our fellow favorably, and interpret his or her conduct and words in a positive light. . . .

The reason why we must judge our fellow favorably is in order to foster peace and harmony among people . . . by eliminating suspicion of one another.

SEFER HACHINUCH

A work on the biblical commandments. Four aspects of every mitzvah are discussed in this work: the definition of the mitzvah; ethical lessons that can be deduced from the mitzvah; basic laws pertaining to the observance of the mitzvah; and who is obligated to perform the mitzvah, and when. The work was composed in the 13th century by an anonymous author who refers to himself as "the Levite of Barcelona." It has been widely thought that this referred to Rabbi Aharon Halevi of Barcelona (Re'ah); however, this view has been contested.

KEY POINTS

1 Jewish law forbids relaying negative information about people unless it is necessary in order to prevent harm to others.

2 Consequently, employers should only be provided with criminal background information about employees on a need-to-know basis. Only information about crimes that have specific relevance to the particular employer should be disclosed, and if the passage of time means the ex-offender no longer presents an elevated risk, information about past offenses should be concealed.

3 Jewish law prohibits discriminating against reformed ex-offenders and stresses the importance of this policy in encouraging offenders to change their ways.

4 For perpetrators of financial crimes, Jewish law requires demonstrable steps of change in order to assess *teshuvah*. Passage of time without re-offense is also an indicator to consider.

5 Jewish ethics call on us to endeavor to judge former offender favorably and afford them a chance.

How likely are you to hire a person with a criminal record? Take a poll at:

MYJLI.COM/CRIME

Additional Readings

A SURVEY OF POLICIES FOR THE INTEGRATION OF EX-OFFENDERS

RABBI ELIEZER GURKOW

This paper surveys policies for the reintegration of ex-offenders into society, specifically, to increase their opportunities of obtaining gainful employment.

The Problem

After completing their sentences and being released from physical confinement, ex-offenders often find themselves incarcerated in the virtual walls of society's rejection. This form of imprisonment is manifest in many roadblocks to opportunities, including housing, employment, education, and access to various benefit programs.[1] Many laws compound the effect as some state statutes deny ex-offenders the right to acquire licenses necessary for many activities. Some states even restrict the ex-offender's right to vote.[2]

This is also true for ex-offenders who were never incarcerated, but are nonetheless stigmatized by criminal records for low-level misdemeanors and violations. Because of the stigma of a criminal record, society will often deny them a fair chance at reintegration.[3]

An element of the problem arises from laws, statutes, or regulations that impose penalties, disabilities, or disadvantages on those convicted for a criminal offense. This paper will address some of these laws, but the primary focus will be on employer discrimination and their reluctance to hire ex-offenders.

RABBI ELIEZER GURKOW

Author and lecturer. Rabbi Gurkow is the spiritual leader of Congregation Beth Tefilah in London, Ontario. He lectures extensively on a variety of Jewish topics, and his articles appear in many print and online publications. Rabbi Gurkow is also a member of the JLI curriculum team, and authored *Portraits in Leadership,* a highly popular JLI course.

Employer discrimination places a harsh burden on ex-offenders. Studies show that ex-offenders earn lower wages and work fewer hours than those without criminal records. This translates into an average loss of nearly $179,000 by the time ex-offenders reach the age of forty-eight.[4] This makes it difficult for ex-offenders to earn an income and keep their family together.

Employer discrimination also places an unfair burden on society. There appears to be a general consensus that barriers to employment significantly increase recidivism rates.[5] Estimates of the number of Americans with criminal records range between 65 and 95 million.[6] Approximately two-thirds of ex-offenders are arrested for a new offense within three years of their release.[7] A staggering eighty-nine percent of those rearrested were unemployed.[8] By contrast, a 2015 study conducted by the Manhattan Institute found that the rates of recidivism for nonviolent[9] ex-offenders who find employment shortly after their release is twenty percent lower than the national average.[10]

The problem of recidivism also increases the burden of the criminal justice system, which must absorb the cost of investigation, prosecution, and incarceration of repeat offenders. It is estimated that the general cost of incarceration to state and federal governments exceeds fifty billion dollars annually.[11] Considering that it costs more than thirty-one thousand dollars, on average, to keep someone in prison for a year,[12] reducing recidivism rates would significantly reduce the cost of incarceration.

Criminal Background Checks

In the United States, every brush with the law results in a record held by the relevant agency. Most court records—of arrests, criminal charges, or convictions—are available to the public under the Freedom of Information Act. In fact, much of this information is freely available online.

It is legal for anyone to access publicly available criminal records. However, collecting enough information to build a dossier about a prospective employee can be difficult for the average employer. Therefore, private companies, known as Consumer Reporting Agencies, build dossiers on prospective employees by combing publicly available records across the country and collating the information into comprehensive reports on an applicant's criminal history.[13]

In addition to publicly available records, state authorities and the FBI maintain comprehensive criminal background records that are not available to the public. However, employers in regulated professions,[14] who are mandated by state law to perform background checks on prospective employees, are granted access to such records. Professions regulated by the state include the obvious, such as doctors and lawyers. However, there are states where professions such as plumbers, electricians, massage therapists and barbers are also regulated, which means that even sealed databases are accessible to a broad spectrum of the public.[15]

Accessing publicly available records doesn't require the subject's consent. However, using such information for employment or rental purposes does require prior consent from the subject. Similarly, access to non-public records (such as those held by the states and the FBI) requires the applicant's prior consent.[16] Applicants may withhold consent, but since employers may refuse an application if consent is withheld, the applicant has little choice but to consent.

Modern technology has made criminal records much easier to access, and this has caused a significant rise in the number of employers that perform criminal background checks.

In the 1990s, only about one-third of employers in the United States performed criminal background checks as a matter of course. A 2010 survey found that seventy-three percent of employers reported checking criminal records for prospective employees. In 2013, eighty-eight percent of employers reported performing criminal background checks—with the percentage being slightly higher among small business owners.[17]

Proposals to solve this problem encounter many obstacles. Chief among them is the obvious reluctance of employers to hire employees with a criminal background.

A study conducted in the 1990s found that sixty-two percent of employers said they would not hire an ex-offender. By comparison, only forty-one percent of employers said they would not hire employees with a spotty work history, and only eighteen percent would not hire employees who had been unemployed for more than a year. It is clear that the existence of a criminal record creates a greater reluctance in potential employers than an inconsistent work record.[18]

When asked why they were reluctant to hire candidates with criminal records, employers reported several concerns. Among them were the safety and security of their clients and employees. There were also concerns about possible theft, embezzlement, and other criminal activity in the workplace. In addition, there were concerns that former criminals might have character flaws, such as a lack of honesty, reliability, punctuality, or a positive work ethic.[19] It appears that the existence of a criminal record creates an impression that the candidate is likely to possess a host of negative traits.

In addition, employers are concerned that hiring ex-offenders could expose them to liability for hiring negligence if the ex-offender that they hired would harm a third party such as a fellow employee or a customer.[20] A key consideration in a determination about whether an employer was negligent in hiring an ex-offender would center on whether the employer performed a reasonable investigation into the background of the employee before hiring. The frequency of such claims has increased in the last few years and the verdicts or settlements can be sizable.[21] This is one reason an increased number of employers perform criminal background checks as a matter of course and are reluctant to hire candidates with criminal records.

Any attempt to improve the reintegration of ex-offenders into society must address the legitimate concerns of prospective employers and the issue of the employer's potential liability. Requiring an employer to hire an ex-offender and then holding them liable if a third party is harmed, places the employer in an untenable position: it forces the employer to assume liability for third-party injury when, the likelihood of third-party injury would likely be lower, had the employer had the option of not hiring an ex-offender.

Suggested Reforms
This paper will now present two different methods of dealing with this problem. First, the paper will survey some of the reforms that have been suggested for the United States penal system. Then, the paper will survey Israeli law which was inspired by traditional Jewish sources.

In a 2014 article, *Employment of Ex-Offenders: The Time Has Come for a True Antidiscrimination Statute*, Sandra J. Mullings provided comprehensive suggestions to reform employers' use of criminal background checks in the United States. Following is a summary of Mullings's suggestions.

The first and most important suggestion is to afford ex-offenders a fair chance at a first interview. Employers should not be provided access to a candidate's criminal records until after the candidate has successfully completed the first interview. This affords candidates a fair chance to be considered on the basis of their qualifications, and to make a positive first impression regardless of their past history.

Many existing statutes and ordinances, under the "Ban the Box" heading, already require this. It means that employers are banned from requiring applicants to fill in a box on the application form indicating whether they have a criminal record. This ban prevents employers from denying candidates as a matter of course merely because a criminal record exists.[22]

However, Mullings argues that these statutes are limited by the fact that they pertain only to public agencies or private contractors who deal with public agencies. They don't relieve the burden for ex-offenders who seek work in the private sector. Even in the public sector, these statutes are of limited value. Many "Ban the Box" regulations do not prevent employers from performing background checks on their own without asking whether applicants have a criminal record. Even in states that have provisions to prevent employers from performing criminal background checks before the initial interview is conducted, there is no restriction on employers accessing criminal records after the first interview. Once an employer gains access to a candidate's criminal record, they are allowed to deny candidates solely on the basis of their criminal past.[23]

"Ban the Box" statutes would work most effectively if they were followed up by parallel statutes that limit how employers are permitted to act on information in the criminal record.

The best way of doing this would be to enact a comprehensive federal law that prohibits the mere existence of a criminal record as a basis for employment decisions. This statute would need to be written clearly to preclude the need for states and courts to argue over the interpretation of this law.

A federal law of this magnitude would likely come in conflict with many state laws. It would therefore need to be written in a way that would allow it to take precedence over all state laws on this matter. However, this is likely to encounter considerable resistance on constitutional grounds, and it is not likely to pass. Even if passed, it would take years to examine all the relevant state statutes because many were written piecemeal and are scattered across the legal code. Mullings therefore suggests that despite the benefits of a federal statute, it might be more effective and constitutional to draft a model statute that can be adopted by the states.[24]

Mullings also suggests that the statute should apply to public agencies, to private employers, and to state and municipal agencies charged with issuing licenses.

Mullings argues that the statute should not present a blanket prohibition against considering a criminal record in making employment decisions, because there are often valid reasons to refuse a particular job to a person convicted of a crime relevant to that job.[25] For example, it is reasonable not to offer a job that requires honesty to someone who was convicted of embezzlement. A candidate convicted of sexual behavior with a child should not be allowed to be employed at a children's school.

Rather, Mullings suggests that the statute provide guidance about how information from a candidate's criminal record may be used when considering a job or license application.

As noted earlier, the statute would begin with a general statement to the effect that employment may never be denied merely because a criminal record exists. This is critical because over time, such pronouncements in federal or state statutes will positively impact society's overall attitude toward ex-offenders.

The statute would then proceed to lay out and regulate the precise fact-specific considerations that lead an employer or license issuer to determine whether a particular candidate may be denied a particular job.

First, the employer or license issuer would consider the specific duties and responsibilities inherent in the potential job or license. This would then be compared to the crime or crimes for which the candidate was convicted to see if these crimes have a direct relationship to the candidate's ability to perform such duties. The employer or license issuer would also consider the seriousness of the offense, how much time has elapsed without re-offense since the crime was committed, the age of the candidate when the crime was committed, and whether the candidate had engaged in rehabilitative efforts since committing the crime.

Conversely, employers or license issuers would also consider the safety of other employees, customers, the public and the protection of property.

After all these factors are given due consideration, employers and license issuers would be able to determine whether the candidate's criminal record should act as a barrier to employment or to the issuance of a license.[26]

To be enforceable, ex-offenders would be allowed to sue for discrimination if their criminal records are abused. The statute would also provide ex-offenders with a government agency to support their lawsuit. The statute would specify the penalties employers would incur such as back or front pay, injunctive relief, or attorney's fees. The statute would require employers to post notices in the workplace about the rights of those subjected to record checks and directions on how to secure counsel or receive guidance from government agencies.[27]

To address the issue of employer liability for negligent hiring in the event that a third party is damaged or injured by the ex-offender, under this statute, employers who comply with the statute's balancing test before hiring would have an affirmative defense to negligent hiring claims. A better option would be to make evidence of the criminal record inadmissible to any such proceeding.

A somewhat more radical suggestion would be the issuance of a certificate of relief to ex-offenders who pass the balancing test. This certificate would protect any potential employer against a charge of negligent hiring. It may also be beneficial to consider a cap on liability for negligent hiring, similar to the caps imposed by some states for medical malpractice liability.[28]

Notwithstanding the improvements from such legislation, several concerns remain.

Will forcing employers to hire ex-offenders cause customers and fellow employees to abandon the company out of fear? Will it result in an increase in workplace violence and fraud? Will potential employers respond by devising alternate ruses under which to reject ex-offenders? Would ex-offenders have the gumption to challenge prospective employers in court? Even if an ex-offender secures employment, will forcing an employer to hire ex-offenders impact their relationship with their employees?

The Israeli Approach

Drawing inspiration from traditional Jewish sources, Israel adopted the Criminal Register and Rehabilitation of Offenders Law in 1991, which takes a radically different approach to criminal records.

Israeli law denies the general public access to criminal records held by any government agency. Private employers in Israel are never permitted access to criminal records, even if hiring for sensitive, trust-based positions.[29] Access is restricted to police, military, and intelligence authorities.[30] Select public agencies, such as the diplomatic corps, are permitted to perform criminal background checks before hiring. But even these agencies are not granted direct access to the records; rather, they must work through the police authorities. In addition, they are not permitted to refuse employment on the mere basis of a criminal record. Rather, they must determine that the candidate's criminal past impacts their ability to serve in the capacity of their prospective employment.[31] If the ex-offender exhibits exemplary behavior and refrains from reoffending, the pool of agencies granted access to the criminal record shrinks over time, until the criminal history is completely stricken from the record.[32]

When considering this law, members of the Knesset, Israel's legislative body, debated the benefits and drawbacks of allowing private sector employers access to criminal records. Those who supported access argued that since dossiers can be compiled by private investigators,[33] restricting legal access would not protect the ex-offender. It would only result in burdening private sector employers with the cost of hiring private investigators. They further argued that restricting such information would create a black market in which unscrupulous members of the police force would be paid to leak criminal records to interested parties. It would be preferable to establish an orderly and effective system through which this information could be transmitted legally. They further argued that it is inappropriate for the state to conspire with criminals to cover up their criminal past.[34]

Those who supported withholding criminal records from private sector employers replied that potential leaks can be controlled by maintaining a registry of those with access to the records. They argued that if criminal records were available to the private sector, employers might abuse the information by rejecting ex-offenders solely because of the existence of a criminal record. Furthermore, once they obtain such records they might share it with unauthorized parties for unscrupulous purposes. Finally, they argued that society is charged with the moral duty to offer ex-offenders a smooth and valid path to rehabilitation.[35]

These arguments are in line with Jewish values. Jewish tradition opposes public access to criminal records on the grounds of *lashon hara*—relaying negative information about another. It is forbidden to share even accurate information with those who have no need to know.[36] However, when there are reasonable grounds to suspect that someone will be harmed by another, it is permissible to convey this information to the potential victim with the caveat that we avoid exaggeration and only share information that is relevant to the potential victim.[37] On this basis,

Jewish tradition would only allow authorities to share aspects of a prospective employee's criminal record that directly impact on the responsibilities they seek to assume.

The laws of *lashon hara* apply to all people, but repentant criminals are entitled to additional consideration. Judaism espouses the value of *takanat hashavim*—the requirement to support repentant criminals in their efforts to repent and in their quest for rehabilitation.[38] Once ex-offenders complete their punishment, enroll in rehabilitation programs, and exhibit a genuine and public desire to change their criminal ways, Jewish law requires that society extend a helping and welcoming hand.[39] We may bar ex-offenders from certain positions of authority and trust until they demonstrate that they have been completely rehabilitated, but society is expected to exhibit a general attitude of acceptance.[40]

Drawing inspiration from these Jewish values, Israeli legislators voted to restrict public access to criminal records. They essentially voted to surrender their right to discovery—even where it is legally and morally defensible—for the benefit of the ex-offender.[41] They determined that it is more important for society to rehabilitate the ex-offender than to engage in fear-based behavior that discriminates against and excludes ex-offenders.[42]

Available evidence shows that this decision did not result in increased violence or strained relations in the workplace. Neither does the Israeli public live in fear that their neighbor might be an ex-offender. Studies show that Israeli employers and the general public, who mix unwittingly with ex-offenders both in the workplace and in their neighborhoods, are more trusting of ex-offenders than the public in the United States, who are isolated from ex-offenders.[43]

We noted earlier that a 2013 study found that eighty-eight percent of employers in the United States perform criminal background checks for all employees. This implies that merely twelve percent of employers in the United States are prepared to hire an ex-offender. When employers in Israel were polled on whether they would hire a released prisoner, nineteen percent replied in the affirmative for any position. Sixty-seven percent replied that they would hire a released prisoner for certain positions. Only fourteen percent said that they would never hire a released prisoner.[44]

The willingness on the part of Israeli employers to hire ex-offenders is representative of the general perception held by the Israeli public. When members of the Israeli public were asked whether they believe prisoners can be rehabilitated, ninety-three percent replied in the affirmative. Seventy-five percent were willing to live next to a released prisoner. Sixty-six percent were willing to rent a room to a released prisoner and forty-two percent were willing to marry a released prisoner. When asked whether the law should be amended to allow public access to criminal records, eighty-two percent of Israelis replied that criminal records should remain sealed.[45]

These results suggest that forcing employers to engage with ex-offenders results in increased tolerance. The less potential employers know about an ex-offender's criminal background, the better they get along. They further suggest that, given the chance, many ex-offenders choose to rehabilitate as law-abiding citizens rather than re-offend.

Conclusion

Mullings's suggestions seek to limit employers' access to criminal records and how they can be used, but they do not completely suggest elimination of access to them. By contrast, the Israeli model denies private citizens any access to this information, and strictly regulates the access of governmental bodies as well.

In balancing the concerns of employers and the fears of society against the interests of ex-offenders, the status quo in the United States today rests heavily in favor of access. Mullings's suggestions attempt to strike a more even balance, while Israeli law strongly favors the rights of ex-offenders.

How society deals with this issue will have far-reaching effects on employers, ex-offenders, and on society as a whole. This is a serious matter that we ought to consider and evaluate carefully.

Endnotes

[1] Deborah N. Archer and Kele S. Williams, "Making America 'The Land of Second Chances': Restoring Socioeconomic Rights for Ex-Offenders," 30 *N.Y.U. Rev. L. & Soc. Change* 527, 2006.

[2] Debbie A. Mukamal and Paul N. Samuels, "Statutory Limitations on Civil Rights of People with Criminal Records," 30 *Ford. Urban L.J.* 1501, 2003.

[3] Sandra J. Mullings, "Employment of Ex-Offenders: The Time Has Come for a True Antidiscrimination Statute," *Syracuse Law Review*, 64, 2014, p. 266.

[4] The Pew Charitable Trusts, *Collateral Costs: Incarceration's Effect on Economic Mobility*, 2010, pp. 11–12.

[5] Mullings, supra note 3, at 267.

[6] Mullings, id.

[7] According to a 2005 study, *3 in 4 Former Prisoners in 30 States Arrested within 5 Years of Release*, by the U.S. Bureau of Justice Statistics. The study found that rates were highest among violent, public order, drug, and property offenders.

[8] Mike Green, "Five Bottom Line Reasons Why Employers Should Hire Ex-Felons," www.huffingtonpost.com/mike-green/five-bottom-line-reasons-_b_8021476.html.

[9] The study found that employment only reduced recidivism rates for violent offenders by two percent.

[10] Aaron Yelowitz and Christopher Bollinger, "Prison-To-Work: The Benefits of Intensive Job-Search Assistance for Former Inmates," www.manhattan-institute.org/html/prison-work-5876.html.

[11] Mullings, supra note 3, at 267.

[12] Peter Cove and Lee Bowes, "Immediate Access to Employment Reduces Recidivism," www.realclearpolitics.com/articles/2015/06/11/immediate_access_to_employment_reduces_recidivism_126939.html.

[13] The information these agencies are permitted to share is regulated by the federal Fair Credit Reporting Act (FCRA) and state laws.

[14] U.S. Department of Justice, "Attorney General's Report on Criminal History Background Checks," June 2006, p. 19.

[15] Over 25 percent of Americans require a license to perform their jobs. "The White House, Occupational Licensing: A Framework for Policymakers," July 2015, p. 3.

[16] Fair Credit Reporting Act (FCRA) 15 U.S.C. § 1681b.

[17] Mullings, supra note 3, p. 272.

[18] Mullings, *id.*, p. 271.

[19] Mullings, *id.*, p. 272.

[20] Mullings, *id.*, p. 273.

[21] Mullings, *id.*, p. 274.

[22] Mullings, *id.*, pp. 281–282.

[23] Mullings, *id.*, pp. 282–283. Mullings argues that evidence suggests Ban the Box initiatives result in employers excluding certain ethnic groups from consideration for employment assuming they have a criminal history.

[24] Mullings, *id.*, pp. 283–288.

[25] Mullings, *id.*, p. 290.

[26] Mullings, *id.*, pp. 290–291.

27 Mullings, *id.*, pp. 289–292.

28 Mullings, *id.*, pp. 292–293.

29 Nachum Rakover, *Takanat Hashavim* (Moreshet Hamishpat LeY-israel, 2007), p. 607.

30 Rakover, *id*, p.603.

31 Rakover, *id.*, p. 606.

32 Rakover, *id.*, p. 604. See p. 606, that the records are sealed rather than erased.

33 Private investigators would not have access to official criminal records, but they could perform background checks by combing media references to the subject, interview acquaintances, and thus recreate a credible history of the subject's past.

34 Rakover, supra note 29, p. 608.

35 Rakover, *id.*

36 Maimonides, *Mishneh Torah*, Laws of Murderers and the Protection of Life 7:6.

37 Rabbi Eliezer Melamed, *Peninei Halachah*, *Likutim* II, *Ben Adam Lechavero* 13.

38 See Rabbi Gershom Me'or Hagolah, *Responsa* 4. Maimonides, *Mishneh Torah*, Laws of Murderers and the Protection of Life 7:6.

39 Determining the precise benchmarks ex-offenders must reach before being recognized as an authentic penitent is beyond the scope of this paper.

40 Rakover, supra note 29, pp. 605–606

41 There are exceptions, such as the Prevention of Employment of Sex Offenders in Specific Institutions Law, passed in 2009, which requires institutions offering services to hapless individuals to obtain permission for employment from police authorities for each employee. See http://www.loc.gov/law/foreign-news/article/israel-prevention-of-employment-of-sex-offenders-in-specific-institutions/ and www.police.gov.il/english_contentPage.aspx?pid=22&menuid=29.

42 Rakover, supra note 29, p. 608.

43 Efrat Shoham and Uri Timor, "Once a Criminal, Always a Criminal? Attitudes Towards Reintegration of Released Prisoners among Israeli Public," *Canadian Social Science*, 10:6, 2014.

44 Shoham and Timor, *id.*, p. 110.

45 Shoham and Timor, *id.*, p. 112.

Lesson

AN OUNCE OF PREVENTION

ADDRESSING CRIME BEFORE IT HAPPENS

The best way to improve the criminal justice system is by keeping people out of it. But before any attempt to prevent crime can be made, its causes and preconditions must be better understood. Judaism has long recognized the role of societal factors in the commission of crime: poverty and unemployment are significant, as are education, values, and personal character. This final lesson discusses the roots of criminality, several specific preventative policy proposals, and the various concerns associated with them.

Grand escalier de Palais de justice, vue de faces (Grand Staircase of the Palace of Justice, view of the facade), from the series *Les Gens de Justice* (*Barristers*), Honoré Daumier, lithograph caricature, Marseille, 1848.

TEXT **1**

MISHNAH, MAKOT 1:10

סַנְהֶדְרִין הַהוֹרֶגֶת אֶחָד בַּשָּׁבוּעַ, נִקְרֵאת חַבְּלָנִית.

A Sanhedrin that executes once every seven years is called a "destructive" court.

MISHNAH

The first authoritative work of Jewish law that was codified in writing. The Mishnah contains the oral traditions that were passed down from teacher to student; it supplements, clarifies, and systematizes the commandments of the Torah. Due to the continual persecution of the Jewish people, it became increasingly difficult to guarantee that these traditions would not be forgotten. Rabbi Yehudah Hanasi therefore redacted the Mishnah at the end of the second century. It serves as the foundation for the Talmud.

Woedende volksmenigte op straat (*Furious Folk Crowd on the Street*), Anonymous, etching, Northern Netherlands, c. 1662–1664. (Rijksmuseum, Amsterdam)

TEXT 2

MIDRASH, *ELIYAHU RABAH*, CH. 11

שֶׁהָיָה לָהֶם לְסַנְהֶדְרֵי גְדוֹלָה שֶׁהִנִּיחַ מֹשֶׁה וִיהוֹשֻׁעַ . . . לֵילֵךְ, וְלִקְשׁוֹר חֲבָלִים שֶׁל בַּרְזֶל בְּמָתְנֵיהֶם, וּלְהַגְבִּיהַּ בִּגְדֵיהֶם לְמַעֲלָה מֵאַרְכּוּבוֹתֵיהֶן, וְיַחֲזְרוּ בְּכָל עֲיָירוֹת יִשְׂרָאֵל, יוֹם אֶחָד לְלָכִישׁ, יוֹם אֶחָד לְבֵית אֵ-ל, יוֹם אֶחָד לְחֶבְרוֹן, יוֹם אֶחָד לִירוּשָׁלַיִם, וְכֵן בְּכָל מְקוֹמוֹת יִשְׂרָאֵל, וִילַמְּדוּ אֶת יִשְׂרָאֵל דֶּרֶךְ אֶרֶץ, בְּשָׁנָה, וּבִשְׁתַּיִם, וּבְשָׁלֹשׁ, עַד שֶׁיִּתְיַישְׁבוּ יִשְׂרָאֵל בְּאַרְצָם . . .

וְהֵם לֹא עָשׂוּ כֵן. אֶלָּא כְּשֶׁנִּכְנְסוּ לְאַרְצָם, כָּל אֶחָד וְאֶחָד מֵהֶם נִכְנַס לְכַרְמוֹ, וּלְיֵינוֹ, וּלְשָׂדֵהוּ, וְאוֹמְרִים שָׁלוֹם עָלֶיךָ נַפְשִׁי, כְּדֵי שֶׁלֹּא לְהַרְבּוֹת עֲלֵיהֶן אֶת הַטּוֹרַח.

TANA DEVEI ELIYAHU

A Midrashic work, sometimes referred to as *Seder Eliyahu*. Midrash is the designation of a particular genre of rabbinic literature usually forming a running commentary on specific books of the Bible. This work deals with the divine precepts, their rationales, and the importance of knowledge of Torah, prayer, and repentance. The work is divided into two sections *(Sedarim)*: *Eliyahu Rabah* and *Eliyahu Zuta*.

The members of the Great Sanhedrin, who were appointed by Moses and Joshua, . . . should have bound iron chains to their loins and raised their garments over their knees and traveled to Lachish, Bethel, Hebron, Jerusalem—to all of the Jewish settlements—in order to teach morality to the Jewish people. They should have done this for the first few years upon their entry to the Land, until the Jews had settled in [and appointed local judges to do this task]. . . .

But the members of the Sanhedrin did not do this. When they came to the Land, each of them occupied themselves with their vineyard, winery, and field, declaring, "I have found peace for myself." They were unwilling to assume this great burden.

TEXT 3

STEVEN P. LAB, "CRIME PREVENTION, POLITICS, AND THE ART OF GOING NOWHERE FAST," *JUSTICE QUARTERLY,* 21:4 (DECEMBER 2004), 681–682

When one raises the issue of crime prevention with virtually any audience, there is universal agreement that preventing crime and victimization is a desired goal. . . . Yet, there is no clear agenda for the prevention of crime in the United States (and many other countries). There is no set crime prevention policy in the United States, except to investigate the crime, arrest and prosecute the offender, and punish the individual for his or her transgression. This is *not* what people expect when they ask for crime prevention. . . .

Where is the prevention policy? Why do we not have a crime prevention agenda?

STEVEN P. LAB, PHD
1955–

Criminologist. Dr. Lab is a member of the criminal justice program at Bowling Green State University, and a nationally recognized expert in the area of crime prevention. He has published extensively on crime prevention and juvenile justice and is a regular consultant on these topics for the National Institute of Justice.

QUESTION FOR DISCUSSION

Why isn't there a sufficient crime prevention policy in our society?

QUESTION FOR DISCUSSION

Which laws, policies, or programs would you support with the aim of preventing crime?

There Was No Other Jail but a Hole in the Ground with Guards over It, Charles M. Russell, ink drawing, c. 1911.
(Amon Carter Museum of American Art, Fort Worth, Texas)

Exercise 1

Together with a partner, read Texts 4 through 7.

What ideas about crime prevention can be gleaned from these texts? Which one resonates most with you?

IDEAS ABOUT CRIME PREVENTION

Watch a panel of experts discuss various ideas to reduce violent crime:

MYJLI.COM/CRIME

TEXT **4**

ETHICS OF THE FATHERS 3:2

הֱוֵי מִתְפַּלֵּל בִּשְׁלוֹמָהּ שֶׁל מַלְכוּת, שֶׁאִלְמָלֵא מוֹרָאָהּ אִישׁ אֶת רֵעֵהוּ חַיִּים בְּלָעוֹ.

Pray for the well-being of the government. For were it not for the fear [of its punishments], people would swallow each other alive.

ETHICS OF THE FATHERS (*PIRKEI AVOT*)

A six-chapter work on Jewish ethics that is studied widely by Jewish communities, especially during the summer. The first five chapters are from the Mishnah, tractate Avot. Avot differs from the rest of the Mishnah in that it does not focus on legal subjects; it is a collection of the sages' wisdom on topics related to character development, ethics, healthy living, piety, and the study of Torah.

A prayer book following the custom of Spanish and Portuguese Jews. (Philadelphia: Sherman & Co., 1838)

190   MORNING SERVICE FOR KIPPUR.

In most places the Reader says here the Prayer for the Government, as follows :

PRAYER FOR THE QUEEN AND ROYAL FAMILY.

May he who dispenseth salvation unto kings, and dominion unto princes ; whose kingdom is an everlasting kingdom ; who delivered his servant David from the destructive sword ; who maketh a way in the sea, and a path in the mighty waters ; bless, preserve, guard, assist, exalt, and raise unto a high eminence, our most gracious Sovereign, QUEEN VICTORIA, ALBERT EDWARD, PRINCE OF WALES, THE PRINCESS OF WALES AND ALL THE ROYAL FAMILY. May the Supreme

TEXT 5

RABBI DON YITSCHAK ABARBANEL, DEUTERONOMY, CH. 21

חֵטְא הָעָם וּפִשְׁעָם . . . כִּי מִיעוּט הַמִּשְׁפָּט בֵּינֵיהֶם יָבִיא אֶל שְׁפִיכוּת דָּמִים, כִּי אִם הָיָה מִשְׁפָּט בָּעִיר קָשֶׁה וּמְדוּקְדָּק כָּרָאוּי לֹא יִגְבַּר יַד הָרוֹצֵחַ לְהָבִיא לַהֲרוֹג נֶפֶשׁ בִּגְבוּל אוֹתָהּ הָעִיר כִּי יִפְחַד לְבָבוֹ מִמִּשְׁפַּט אוֹתָהּ הָעִיר וְשׁוֹפְטֶיהָ שֶׁיִּרְדְּפוּ אַחֲרָיו וְיַשִּׂיגוּהוּ וְיִרְמְסוּ לָאָרֶץ חַיָּיו.

The sin of the people...is that their laxity in administering punishment enabled this murder. If the city had an appropriately strict and consistent system of justice, the murderer would not have had the audacity to kill in its jurisdiction. He would have been deterred by the law of the city, and by its judges, fearing that they would pursue him, apprehend him, and punish him harshly.

RABBI DON YITSCHAK ABARBANEL
1437–1508

Biblical exegete and statesman. Abarbanel was born in Lisbon, Portugal, and served as a minister in the court of King Alfonso V of Portugal. After intrigues at court led to accusations against him, he fled to Spain, where he once again served as a counselor to royalty. It is claimed that Abarbanel offered King Ferdinand and Queen Isabella large sums of money for the revocation of their Edict of Expulsion of 1492, but to no avail. After the expulsion, he eventually settled in Italy where he wrote a commentary on Scripture, as well as other venerated works.

TEXT 6a

TALMUD, KIDUSHIN 29A

כָּל שֶׁאֵינוֹ מְלַמֵּד אֶת בְּנוֹ אוּמָנוּת . . . כְּאִילוּ מְלַמְדוֹ לִיסְטוּת.

When people don't teach their child a trade . . . it's as though they taught the child thievery.

BABYLONIAN TALMUD

A literary work of monumental proportions that draws upon the legal, spiritual, intellectual, ethical, and historical traditions of Judaism. The 37 tractates of the Babylonian Talmud contain the teachings of the Jewish sages from the period after the destruction of the Second Temple through the fifth century CE. It has served as the primary vehicle for the transmission of the Oral Law and the education of Jews over the centuries; it is the entry point for all subsequent legal, ethical, and theological Jewish scholarship.

TEXT 6b

RASHI, AD LOC.

כְּאִילוּ מְלַמְדוֹ לִיסְטוּת - דְּכֵיוָן דְּאֵין לוֹ אוּמָנוּת, וְיֶחְסַר לַחֲמוֹ, יֵלֵךְ בְּפָרָשַׁת דְּרָכִים וִילַסְטֵם אֶת הַבְּרִיּוֹת.

Because these children will not have a trade with which to feed themselves, they will take to the highways and rob others.

RABBI SHLOMO YITSCHAKI (RASHI) 1040–1105

Most noted biblical and Talmudic commentator. Born in Troyes, France, Rashi studied in the famed *yeshivot* of Mainz and Worms. His commentaries on the Pentateuch and the Talmud, which focus on the straightforward meaning of the text, appear in virtually every edition of the Talmud and Bible.

TEXT 7

MIDRASH, *TANCHUMA, KI TETSEI* 1:1

"כִּי תִהְיֶיןָ לְאִישׁ שְׁתֵּי נָשִׁים" וְגוֹ' (דְּבָרִים כא, טו) - שְׁתַּיִם בַּבַּיִת מְרִיבָה בַּבַּיִת.

וְלֹא עוֹד, "אַחַת אֲהוּבָה וְאַחַת שְׂנוּאָה" - אוֹ שְׁתֵּיהֶן שְׂנוּאוֹת.

מַה כְּתִיב אַחֲרָיו? "כִּי יִהְיֶה לְאִישׁ בֵּן סוֹרֵר וּמוֹרֶה" (דְּבָרִים כא, יח).

MIDRASH TANCHUMA

A Midrashic work bearing the name of Rabbi Tanchuma, a 4th-century Talmudic sage quoted often in this work. Midrash is the designation of a particular genre of rabbinic literature usually forming a running commentary on specific books of the Bible. *Midrash Tanchuma* provides textual exegeses, expounds upon the biblical narrative, and develops and illustrates moral principles. *Tanchuma* is unique in that many of its sections commence with a halachic discussion, which subsequently leads into non-halachic teachings.

"If a man has two wives . . ." (DEUTERONOMY 21:15): A home with two wives is a home with conflict.

In fact, [as the verse continues, the best case scenario is] "one who is loved and one who is hated." But it is also possible that both will be hated.

And what is the result? Immediately thereafter it says, "If one has a rebellious child . . ." (DEUTERONOMY 21:18)

*Watch **Professor Rona Novick** discuss risk factors that can lead to criminal activity and what we can do to help mitigate them:*

MYJLI.COM/CRIME

TEXT 8

JESSICA LAHEY, "THE BENEFITS OF CHARACTER EDUCATION," *THE ATLANTIC*,
MAY 6, 2013

The founders of this country, including John and Abigail Adams, Thomas Jefferson, James Madison, and Benjamin Franklin wrote about the importance of character education in maintaining the new republic. Those founders would likely be horrified by the loss of this goal, as they all cite character education as the way to create an educated and virtuous citizenry.

As Gallup polls show that over ninety percent of American adults support the teaching of honesty, democracy, acceptance of people of different races and ethnic backgrounds, patriotism, caring for friends and family members, moral courage, and the Golden Rule in public schools, it seems odd that this facet of American education has disappeared from public debate over curriculum and academic content.

JESSICA LAHEY

Teacher and writer. Jessica Lahey writes and speaks about education, parenting, and child welfare. She has written about these topics for *The Atlantic and The New York Times, and* is the author of the best-selling book, *The Gift of Failure: How the Best Parents Learn to Let Go So Their Children Can Succeed.*

TEXT 9

THE REBBE, RABBI MENACHEM MENDEL SCHNEERSON, APRIL 15, 1981 (11 NISAN 5741), *SICHOT KODESH* 5741, 3:109–110

דֶער חִינוּךְ אִיז אַוועקגעשטעלט געווארן, אַז צו חִינוּךְ אִיז גענוג אַז מ'קלייבט צוזאמען ידיעות, אַבִּי מ'גִיט ידיעות אִין פַאַרשִידענע עִנְיָנִים - אָט דָאס הייסט חִינוּךְ. אוּן דֶער צוזאמענקלייבּן ידיעות אִיז נִיט פַאַרבּוּנדְן מִיט אַ מַטָרָה, מִיט דִי מַטָרָה פוּן אַראפּבְּרֵיינגען טוֹב אֲמִיתִּי פַאַר זִיךְ, אוּן טוֹב פַאַר דֶער אַרוּם.

דֶער מַטָרָה וואס אִיז דָא אִיז כְּדֵי בַּאווייזן אַז "אֲנִי וְאַפְסִי עוֹד". אוּן מ'אִיז אִים מְחַנֵךְ אִין אַן אוֹפֶן אַז "אֲנִי וְאַפְסִי עוֹד".

ס'אִיז כְּאִילוּ אַז מ'האַלט פוּן "לִיבֶּעראַלִיזְם", האַלט מען אַז מ'טאַר זִיךְ נִיט מִישְׁן אִין דֶעם לֶעבְּן פוּן אַ קִינד, נָאר מ'דאַרף אִים לָאזן גֵיין לְנַפְשׁוֹ. אוּן אָט דָאס וואס "עַיִר פֶּרֶא אָדָם יִוָלֵד" (אִיוֹב יא, יב) - דָאס אִיז וואס דֶער אוֹיבֶּערשְׁטֶער האָט אִים אַזוֹי בַּאשאַפְן, בְּמֵילָא האָט דָאס צוּ דֶער פאַטֶער אוּן דֶער מוּטֶער קֵיין שַׁיְיכוּת נִיט, אוּן זֵיי לָאזן אִים זִיךְ פַאשְׁן אוּן פִירן זִיךְ ווי בַּיי אִים קוּמט אוֹיס.

אוּן אַף עַל פִּי אַז ס'אִיז דָא דֶער חוֹק הַמְּדִינָה אַז מ'דאַרף גֵיין אִין בֵּית הַסֵּפֶר, אִיז כָּאמוֹר, דֶער בֵּית סֵפֶר אִיז מְיֻסָּד אוּן דוּרכגענוּמען מִיט דִי הַנָחָה אַז וואס דאַרף געבּן אַ בֵּית סֵפֶר - ידיעות. נִיט אַ בֵּית סֵפֶר דאַרף אוֹיסְפּוּרְעמען, אוֹיפְטָאן אוּן אוֹיפְמאַכן דֶעם "יֵצֶר לֵב הָאָדָם" אַז עֶר זָאל זַיין מִיט מִדּוֹת טוֹבוֹת, אוּן זָאל וויסן אַז אֱמֶת טאַקע עֶר גֵייט אוּן לֶערְנט אִין דֶעם בֵּית סֵפֶר, אָבֶּער דֶער עִיקָר לֶערְנֶען זֵיינֶער אִיז ווי אַזוֹי צוּ טָאן טוֹב אַרוּם זִיךְ, אוּן דָאס אִיז דֶער טוֹב הָאֲמִיתִּי פַאַר זִיךְ. אִיז דָאס אַריין נִיט אִינגאַנצן נִיט דֶער תַּכְנִית אוּן אִין דֶער פּראָגראַם פוּן דֶעם בֵּית סֵפֶר... וואס אַזַא חִינוּךְ אִיז דֶער שׁוֹרֶשׁ פוּן מַעֲשִׂים וְהַנְהָגָה בִּלְתִּי רְצוּיָה...

אוּן אוֹיךְ דָאס וואס גֵייט אַריין אִין דֶער חִינוּךְ אִין בֵּית סֵפֶר, דֶער עִנְיָן פוּן יִרְאַת הָעוֹנֶשׁ, אַז טאַמֶער וועט עֶר זַיין אַ נַעַר אוּן וועט זִיךְ לָאזן כַאפְּן וועט מֶען אִים דֶערנאָךְ מַעֲנִישׁ זַיין, אִיז דָאס גוּפָא - וְעַל פִּי דֶעם וואס מ'גִיט אִים פְּרִיעֶר דִי הַכָּרָה אַז עֶר אִיז עוֹמֵד לְנַפְשׁוֹ, אוּן אַז

RABBI MENACHEM MENDEL SCHNEERSON
1902–1994
The towering Jewish leader of the 20th century, known as "the Lubavitcher Rebbe," or simply as "the Rebbe." Born in southern Ukraine, the Rebbe escaped Nazi-occupied Europe, arriving in the U.S. in June 1941. The Rebbe inspired and guided the revival of traditional Judaism after the European devastation, impacting virtually every Jewish community the world over. The Rebbe often emphasized that the performance of just one additional good deed could usher in the era of Mashiach. The Rebbe's scholarly talks and writings have been printed in more than 200 volumes.

עֶר אִיז דֶער רֹאשׁ לְכָל מַדְגִישׁ, אַז סְ'אִיז אַ זִיכֶערֶע זַאך אַז עֶר וֶועט
קֶענֶען אִיבֶּערְקָלַייבֶּן אוּן גֶעפִינֶען אַ תַּחְבּוּלָה אוֹיף אַרוֹיסְדְרֵייעֶן זִיך פֿוּן
דֶעם עוֹנֶשׁ. וְאַדְרַבָּה וֶוען בַּאוַוייזְט עֶר זַיין גְרוֹיסְקַייט, בִּשְׁעַת עֶר טוּט
אַן עִנְיָן וָואס אִיז פֿאַרְבּוּנְדְן מִיט אַ צָרָה אוּן מִיט אַ נֶזֶק וְכוּ', אוּן בַּאוַוייזְט
אַז עֶר הָאט זִיך נִיט וָואס צוּ רֶעכֶענֶען מִיט דֶער אַרוּם זִיך.

The modern secular educational system is premised on the notion that it is sufficient for children to accumulate knowledge about numerous disciplines. What the educational system fails to teach is that the purpose behind the accumulation of all this knowledge is to bring goodness to others, which is also *true* goodness for oneself.

In fact, the system is such that students see the goal of their learning as a means to pursue their own careers and display their own prowess, leading to a sense of self-centeredness and narcissism.

This reality is due to the assumption that we may not interfere with the lives of children but must allow them to develop autonomously. Although humans are born with negative impulses, many assume that parents have no responsibility to change this but should allow children to develop as they see fit.

To be sure, children are legally required to attend school; but as noted, modern schools operate as though their sole task is to provide children with knowledge. The assumption is that schools need not teach students how to be a *mentsh*, how to be a decent citizen, how to develop virtuous character traits, and how the primary object of all learning is to promote goodness in one's surroundings. . . . This sort of education is a cause for criminal activity later in life. . . .

In fact, one message that children often hear in school is that they ought to behave properly because of the threat of punishment. . . . But education anchored in the fear of punishment—coupled with the aforementioned narcissism—can lead students to the conclusion that they can outsmart the system and avoid any punishment. In fact, they may even engage in harmful activity in order to express how independent-minded they are—that they can completely disregard all others, both their victims and the criminal justice system.

A 20th-century public school classroom in the United States. (Museum of the City of New York)

TEXT **10**

THE REBBE, RABBI MENACHEM MENDEL SCHNEERSON, JULY 14, 1981
(12 TAMUZ 5741), *SICHOT KODESH* 5741, 4:152–154

וּמַה רוֹאֶה הַיֶּלֶד בְּמַכְשִׁיר הַהוּא - שֶׁכַּאֲשֶׁר הוּא פִּיקֵחַ, כְּפִי שֶׁהוֹרָיו מַכְנִיסִים לוֹ לָרֹאשׁ שֶׁהוּא פִּיקֵחַ שֶׁאֵין כָּמוֹהוּ, יָכוֹל הוּא לְהַשִּׂיג כָּל מַה שֶׁלִּבּוֹ חָפֵץ.

עַל יְדֵי זֶה מְחַנְּכִים אֶת הַיֶּלֶד שֶׁיִּהְיֶה גַּנָּב וְגַזְלָן. כִּי מְחַנְּכִים אוֹתוֹ בְּאוֹפֶן כָּזֶה שֶׁהוּא צָרִיךְ לְהַשִּׂיג כָּל מַה שֶׁלִּבּוֹ חָפֵץ, וַהֲרֵי הַטֶּבַע שֶׁל בָּשָׂר וָדָם הוּא שֶׁכָּל מַה שֶׁנּוֹתְנִים לוֹ יוֹתֵר, הֲרֵי הוּא רוֹצֶה וְדוֹרֵשׁ יוֹתֵר [זוֹ מַכַּת מְדִינָה רַחֲמָנָא לִיצְלַן] עַד שֶׁבַּסּוֹף הֲרֵי הוּא נַעֲשֶׂה לְגַנָּב וְגַזְלָן כְּדֵי שֶׁיּוּכַל לְהַשִּׂיג כָּל מַה שֶׁלִּבּוֹ חָפֵץ.

הֶעֱמִידוּ אֱלִיל שֶׁל עֲבוֹדָה זָרָה - שֶׁאָסוּר לִפְגּוֹעַ בְּחוֹפֶשׁ הַפְּרָט, וְלָכֵן אָסוּר לִמְנוֹעַ מֵהַיֶּלֶד לַעֲשׂוֹת כָּל מַה שֶׁלִּבּוֹ חָפֵץ, כִּי עַל יְדֵי זֶה פּוֹגְעִים בְּחוֹפֶשׁ הַפְּרָט. וְכַאֲשֶׁר הוּא מִתְנַהֵג בְּאוֹפֶן דְּ"שֶׁלִּי שֶׁלָּךְ וְשֶׁלָּךְ שֶׁלִּי" - אָסוּר לוֹמַר לוֹ מְאוּמָה, וַאֲפִילוּ אִם רוֹצִים לְהָעִיר לוֹ עַל זֶה, צָרִיךְ לַעֲשׂוֹת זֹאת בִּנְחִיתוּתָא, וְלֹא לוֹמַר לוֹ שֶׁאִם יִתְנַהֵג בְּאוֹפֶן כָּזֶה, יִהְיֶה אֵיזֶה עִנְיָן בִּלְתִּי רָצוּי.

לֹא צְרִיכִים לְחַנֵּךְ אֶת הַיֶּלֶד וְלוֹמַר לוֹ בְּפֵירוּשׁ שֶׁיֵּלֵךְ וְיִקַּח חֲפָצָיו שֶׁל חֲבֵירוֹ ("שֶׁלִּי שֶׁלִּי וְשֶׁלָּךְ שֶׁלִּי"). מַסְפִּיק רַק שֶׁמְּחַנְּכִים אוֹתוֹ בְּאוֹפֶן שֶׁיֵּדַע שֶׁ"אֲנִי וְאַפְסִי עוֹד", וְזֶהוּ הֲכָנָה קְרוֹבָה לְכָל הָעִנְיָנִים הַמִּסְתַּעֲפִים מִזֶּה, כְּפִי שֶׁרוֹאִים בְּפוֹעַל . . .

לֹא צְרִיכִים לָתֵת לַיֶּלֶד אֶת כָּל מַה שֶׁלִּבּוֹ חָפֵץ . . . מַסְבִּירִים לוֹ שֶׁלְּטוֹבָתוֹ לֹא כְּדַאי שֶׁיֵּלֵךְ אַחַר תַּאֲוֹותָיו וְיַעֲשֶׂה כָּל מַה שֶׁלִּבּוֹ חָפֵץ.

וּכְפִי שֶׁרוֹאִים בִּפְשִׁיטוּת בְּנוֹגֵעַ לִבְרִיאוּת הַגּוּף, כַּאֲשֶׁר בָּא רוֹפֵא וְאוֹמֵר לַיֶּלֶד שֶׁאָסוּר לוֹ לֶאֱכוֹל מַאֲכָלִים מְסוּיָמִים, כִּי אַף עַל פִּי שֶׁכְּלַפֵּי חוּץ נִרְאִים מַאֲכָלִים אֵלּוּ טוֹבִים, הֵם מְצוּפִּים עִם סוּכָּר וּדְבַשׁ וְנוֹפֶת בַּר, אַף עַל פִּי כֵן אִם מַאֲכָלִים אֵלּוּ יִהְיוּ דָם וּבָשָׂר כִּבְשָׂרוֹ, הֲרֵי זֶה יַזִּיק לִבְרִיאוּתוֹ, וְעַד שֶׁיִּהְיֶה מִזֶּה חוֹלִי שֶׁיֵּשׁ בּוֹ סַכָּנָה. הֲרֵי בְּוַדַּאי שֶׁיִּתְנַהֵג כְּהוֹרָאַת הָרוֹפֵא, וְלֹא בִּגְלַל שֶׁהוּא (הַיֶּלֶד) לָמַד וְיוֹדֵעַ חָכְמַת הָרְפוּאָה, אֶלָּא הוּא מִסְתַּמֵּךְ עַל יְדִיעַת הָרוֹפֵא, שֶׁהָרוֹפֵא הִשְׁקִיעַ רִיבּוּי שָׁנִים בְּלִימּוּד חָכְמָה זוֹ, וְאוֹפֶן לִימּוּדוֹ הָיָה לָדַעַת אֶת אֲמִיתִּית הָעִנְיָן וְלֹא כְּפִי שֶׁנּוֹחַ לוֹ.

וְעַל אַחַת כַּמָּה וְכַמָּה שֶׁכָּךְ צָרִיךְ לִהְיוֹת בְּנוֹגֵעַ לִבְרִיאוּת הַנֶּפֶשׁ.

One message that children often absorb from modern entertainment is that they ought to pursue whatever their hearts desire, and that if they are clever—and their parents have told them that they are—they will be able to satisfy these desires successfully.

But this messaging can ultimately lead to criminal activity. It is human nature to be unsatisfied with what one has and to incessantly desire more. Accordingly, if we teach children that they must obtain their every whim, the result will be citizens who are even willing to steal to satisfy their desires. Unfortunately, this is a common problem in this country.

Our society has propped up a sacred but ultimately false value—that we cannot interfere in the lives of others, which is why we cannot stop children from doing what they want. In this climate, even when one chooses to reprimand a child for selfish or harmful activity, it is often done quite mildly, without disciplining the child.

One need not teach a child to steal to raise a generation of thieves. It is sufficient that we teach our children to be self-centered, and this can be a direct cause of criminal activity. . . .

We need not give our children everything they desire. We have to explain to them that it is in their interest that they not pursue or obtain each and every one of their whims.

After all, when physicians instruct children to refrain from certain foods, warning that consuming these foods will be dangerous, even life-threatening, the children listen to these instructions, even if the foods are tempting and coated with sugar. They listen not because they understand the medical reality, but because they are happy to trust the physician who invested many years studying medicine.

We must convey the same message to our children, in order to ensure the well-being of their character.

Portret van een jonge scholier (*Portrait of a Young Scholar*), artist not certain but generally attributed to Jan van Scorel, oil on panel, 1531. (Museum Boijmans Van Beuningen, Rotterdam)

Figure 6.1

Excerpts from the 2012 *Josephson Report Card on the Ethics of American Youth*

	DISAGREE	AGREE
When it comes to doing what is right, I am better than most people I know.	19%	81%
In personal relationships, trust and honesty are essential.	2%	98%
In the real world, successful people do what they have to do to win, even if others consider it cheating.	43%	57%
A person has to lie or cheat sometimes in order to succeed.	64%	36%
I sometimes lie to save money.	62%	38%
People who are willing to lie, cheat, or break the rules are more likely to succeed than people who are not.	78%	22%
It's not worth it to lie or cheat, because it hurts your character.	14%	86%
It's sometimes OK to hit or threaten a person who makes me very angry.	76%	24%
Physical violence (fighting, bullying, intimidation) is a big problem at my school.	69%	31%
If I wanted to, I could get drugs.	41%	59%
It's not cheating if everyone is doing it.	85%	15%
I frequently volunteer to help others or perform charity work.	37%	63%

JOSEPHSON INSTITUTE, CENTER FOR YOUTH ETHICS

QUESTIONS FOR DISCUSSION

1 What is your reaction to these statistics?

2 Which statistic, if any, is most bothersome to you?

3 Which statistic, if any, is most encouraging to you?

TEXT **11**

ETHICS OF THE FATHERS 2:1

הִסְתַּכֵּל בִּשְׁלֹשָׁה דְבָרִים וְאֵין אַתָּה בָא לִידֵי עֲבֵרָה:
דַּע מַה לְמַעְלָה מִמָּךְ, עַיִן רוֹאָה וְאֹזֶן שׁוֹמַעַת, וְכָל מַעֲשֶׂיךָ בַּסֵּפֶר נִכְתָּבִין.

Contemplate three things and you will not come to a transgression:

Know what is above you—a seeing eye, a listening ear, and all your deeds are written in a book.

*Watch excerpts from **Professor Dan Ariely**'s film about dishonesty and an exclusive interview about his findings:*

MYJLI.COM/CRIME

Bust of a Young Jew (The young man is depicted wearing a *kipah*, traditionally worn as a sign of reverence for G-d.), Rembrandt van Rijn, oil on canvas, 1663. (Kimbell Art Museum, Fort Worth, Texas)

TEXT 12

THE REBBE, RABBI MENACHEM MENDEL SCHNEERSON,
LETTER DATED 26 NISAN, 5724 (APRIL 8, 1964) (ii)

In my opinion, this acknowledgment is absolutely necessary in order to impress upon the minds of our growing-up generation that the world in which they live is not a jungle, where brute force, cunning and unbridled passion rule supreme, but that it has a Master Who is not an abstraction, but a personal G-d; that this Supreme Being takes a "personal interest" in the affairs of each and every individual, and to Him everyone is accountable for one's daily conduct.

Juvenile delinquency, the tragic symptom of the disillusionment, insecurity and confusion of the young generation, has not abated; rather the reverse is the case. Obviously, it is hard to believe that the police and law-enforcement agencies will succeed in deterring delinquency and crime, not to mention completely eliminating them at the root, even if there were enough police officers to keep an eye on every recalcitrant child. Besides, this would not be the right way to remedy the situation. The remedy lies in removing the cause, not in merely treating the symptoms. It will not suffice to tell the juvenile delinquent that crime does not pay, and that he will eventually land in jail (if he is not smart enough). Nor will he be particularly impressed if he is admonished that law-breaking is an offense against society. It is necessary to engrave upon the child's mind the idea that any wrongdoing is an offense against the Divine authority and order. . . .

Does morality require G-d? **Rabbis Yitzchak Breitowitz, Manis Friedman,** *and* **Yitzchok Schochet** *address this question:*

MYJLI.COM/CRIME

TEXT 13

THE REBBE, RABBI MENACHEM MENDEL SCHNEERSON, APRIL 12, 1984 (11 NISAN 5744)
TORAT MENACHEM 5744, 3:1432–1433

בְּכָל בָּתֵּי-הַסֵּפֶר שֶׁבָּהֶם מְחַנְּכִים אֶת הַנּוֹעַר - יֵשׁ לְבַסֵּס אֶת הַחִינּוּךְ עַל הַהַכָּרָה וְהַקֶּשֶׁר עִם בּוֹרֵא עוֹלָם וּמַנְהִיגוֹ, וְזֹאת - **לִפְנֵי** כָּל הַלִּימּוּדִים הַקְּשׁוּרִים עִם תּוֹעֶלֶת גַּשְׁמִית, מִכֵּיוָן שֶׁזֶּהוּ הַדָּבָר הָעִיקָּרִי בְּחִינּוּךְ לְצֶדֶק וְיוֹשֶׁר. וּלְשֵׁם כַּךְ - יֵשׁ לִקְבּוֹעַ "חוֹק" שֶׁיֵּשׁ לִפְתּוֹחַ אֶת יוֹם הַלִּימּוּדִים עִם "רֶגַע שֶׁל שְׁתִיקָה", שֶׁיִּהְיֶ' מְיוּעָד לְמַחֲשָׁבָה אוֹדוֹת בּוֹרֵא עוֹלָם וּמַנְהִיגוֹ . . .

וְיֵשׁ לַעֲשׂוֹת עִנְיָן זֶה עַל יְדֵי "רֶגַע שֶׁל **שְׁתִיקָה**" דַּוְקָא:

כַּאֲשֶׁר נִגָּשִׁים לַעֲשׂוֹת פְּעוּלָּה שֶׁתַּכְלִיתָהּ מִילּוּי רָצוֹן הַבּוֹרֵא - יֵשׁ לִזְכּוֹר שֶׁרְצוֹנוֹ שֶׁל הַבּוֹרֵא שֶׁיַּעֲשׂוּ זֹאת בְּדַרְכֵי נוֹעַם וּבְדַרְכֵי שָׁלוֹם, מִתּוֹךְ קֵירוּב הַלְּבָבוֹת, וּבְוַדַּאי שֶׁלֹּא מִתּוֹךְ מִלְחָמָה וְנִצָּחוֹן כו', וּבִפְרָט כַּאֲשֶׁר יְכוֹלִים לִמְנוֹעַ זֹאת **בְּקַלּוּת** . . .

כַּאֲשֶׁר מְדוּבָּר אוֹדוֹת עִנְיָן שֶׁל דִּיבּוּר - מַתְחִיל מִיָּד דִּין וּדְבָרִים וְשַׁקְלָא וְטַרְיָא בְּקֶשֶׁר לְהִתְעָרְבוּת בֶּאֱמוּנָתוֹ שֶׁל בֶּן דָּת מְסוּיֶּימֶת וְכו': מַה שֶׁאֵין כֵּן כַּאֲשֶׁר יִקְבַּע "רֶגַע שֶׁל **שְׁתִיקָה**", לֹא בְּדִיבּוּר כִּי אִם בְּמַחֲשָׁבָה בִּלְבָד, הֲרֵי כָּל אֶחָד וְאֶחָד יָכוֹל לַחֲשׁוֹב מַה שֶּׁרוֹצֶה, שֶׁהֲרֵי אַף אֶחָד אֵינוֹ יוֹדֵעַ אֶת מַחֲשַׁבְתּוֹ שֶׁל הַשֵּׁנִי, כַּךְ שֶׁעַל יְדֵי זֶה מַשִּׂיגִים אֶת תַּכְלִית וּמַטְרַת הַדָּבָר (הַכָּרָה בַּבּוֹרֵא הָעוֹלָם) בְּדַרְכֵי נוֹעַם וּבְדַרְכֵי שָׁלוֹם.

וּמוּבָן - שֶׁכַּאֲשֶׁר מְדוּבָּר אוֹדוֹת עִנְיָן שֶׁל דִּיבּוּר - הֲרֵי גַם לְאַחֲרֵי כָּל הַהַבְטָחוֹת שֶׁלֹּא יִפְעֲלוּ שׁוּם לַחַץ וְלֹא יִתְעָרְבוּ בֶּאֱמוּנָה שֶׁל הַשֵּׁנִי, אִי אֶפְשָׁר לִהְיוֹת סוֹמְכִים וּבְטוּחִים שֶׁהַהַבְטָחָה זוֹ תִּתְקַיֵּים בִּשְׁלֵימוּתָהּ,

מִכֵּיוָן שֶׁזֶּהוּ נִסָּיוֹן גָּדוֹל בְּיוֹתֵר עֲבוּר הַ"מְנַהֵל" אוֹ הַ"מּוֹרֶה", שֶׁלְּמָרוֹת
שֶׁמְּדַבֵּר עִם הַתַּלְמִידִים אוֹדוֹת עִנְיָנִים הַקְּשׁוּרִים עִם אֱמוּנָה, יִתְאַפֵּק
שֶׁלֹּא לְהַזְכִּיר שׁוּם דָּבָר הַקָּשׁוּר לָאֱמוּנָה שֶׁלּוֹ (שֶׁאֵינָהּ תּוֹאֶמֶת אֶת
הָאֱמוּנָה שֶׁל בֶּן דַּת אַחֶרֶת) וְכָךְ יִתְנַהֵג מִדֵּי יוֹם בְּיוֹמוֹ! ...

הָעֵצָה לָזֶה - שֶׁיִּקָּבַע "רֶגַע שֶׁל שְׁתִיקָה" דַּוְקָא, לְלֹא עִנְיָן שֶׁל דִּיבּוּר
כְּלָל ...

It is imperative to base school education on the cognizance of a Supreme Being. And because it is such a basic element in education, it should be done before all other lessons. A law should therefore be passed establishing that the school day open with "a moment of silence," in which students will think about the Creator and Ruler of the world. . . .

Why should this be done with a "moment of silence," specifically? Because when fulfilling G-d's will, one must keep in mind that G-d wants it done pleasantly and peacefully, not with quarrels and strife, especially when it can be easily avoided.

A proposal for a spoken acknowledgment of G-d in school immediately leads to arguments about interference with an individual's religious beliefs, etc. And even with full provisions for non-coercion and neutrality concerning any particular religion, nothing can assure that the teacher or principal will not exert some pressure on the students concerning a particular religious belief. For it is extremely difficult for a teacher or principal to talk to students about matters of faith, and simultaneously not mention anything about their own particular beliefs—and to do so day in and day out!

Concerning a "moment of silence," in contrast—consisting of thinking instead of speaking—students can think freely without any external pressure, and thus the goal of acknowledging G-d is achieved pleasantly and peacefully. . . .

*Watch **Professor Jonathan Sarna**, prominent historian of American Judaism, explain the historical background and debate surrounding the moment of silence:*

MYJLI.COM/CRIME

KEY POINTS

1 From a Jewish perspective, the primary method of dealing with crime is to proactively take measures that prevent crime before it occurs.

2 To prevent crime in ancient Israel, it was incumbent upon members of the Sanhedrin to assume the burden of extensive travel in order to teach morality to the masses. This indicates that we must bear any burden in drawing up an effective crime-prevention strategy.

3 While one goal of crime prevention is to reduce the suffering of victims, a second goal is to prevent potential criminals from ruining themselves. Crime prevention is not a zero-sum game where law-abiding citizens are protected at the expense of others, but rather, a boon for everyone.

4 A number of ideas about crime prevention are found in Talmudic literature. These include sentences that will have a deterrent effect, strategies that reduce poverty and unemployment, and ensuring that children are raised in a loving and peaceful environment.

5 Human beings outgrow their untamed and selfish traits, or at least learn to control them, through an education that focuses on virtues, values, and character development. Schools should therefore incorporate these goals into their curricula. Students should

*Is legislative prayer good for the Jews? Watch attorney **Nathan Lewin** and **Professor Sheldon Nahmod** debate this matter:*

MYJLI.COM/CRIME

learn that the primary objective of their learning is to unleash their knowledge to promote goodness in their surroundings. This will result in adults who—due to their self-control, their heightened sense of empathy, and their personal integrity—are less inclined to engage in criminal activity.

6 Humans often employ a "fudge factor" that rationalizes different forms of dishonesty. Moral behavior, therefore, requires the recognition that we are not the final arbiter of right and wrong, and that something beyond us renders certain actions off-limits. This is why the Torah insists that "Do not kill" and "Do not steal" must be rooted in a recognition of G-d.

7 If enacted properly, a moment of silence to begin each school day is constitutional and does not impose any specific set of beliefs on children. This practice will encourage children to have discussions with their parents about their families' values and beliefs, and parents will instruct their children on what to think about during this moment of reflection. Those children who choose to think about a Supreme Being, Who created them to promote goodness in their surroundings, will root all of their learning in something absolute and timeless.

Additional Readings

MOMENT OF SILENCE, RELIGION AND STATE, AND THE AMERICAN SUPREME COURT

FROM VINCENT PHILLIP MUÑOZ, *RELIGIOUS LIBERTY AND THE AMERICAN SUPREME COURT*

Wallace v. Jaffree, 472 U.S. 38 (1985)
Vote: 6—Brennan, Marshall, Blackmun, Powell, Stevens, O'Connor
3—Burger, White, Rehnquist
Opinion announcing the opinion of the Court: Stevens
Concurring opinion: Powell
Opinion concurring in the judgment: O'Connor
Dissenting opinions: Burger, White, Rehnquist

In 1978, subsequent to Supreme Court decisions finding prayer in public schools unconstitutional, the state of Alabama passed legislation authorizing a one-minute period of silence in public elementary schools "for meditation." The 1978 statute (§ 16-1-20) specified, "At the commencement of the first class each day in the first through the sixth grades in all public schools, the teacher in charge of the room in which each such class is held shall announce that a period of silence, not to exceed one minute in duration, shall be observed for meditation, and during any such period silence shall be maintained and no activities engaged in."

In 1981, the Alabama state legislature amended § 16-1-20 to authorize a period of silence "for meditation or voluntary prayer" in all grades. The 1981 statute (§ 16-1-20.1) specified, "At the commencement of the first class of each day in all grades in all public schools the

VINCENT PHILLIP MUÑOZ

American political scientist. Muñoz is the Tocqueville associate professor of Religion & Public Life in the Department of Political Science at the University of Notre Dame. He is the author of an award-winning book on 3 of the Founding Fathers' views on the separation of church and state in the United States and the editor of a second book on Supreme Court cases on religious liberty.

teacher in charge of the room in which each class is held may announce that a period of silence not to exceed one minute in duration shall be observed for meditation or voluntary prayer, and during any such period no other activities shall be engaged in."

In 1982, the Alabama state legislature further amended its moment-of-silence law to authorize public school teachers to lead "willing students" in a prescribed prayer. The 1982 amendment (§ 16-1-20.2) specified:

> From henceforth, any teacher or professor in any public educational institution within the state of Alabama, recognizing that the L-rd G-d is one, at the beginning of any homeroom or any class, may pray, may lead willing students in prayer, or may lead the willing students in the following prayer to G-d:
> "Al-mighty G-d, You alone are our G-d. We acknowledge You as the Creator and Supreme Judge of the world. May Your justice, Your truth, and Your peace abound this day in the hearts of our countrymen, in the counsels of our government, in the sanctity of our homes and in the classrooms of our schools in the name of our L-rd. Amen."

The federal district court opinion in this case was particularly notable. After a four-day trial in 1982 that pertained primarily to activities that occurred during the 1981-1982 academic year and the 1981 Alabama statute (§ 16-1-20.1) authorizing a moment of silence for "meditation or voluntary prayer," federal district court Judge W. Brevard Hand concluded that "the establishment clause of the first amendment to the United States Constitution does not prohibit the state from establishing a religion." Jaffree v. Board of Commissioners of Mobile County, 554 F. Supp. 1104, 1128 (S.D.

Ala. 1983). Citing the legislative history surrounding the adoption of both the First Amendment and the Fourteenth Amendment and the plain language of those amendments, Judge Hand found that the Constitution established a federal arrangement on matters of establishment of religion, restricting only the national government from establishing a religion.

The Eleventh Circuit Court of Appeals reversed the district court opinion, holding that both § 16-1-20.1 and § 16-1-20.2 violated the Establishment Clause. The Supreme Court reviewed the circuit court's decision concerning § 16-1-20.1, the "for meditation or voluntary prayer" provision.

STEVENS, J., delivered the opinion of the Court, in which BRENNAN, MARSHALL, BLACKMUN, and POWELL, JJ., joined.

. . . [55] When the Court has been called upon to construe the breadth of the Establishment Clause, it has examined the criteria developed over a period of many years. Thus, in *Lemon v. Kurtzman,* 403 U.S. 602, 612-613 (1971), we wrote:

> *"Every analysis in this area must begin with consideration of the cumulative criteria developed by the Court over many years. Three such tests may be gleaned from our cases. First, the statute must have a secular legislative purpose; second, its principal or primary effect must be one that neither advances nor inhibits religion; finally, the statute must not foster 'an excessive [56] government entanglement with religion.'"*

It is the first of these three criteria that is most plainly implicated by this case. As the District Court correctly recognized, no consideration of the second or third criteria is necessary if a statute does not have a clearly secular purpose. For even though a statute that is motivated in part by a religious purpose may satisfy the first criterion, the First Amendment requires that a statute must be invalidated if it is entirely motivated by a purpose to advance religion.

In applying the purpose test, it is appropriate to ask "whether government's actual purpose is to endorse or disapprove of religion." In this case, the answer to that question is dispositive. For the record not only provides us with an unambiguous affirmative answer, but it also reveals that the enactment of § 16-1-20.1 was not motivated by any clearly secular purpose—indeed, the statute had no secular purpose.

The sponsor of the bill that became § 16-1-20.1, Senator Donald Holmes, inserted into the legislative record—apparently [57] without dissent—a statement indicating that the legislation was an "effort to return voluntary prayer" to the public schools.[1] Later Senator Holmes confirmed this purpose before the District Court. In response to the question whether he had any purpose for the legislation other than returning voluntary prayer to public schools, he stated: "No, I did not have no other purpose in mind." The State did not present evidence of any secular purpose.

[58] The unrebutted evidence of legislative intent contained in the legislative record and in the testimony of the sponsor of § 16-1-20.1 is confirmed by a consideration of the relationship between this statute and the two other measures that were considered in this case. The District Court found that the 1981 statute and its 1982 sequel had a common, nonsecular purpose. The wholly religious character of the later enactment is plainly evident from its text. When the differences between § 16-1-20.1 and its 1978 predecessor, § 16-1-20, are examined, it is equally clear that the 1981 statute has the same wholly religious character.

There are only three textual differences between § 16-1-20.1 and § 16-1-20: (1) the earlier statute applies only to grades one through six, whereas § 16-1-20.1 applies to all grades; (2) the earlier statute uses the word "shall" whereas § 16-1-20.1 uses the word "may"; (3) the earlier statute refers [59] only to "meditation" whereas § 16-1-20.1 refers to "meditation or voluntary prayer." The first difference is of no relevance in this litigation because the minor appellees were in kindergarten or second grade during the 1981-1982 academic year. The second difference would also have no impact on this litigation because the mandatory language of § 16-1-20 continued to apply to grades one through six. Thus, the only significant textual difference is the addition of the words "or voluntary prayer."

The legislative intent to return prayer to the public schools is, of course, quite different from merely protecting every student's right to engage in voluntary prayer during an appropriate moment of silence during the schoolday. The 1978 statute already protected that right, containing nothing that prevented any student from engaging in voluntary prayer during a silent minute of meditation. Appellants have not identified any secular purpose that was not fully served by § 16-1-20 before the enactment of § 16-1-20.1. Thus, only two conclusions are consistent with the text of § 16-1-20.1: (1) the statute was enacted to convey a message of state endorsement and promotion of prayer; or (2) the statute was enacted for no purpose. No one suggests that the statute was nothing but a meaningless or irrational act.

We must, therefore, conclude that the Alabama Legislature intended to change existing law and that it was motivated [60] by the same purpose that the Governor's answer to the second amended complaint expressly admitted; that the statement inserted in the legislative history revealed; and that Senator Holmes' testimony frankly described. The legislature enacted § 16-1-20.1, despite the existence of § 16-1-20 for the sole purpose of expressing the State's endorsement of prayer activities for one minute at the beginning of each schoolday. The addition of "or voluntary prayer" indicates that the State intended to characterize prayer as a favored practice. Such an endorsement is not consistent with the established principle that the government must pursue a course of complete neutrality toward religion.

The importance of that principle does not permit us to treat this as an inconsequential case involving nothing more than a few words of symbolic speech on behalf of the political majority. For whenever the State itself speaks on a religious [61] subject, one of the questions that we must ask is "whether the government intends to convey a message of endorsement or disapproval of religion." The well-supported concurrent findings of the District Court and the Court of Appeals—that § 16-1-20.1 was intended to convey a message of state approval of prayer activities in the public schools—make it unnecessary, and indeed inappropriate, to evaluate the practical significance of the addition of the words "or voluntary prayer" to the statute. Keeping in mind, as we must, "both the fundamental place held by the Establishment Clause in our constitutional scheme and the myriad, subtle ways in which Establishment Clause values can be eroded," we conclude that § 16-1-20.1 violates the First Amendment. . . .

**[67] JUSTICE O'CONNOR,
concurring in the judgment.**
Nothing in the United States Constitution as interpreted by this Court or in the laws of the State of Alabama prohibits public school students from voluntarily praying at any time before, during, or after the schoolday. Alabama has facilitated voluntary silent prayers of students who are so inclined by enacting Ala. Code § 16-1-20 (Supp. 1984), which provides a moment of silence in appellees' schools each day. The parties to these proceedings concede the validity of this enactment. At issue in these appeals is the constitutional validity of an additional and subsequent Alabama statute, Ala. Code § 16-1-20.1 (Supp. 1984), which both the District Court and the Court of Appeals concluded was enacted solely to officially encourage prayer during the moment of silence. I agree with the judgment of the Court that, in light of the findings of the courts below and the history of its enactment, § 16-1-20.1 of the Alabama Code violates the Establishment Clause of the First Amendment. In my view, there can be little doubt that the purpose and likely effect of this subsequent enactment is to endorse and sponsor voluntary prayer in the public schools. I write separately to identify the peculiar features of the Alabama law that render it invalid, and to explain why moment of silence laws in other States do not necessarily manifest the same infirmity. I also write to explain why neither history nor the Free Exercise Clause of the First Amendment validates the Alabama law struck down by the Court today.

The Religion Clauses of the First Amendment, coupled with the Fourteenth Amendment's guarantee of ordered liberty, preclude both the Nation and the States from making any law respecting an establishment of religion or prohibiting [68] the free exercise thereof. Although a distinct jurisprudence has enveloped each of these Clauses, their common purpose is to secure religious liberty. On these principles the Court has been and remains unanimous.

As these cases once again demonstrate, however, "it is far easier to agree on the purpose that underlies the First Amendment's Establishment and Free Exercise Clauses than to obtain agreement on the standards that should govern their application." *Walz v. Tax Comm'n,* 397 U.S. 664, 694 (1970) (opinion of Harlan, J.). It once appeared that the Court had developed a workable standard by which to identify impermissible government establishments of religion. Under the now familiar *Lemon* test, statutes must have both a secular legislative purpose and a principal or primary effect that neither advances nor inhibits religion, and in addition they must not foster excessive government entanglement with religion. Despite its initial promise, the *Lemon* test has proved problematic. The required inquiry into "entanglement" has been modified and questioned, see *Mueller v. Allen,* 463 U.S. 388, 403, n. 11 (1983), and in one case we have upheld state action against an Establishment Clause challenge without applying the *Lemon* test at all. *Marsh v. Chambers* (1983). The author of *Lemon* himself apparently questions the test's general applicability. See *Lynch v. Donnelly,* 465 U.S. 668, 679 (1984). JUSTICE REHNQUIST today suggests that we abandon *Lemon* entirely, and in the process limit the reach of the Establishment Clause to state discrimination between sects and government designation of a particular church as a "state" or "national" one. *Post,* at 108-113.

Perhaps because I am new to the struggle, I am not ready to abandon all aspects of the *Lemon* test. I do believe, however, that the standards announced in *Lemon* should be [69] reexamined and refined in order to make them more useful in achieving the underlying purpose of the First Amendment. We must strive to do more than erect a constitutional "signpost," to be followed or ignored in a particular case as our predilections may dictate. Instead, our goal should be "to frame a principle for constitutional adjudication that is not only grounded in the history and language of the first amendment, but one that is also capable of consistent application to the relevant problems." Choper, *Religion in the Public Schools: A Proposed Constitutional Standard,* 47 Minn. L. Rev. 329, 332-333 (1963). Last Term, I proposed a refinement of the *Lemon* test with this goal in mind. *Lynch v. Donnelly,* 465 U.S., at 687-689 (concurring opinion).

The *Lynch* concurrence suggested that the religious liberty protected by the Establishment Clause is infringed when the government makes adherence to religion relevant to a person's standing in the political community. Direct government action endorsing religion or a particular religious practice is invalid under this approach because it "sends a message to nonadherents that they are outsiders, not full members of the political community, and an accompanying message to adherents that they are insiders, favored members of the political community." Under this view, *Lemon's* inquiry as to the purpose and effect of a statute requires courts to examine whether government's purpose is to endorse religion and whether the statute actually conveys a message of endorsement.

The endorsement test is useful because of the analytic content it gives to the *Lemon*-mandated inquiry into legislative purpose and effect. In this country, church and state must necessarily operate within the same community. Because of this coexistence, it is inevitable that the secular interests of government and the religious interests of various sects and their adherents will frequently intersect, conflict, and combine. A statute that ostensibly promotes a secular interest [70] often has an incidental or even a primary effect of helping or hindering a sectarian belief. Chaos would ensue if every such statute were invalid under the Establishment Clause. For example, the State could not criminalize murder for fear that it would thereby promote the Biblical command against killing. The task for the Court is to sort out those statutes and government practices whose purpose and effect go against the grain of religious liberty protected by the First Amendment.

The endorsement test does not preclude government from acknowledging religion or from taking religion into account in making law and policy. It does preclude government from conveying or attempting to convey a message that religion or a particular religious belief is favored or preferred. Such an endorsement infringes the religious liberty of the nonadherent, for "[when] the power, prestige and financial support of government is placed behind a particular religious belief, the indirect coercive pressure upon religious minorities to conform to the prevailing officially approved religion is plain." *Engel v. Vitale,* at 431. At issue today is whether state moment of silence statutes in general, and Alabama's moment of silence statute in particular, embody an impermissible endorsement of prayer in public schools.

A

Twenty-five states permit or require public school teachers to have students observe a moment of silence in their classrooms. . . .

[72] A state-sponsored moment of silence in the public schools is different from state-sponsored vocal prayer or Bible reading. First, a moment of silence is not inherently religious. Silence, unlike prayer or Bible reading, need not be associated with a religious exercise. Second, a pupil who participates in a moment of silence need not compromise his or her beliefs. During a moment of silence, a student who objects to prayer is left to his or her own thoughts, and is not compelled to listen to the prayers or thoughts of others. For these simple reasons, a moment of silence statute does not stand or fall under the Establishment Clause according to how the Court regards vocal prayer or Bible reading. Scholars and at least one Member of this Court have recognized the distinction and suggested that a moment of silence in public schools would be constitutional. See *Abington,* at 281 (BRENNAN, J., concurring) ("[The] observance of a moment [73] of reverent silence at the opening of class" may serve "the solely secular purposes of the devotional activities without jeopardizing either the religious liberties of any members of the community or the proper degree of separation between the spheres of religion and government"). As a general matter, I agree. It is difficult to discern a serious threat to religious liberty from a room of silent, thoughtful schoolchildren.

By mandating a moment of silence, a State does not necessarily endorse any activity that might occur during the period. Even if a statute specifies that a student may choose to pray silently during a quiet moment,

the State has not thereby encouraged prayer over other specified alternatives. Nonetheless, it is also possible that a moment of silence statute, either as drafted or as actually implemented, could effectively favor the child who prays over the child who does not. For example, the message of endorsement would seem inescapable if the teacher exhorts children to use the designated time to pray. Similarly, the face of the statute or its legislative history may clearly establish that it seeks to encourage or promote voluntary prayer over other alternatives, rather than merely provide a quiet moment that may be dedicated to prayer by those so inclined. The crucial question is whether the State has conveyed or attempted to convey the message that children should use the moment of silence for prayer. [74] This question cannot be answered in the abstract, but instead requires courts to examine the history, language, and administration of a particular statute to determine whether it operates as an endorsement of religion.

Before reviewing Alabama's moment of silence law to determine whether it endorses prayer, some general observations on the proper scope of the inquiry are in order. First, the inquiry into the purpose of the legislature in enacting a moment of silence law should be deferential and limited. In determining whether the government intends a moment of silence statute to convey a message of endorsement or disapproval of religion, a court has no license to psychoanalyze the legislators. If a legislature expresses a plausible secular purpose for a moment of silence statute in either the text or the legislative history, or if the statute disclaims an intent to encourage prayer over alternatives during a moment of silence, then courts should generally [75] defer to that stated intent. It is particularly troublesome to denigrate an expressed secular purpose due to postenactment testimony by particular legislators or by interested persons who witnessed the drafting of the statute. Even if the text and official history of a statute express no secular purpose, the statute should be held to have an improper purpose only if it is beyond purview that endorsement of religion or a religious belief "was and is the law's reason for existence."

Epperson v. Arkansas, 393 U.S. 97, 108 (1968). Since there is arguably a secular pedagogical value to a moment of silence in public schools, courts should find an improper purpose behind such a statute only if the statute on its face, in its official legislative his tory, or in its interpretation by a responsible administrative agency suggests it has the primary purpose of endorsing prayer.

JUSTICE REHNQUIST suggests that this sort of deferential inquiry into legislative purpose "means little," because "it only requires the legislature to express any secular purpose and omit all sectarian references." *Post,* at 108. It is not a trivial matter, how ever, to require that the legislature manifest a secular purpose and omit all sectarian endorsements from its laws. That requirement is precisely tailored to the Establishment Clause's purpose of assuring that government not intentionally endorse religion or a religious practice. It is of course possible that a legislature will enunciate a sham secular purpose for a statute. I have little doubt that our courts are capable of distinguishing a sham secular purpose from a sincere one, or that the *Lemon* inquiry into the effect of an enactment would help decide those close cases where the validity of an expressed secular purpose is in doubt. While the secular purpose requirement alone may rarely be determinative in striking down a statute, it nevertheless serves an important function. It reminds government that [76] when it acts it should do so without endorsing a particular religious belief or practice that all citizens do not share. In this sense the secular purpose requirement is squarely based in the text of the Establishment Clause it helps to enforce.

Second, the *Lynch* concurrence suggested that the effect of a moment of silence law is not entirely a question of fact:

> *"[Whether] a government activity communicates endorsement of religion is not a question of simple historical fact. Although evidentiary submissions may help answer it, the question is, like the question whether racial or sex-based classifications communicate an invidious message, in large part a legal question to be answered on the basis of judicial interpretation of social facts." 465 U.S., at 693-694.*

The relevant issue is whether an objective observer, acquainted with the text, legislative history, and implementation of the statute, would perceive it as a state endorsement of prayer in public schools. A moment of silence law that is clearly drafted and implemented so as to permit prayer, meditation, and reflection within the prescribed period, without endorsing one alternative over the others, should pass this test.

B

The analysis above suggests that moment of silence laws in many States should pass Establishment Clause scrutiny because they do not favor the child who chooses to pray during a moment of silence over the child who chooses to meditate [77] or reflect. Alabama Code § 16-1-20.1 (Supp. 1984) does not stand on the same footing. However deferentially one examines its text and legislative history, however objectively one views the message attempted to be conveyed to the public, the conclusion is unavoidable that the purpose of the statute is to endorse prayer in public schools. I accordingly agree with the Court of Appeals that the Alabama statute has a purpose which is in violation of the Establishment Clause, and cannot be upheld.

In finding that the purpose of § 16-1-20.1 is to endorse voluntary prayer during a moment of silence, the Court relies on testimony elicited from State Senator Donald G. Holmes during a preliminary injunction hearing. Senator Holmes testified that the sole purpose of the statute was to return voluntary prayer to the public schools. For the reasons expressed above, I would give little, if any, weight to this sort of evidence of legislative intent. Nevertheless, the text of the statute in light of its official legislative history leaves little doubt that the purpose of this statute corresponds to the purpose expressed by Senator Holmes at the preliminary injunction hearing.

First, it is notable that Alabama already had a moment of silence statute before it enacted § 16-1-20.1. See Ala. Code § 16-1-20 (Supp. 1984). Appellees do not challenge this statute—indeed, they concede its validity. The only significant addition made by § 16-1-20.1 is to specify expressly that voluntary prayer is one of the authorized activities during a moment of silence. Any doubt as to the legislative purpose of that addition is removed by the official legislative history. The sole purpose reflected in the official history is "to return voluntary prayer to our public schools." Nor does anything in the legislative history contradict an intent to encourage children to choose prayer over other alternatives during the moment of silence. Given this legislative history, it is not surprising that the State of Alabama conceded in the [78] courts below that the purpose of the statute was to make prayer part of daily classroom activity, and that both the District Court and the Court of Appeals concluded that the law's purpose was to encourage religious activity. In light of the legislative history and the findings of the courts below, I agree with the Court that the State intended § 16-1-20.1 to convey a message that prayer was the endorsed activity during the state-prescribed moment of silence.[2] While it is therefore unnecessary also to determine the effect of the statute, it also seems likely that the message actually conveyed to objective observers by § 16-1-20.1 is approval of the child who selects prayer over other alternatives during a moment of silence.

I also disagree with THE CHIEF JUSTICE's suggestion that the Court's opinion invalidates any moment of silence statute that includes the word "prayer." *Post,* at 85. As noted *supra,* at 73, "[even] if a statute specifies that a student may choose to pray silently during a quiet moment, the State has not thereby encouraged prayer over other specified alternatives."

Given this evidence in the record, candor requires us to admit that this Alabama statute was intended to convey a message of state encouragement and endorsement of religion. In *Walz v. Tax Comm'n,* 397 U.S., at 669, the Court stated that the Religion Clauses of the First Amendment are flexible enough to "permit religious exercise to exist without sponsorship and without interference." Alabama Code § 16-1-20.1 (Supp. 1984) does more than permit prayer to occur during a moment of silence "without interference." It [79] endorses the decision to pray during a moment of silence, and accordingly sponsors a religious exercise. For that reason, I concur in the judgment of the Court. . . .

CHIEF JUSTICE BURGER, dissenting.

[84] Some who trouble to read the opinions in these cases will find it ironic—perhaps even bizarre—that on the very day we heard arguments in the cases, the Court's session opened with an invocation for Divine protection. Across the park a few hundred yards away, the House of Representatives and [85] the Senate regularly open each session with a prayer. These legislative prayers are not just one minute in duration, but are extended, thoughtful invocations and prayers for Divine guidance. They are given, as they have been since 1789, by clergy appointed as official chaplains and paid from the Treasury of the United States. Congress has also provided chapels in the Capitol, at public expense, where Members and others may pause for prayer, meditation—or a moment of silence.

Inevitably some wag is bound to say that the Court's holding today reflects a belief that the historic practice of the Congress and this Court is justified because members of the Judiciary and Congress are more in need of Divine guidance than are schoolchildren. Still others will say that all this controversy is "much ado about nothing," since no power on earth—including this Court and Congress—can stop any teacher from opening the schoolday with a moment of silence for pupils to meditate, to plan their day—or to pray if they voluntarily elect to do so.

I make several points about today's curious holding.

(a) It makes no sense to say that Alabama has "endorsed prayer" by merely enacting a new statute "to specify expressly that voluntary prayer is *one* of the authorized activities during a moment of silence," *ante,* at 77 (O'CONNOR, J., concurring in judgment) (emphasis added). To suggest that a moment-of-silence statute that includes the word "prayer" unconstitutionally endorses religion, while one that simply provides for a moment of silence does not, manifests not neutrality but hostility toward religion. For decades our opinions have stated that hostility toward any religion or toward all religions is as much forbidden by the Constitution as is an official establishment of religion. The Alabama Legislature has no more "endorsed" religion than a state or the Congress does when it provides for legislative chaplains, or than this Court does when it opens each session with an invocation to [86] G-d. Today's decision recalls the observations of Justice Goldberg:

> *"[Untutored] devotion to the concept of neutrality can lead to invocation or approval of results which partake not simply of that noninterference and noninvolvement with the religious which the Constitution commands, but of a brooding and pervasive dedication to the secular and a passive, or even active, hostility to the religious. Such results are not only not compelled by the Constitution, but, it seems to me, are prohibited by it."* Abington School District v. Schempp, *374 U.S. 203, 306 (1963) (concurring opinion).*

(b) The inexplicable aspect of the foregoing opinions, however, is what they advance as support for the holding concerning the purpose of the Alabama Legislature. Rather than determining legislative purpose from the face of the statute as a whole, the opinions rely on three factors in concluding that the Alabama Legislature had a "wholly religious" purpose for enacting the statute under review, Ala. Code § 16-1-20.1 (Supp.

1984): (i) statements of the statute's sponsor, (ii) admissions in Governor James' answer to the second amended complaint, and (iii) the difference between § 16-1-20.1 and its predecessor statute.

Curiously, the opinions do not mention that all of the sponsor's statements relied upon—including the statement "inserted" into the Senate Journal—were made after the legislature had passed the statute; indeed, the testimony that the Court finds critical was given well over a year after the statute was enacted. As even the appellees concede there is not a shred of evidence that [87] the legislature as a whole shared the sponsor's motive or that a majority in either house was even aware of the sponsor's view of the bill when it was passed. The sole relevance of the sponsor's statements, therefore, is that they reflect the personal, subjective motives of a single legislator. No case in the 195-year history of this Court supports the disconcerting idea that postenactment statements by individual legislators are relevant in determining the constitutionality of legislation.

Even if an individual legislator's after-the-fact statements could rationally be considered relevant, all of the opinions fail to mention that the sponsor also testified that one of his purposes in drafting and sponsoring the moment-of-silence bill was to clear up a widespread misunderstanding that a schoolchild is legally prohibited from engaging in silent, individual prayer once he steps inside a public school building. That testimony is at least as important as the statements the Court relies upon, and surely that testimony manifests a permissible purpose.

The Court also relies on the admissions of Governor James' answer to the second amended complaint. Strangely, however, the Court neglects to mention that there was no trial bearing on the constitutionality of the Alabama statutes; trial became unnecessary when the District Court held that the Establishment Clause does not apply to the states. The absence of a trial on the issue of the constitutionality of § 16-1-20.1 is significant be cause the answer filed by the State Board and Superintendent of Education did not make the same admissions that the Governor's answer made. The Court cannot know whether, if these cases had been tried, those state officials would have offered evidence to contravene appellees' allegations concerning legislative purpose. Thus, it is completely inappropriate to accord any relevance to the admissions in the Governor's answer.

(88) The several preceding opinions conclude that the principal difference between § 16-1-20.1 and its predecessor statute proves that the sole purpose behind the inclusion of the phrase "or voluntary prayer" in § 16-1-20.1 was to endorse and promote prayer. This reasoning is simply a subtle way of focusing exclusively—on the religious component of the statute rather than examining the statute as a whole. Such logic—if it can be called that—would lead the Court to hold, for example, that a state may enact a statute that provides reimbursement for bus transportation to the parents of all schoolchildren, but may not add parents of parochial school students to an existing program providing reimbursement for parents of public school students. Congress amended the statutory Pledge of Allegiance 31 years ago to add the words "under G-d."

Act of June 14, 1954, Pub. L. 396, 68 Stat. 249. Do the several opinions in support of the judgment today render the Pledge unconstitutional? That would be the consequence of their method of focusing on the difference between § 16-1-20.1 and its predecessor statute rather than examining § 16-1-20.1 as a whole.[3] Any such holding would of course make a mockery of our decision making in Establishment Clause cases. And even were the Court's method correct, the inclusion of the words "or voluntary prayer" in § 16-1-20.1 is wholly consistent with the clearly permissible purpose of clarifying that silent, voluntary prayer is not forbidden in the public school building.

(89) (c) The Court's extended treatment of the "test" of *Lemon v. Kurtzman* (1971) suggests a naive preoccupation with an easy, bright-line approach for addressing constitutional issues. We have repeatedly cautioned that *Lemon* did not establish a rigid caliper capable of resolving every Establishment Clause issue, but that it sought only to provide "signposts." "In each [Establishment Clause] case, the inquiry calls for line-drawing; no fixed, per se rule can be framed." *Lynch v. Donnelly,* 465 U.S. 668, 678 (1984). In any event, our responsibility is not to apply tidy formulas by rote; our duty is to determine whether the statute or practice at issue is a step toward establishing a state religion. Given today's decision, however, perhaps it is understandable that the opinions in support of the judgment all but ignore the Establishment Clause itself and the concerns that underlie it.

(d) The notion that the Alabama statute is a step toward creating an established church borders on, if it does not trespass into, the ridiculous. The statute does not remotely threaten religious liberty; it affirmatively furthers the values of religious freedom and tolerance that the Establishment Clause was designed to protect. Without pressuring those who do not wish to pray, the statute simply creates an opportunity to think, to plan, or to pray if one wishes—as Congress does by providing chaplains and chapels. It accommodates the purely private, voluntary religious choices of the individual pupils who wish to pray while at the same time creating a time for nonreligious reflection for those who do not choose to pray. The statute also provides a meaningful opportunity for schoolchildren to appreciate the absolute constitutional right of each individual to worship and believe as the individual wishes. The statute "endorses" only the view that the religious observances of others should be tolerated and, [90] where possible, accommodated. If the government may not accommodate religious needs when it does so in a wholly neutral and noncoercive manner, the "benevolent neutrality" that we have long considered the correct constitutional standard will quickly translate into the "callous indifference" that the Court has consistently held the Establishment Clause does not require.

The Court today has ignored the wise admonition of Justice Goldberg that "the measure of constitutional adjudication is the ability and willingness to distinguish between real threat and mere shadow." *Abington School District v. Schempp,* 374 U.S., at 308 (concurring opinion). The innocuous statute that the Court strikes down does not even rise to the level of "mere shadow." JUSTICE O'CONNOR paradoxically acknowledges: "It is difficult to discern a serious threat to religious liberty from a room of silent, thoughtful schoolchildren." *Ante,* at 73. I would add to that, "even if they choose to pray."

The mountains have labored and brought forth a mouse.[4]

[91] JUSTICE REHNQUIST, dissenting.
Thirty-eight years ago this Court, in *Everson v. Board of Education,* 330 U.S. 1, 16 (1947), summarized its exegesis of Establishment Clause doctrine thus:

> *"In the words of Jefferson, the clause against establishment of religion by law was intended to erect 'a wall of separation between church and State.'* Reynolds v. United States, *[98 U.S. 145, 164 (1879)]."*

This language from *Reynolds,* a case involving the Free Exercise Clause of the First Amendment rather than the Establishment Clause, quoted from Thomas Jefferson's letter to the Danbury Baptist Association the phrase "I contemplate with sovereign reverence that act of the whole American people which declared that their legislature should 'make no law respecting an establishment of religion, or prohibiting the free exercise thereof,' thus building a wall of separation [92] between church and State."[5]

It is impossible to build sound constitutional doctrine upon a mistaken understanding of constitutional history, but unfortunately the Establishment Clause has been expressly freighted with Jefferson's misleading metaphor for nearly 40 years. Thomas Jefferson was of course in France at the time the constitutional Amendments known as the Bill of Rights were passed by Congress and ratified by the States. His letter to the Danbury Baptist Association was a short note of courtesy, written 14 years after the Amendments were passed by Congress. He would seem to any detached observer as a less than ideal source of contemporary history as to the meaning of the Religion Clauses of the First Amendment.

Jefferson's fellow Virginian, James Madison, with whom he was joined in the battle for the enactment of the Virginia Statute of Religious Liberty of 1786, did play as large a part as anyone in the drafting of the Bill of Rights. He had two advantages over Jefferson in this regard: he was present in the United States, and he was a leading Member of the First Congress. But when we turn to the record of the proceedings in the First Congress leading up to the adoption of the Establishment Clause of the Constitution, including Madison's significant contributions thereto, we see a far different picture of its purpose than the highly simplified "wall of separation between church and State."

During the debates in the Thirteen Colonies over ratification of the Constitution, one of the arguments frequently used by opponents of ratification was that without a Bill of Rights guaranteeing individual liberty the new general Government [93] carried with it a potential for tyranny. The typical response to this argument on the part of those who favored ratification was that the general Government established by the Constitution had only delegated powers, and that these delegated powers were so limited that the Government would have no occasion to violate individual liberties. This response satisfied some, but not others, and of the 11 Colonies which ratified the Constitution by early 1789, 5 proposed one or another amendments guaranteeing individual liberty. Three—New

Hampshire, New York, and Virginia—included in one form or another a declaration of religious freedom. Rhode Island and North Carolina flatly refused to ratify the Constitution in the absence of amendments in the nature of a Bill of Rights. Virginia and North Carolina proposed identical guarantees of religious freedom:

"[All] men have an equal, natural and unalienable right to the free exercise of religion, ac cording to the dictates of conscience, and . . . no particular religious sect or society ought to be favored or established, by law, in preference to others."[6]

On June 8, 1789, James Madison rose in the House of Representatives and "reminded the House that this was the day that he had heretofore named for bringing forward amendments to the Constitution." 1 Annals of Cong. 424. Madison's subsequent remarks in urging the House to adopt his drafts of the proposed amendments were less those of a dedicated advocate of the wisdom of such measures than those of a prudent statesman seeking the enactment of measures [94] sought by a number of his fellow citizens which could surely do no harm and might do a great deal of good. He said, *inter alia:*

"It appears to me that this House is bound by every motive of prudence, not to let the first session pass over without proposing to the State Legislatures, some things to be incorporated into the Constitution, that will render it as acceptable to the whole people of the United States, as it has been found acceptable to a majority of them. I wish, among other reasons why something should be done, that those who had been friendly to the adoption of this Constitution may have the opportunity of proving to those who were opposed to it that they were as sincerely devoted to liberty and a Republican Government, as those who charged them with wishing the adoption of this Constitution in order to lay the foundation of an aristocracy or despotism. It will be a desirable thing to extinguish from the bosom of every member of the community, any apprehensions that there are those among his countrymen who wish to deprive them of the liberty for which they valiantly fought and honorably bled. And if there are amendments desired of such a nature as will not injure the Constitution, and they can be ingrafted so as to give satisfaction to the doubting part of our fellow-citizens, the friends of the Federal Government will evince that spirit of deference and concession for which they have hitherto been distinguished." *Id.*, at 431-432.

The language Madison proposed for what ultimately became the Religion Clauses of the First Amendment was this:

> "*The civil rights of none shall be abridged on account of religious belief or worship, nor shall any national religion be established, nor shall the full and equal rights of conscience be in any manner, or on any pretext, infringed.*" Id., *at 434.*

[95] On the same day that Madison proposed them, the amendments which formed the basis for the Bill of Rights were referred by the House to a Committee of the Whole, and after several weeks' delay were then referred to a Select Committee consisting of Madison and 10 others. The Committee revised Madison's proposal regarding the establishment of religion to read:

> "*[No] religion shall be established by law, nor shall the equal rights of conscience be infringed.*" Id., *at 729.*

The Committee's proposed revisions were debated in the House on August 15, 1789. The entire debate on the Religion Clauses is contained in two full columns of the "Annals," and does not seem particularly illuminating. See *id.*, at 729-731. Representative Peter Sylvester of New York expressed his dislike for the revised version, because it might have a tendency "to abolish religion altogether." Representative John Vining suggested that the two parts of the sentence be transposed; Representative Elbridge Gerry thought the language should be changed to read "that no religious doctrine shall be established by law." *Id.*, at 729. Roger Sherman of Connecticut had the traditional reason for opposing provisions of a Bill of Rights—that Congress had no delegated authority to "make religious establishments"—and therefore he opposed the adoption of the amendment. Representative Daniel Carroll of Maryland thought it desirable to adopt the words proposed, saying "[he] would not contend

with gentlemen about the phraseology, his object was to secure the substance in such a manner as to satisfy the wishes of the honest part of the community."

Madison then spoke, and said that "he apprehended the meaning of the words to be, that Congress should not establish a religion, and enforce the legal observation of it by law, nor compel men to worship G-d in any manner contrary to their conscience." *Id.*, at 730. He said that some of the state conventions had thought that Congress might rely on [96] the Necessary and Proper Clause to infringe the rights of conscience or to establish a national religion, and "to prevent these effects he presumed the amendment was intended, and he thought it as well expressed as the nature of the language would admit." *Ibid.*

Representative Benjamin Huntington then expressed the view that the Committee's language might "be taken in such latitude as to be extremely hurtful to the cause of religion. He understood the amendment to mean what had been expressed by the gentleman from Virginia; but others might find it convenient to put another construction upon it." Huntington, from Connecticut, was concerned that in the New England States, where state-established religions were the rule rather than the exception, the federal courts might not be able to entertain claims based upon an obligation under the bylaws of a religious organization to contribute to the support of a minister or the building of a place of worship. He hoped that "the amendment would be made in such a way as to secure the rights of conscience, and a free exercise of the rights of religion, but not to patronise those who professed no religion at all." *Id.*, at 730-731.

Madison responded that the insertion of the word "national" before the word "religion" in the Committee version should satisfy the minds of those who had criticized the language. "He believed that the people feared one sect might obtain a pre-eminence, or two combine together, and establish a religion to which they would compel others to conform. He thought that if the word 'national' was introduced, it would point the amendment directly to the object it was intended to prevent." *Id.*, at 731. Representative Samuel Livermore expressed himself as dissatisfied with Madison's proposed amendment, and thought it would be better if the Committee language were altered to read that "Congress shall make no laws touching religion, or infringing the rights of conscience." *Ibid.*

Representative Gerry spoke in opposition to the use of the word "national" because of strong feelings expressed during [97] the ratification debates that a federal government, not a national government, was created by the Constitution. Madison thereby withdrew his proposal but insisted that his reference to a "national religion" only referred to a national establishment and did not mean that the Government was a national one. The question was taken on Representative Livermore's *motion,* which passed by a vote of 31 for and 20 against. *Ibid.*

The following week, without any apparent debate, the House voted to alter the language of the Religion Clauses to read "Congress shall make no law establishing religion, or to prevent the free exercise thereof, or to infringe the rights of conscience." *Id.,* at 766. The floor debates in the Senate were secret, and therefore not reported in the Annals. The Senate on September 3, 1789, considered several different forms of the Religion Amendment, and reported this language back to the House:

> *"Congress shall make no law establishing articles of faith or a mode of worship, or prohibiting the free exercise of religion." C. Antieau, A. Downey, &. E. Roberts,* Freedom from Federal Establishment *130 (1964).*

The House refused to accept the Senate's changes in the Bill of Rights and asked for a conference; the version which emerged from the conference was that which ultimately found its way into the Constitution as a part of the First Amendment.

> *"Congress shall make no law respecting an establishment of religion, or prohibiting the free exercise thereof."*

The House and the Senate both accepted this language on successive days, and the Amendment was proposed in this form.

On the basis of the record of these proceedings in the House of Representatives, James Madison was undoubtedly the most important architect among the Members of the [98] House of the Amendments which became the Bill of Rights, but it was James Madison speaking as an advocate of sensible legislative compromise, not as an advocate of incorporating the Virginia Statute of Religious Liberty into the United States Constitution. During the ratification debate in the Virginia Convention, Madison had actually opposed the idea of any Bill of Rights.[7] His sponsorship of the Amendments in the House was obviously not that of a zealous believer in the necessity of the Religion Clauses, but of one who felt it might do some good, could do no harm, and would satisfy those who had ratified the Constitution on the condition that Congress propose a Bill of Rights:' His original language "nor shall any national religion be established" obviously does not conform to the "wall of separation" between church and State idea which latter-day commentators have ascribed to him. His explanation on the floor of the meaning of his language—"that Congress should not establish a religion, and enforce the legal observation of it by law"—is of the same ilk. When he replied to Huntington in the debate over the proposal which came from the Select Committee of the House, he urged that the language "no religion shall be established by law" should be amended by inserting the word "national" in front of the word "religion."

It seems indisputable from these glimpses of Madison's thinking, as reflected by actions on the floor of the House in 1789, that he saw the Amendment as designed to prohibit the establishment of a national religion, and perhaps to prevent discrimination among sects. He did not see it as requiring neutrality on the part of government between religion and irreligion. Thus the Court's opinion in *Everson*—while correct in bracketing Madison and Jefferson together in their exertions in their home State leading to the enactment of the [99] Virginia Statute of Religious Liberty—is totally incorrect in suggesting that Madison carried these views onto the floor of the United States House of Representatives when he proposed the language which would ultimately become the Bill of Rights.

The repetition of this error in the Court's opinion in *Illinois ex rei. McCollum v. Board of Education* (1948), and, *inter alia, Engel v. Vitale* (1962), does not make it any sounder historically. Finally, in *Abington School District v. Schempp,* 374 U.S. 203, 214 (1963), the Court made the truly remarkable statement that "the views of Madison and Jefferson, preceded by Roger Williams, came to be incorporated not only in the Federal Constitution but likewise in those of most of our States." On the basis of what evidence we have, this statement is demonstrably incorrect as a matter of history.[8] And its repetition in varying forms in succeeding opinions of the Court can give it no more authority than it possesses as a matter of fact; *stare decisis* may bind courts as to matters of law, but it cannot bind them as to matters of history.

None of the other Members of Congress who spoke during the August 15th debate expressed the slightest indication that they thought the language before them from the Select Committee, or the evil to be aimed at, would require that the Government be absolutely neutral as between religion and irreligion. The evil to be aimed at, so far as those who spoke were concerned, appears to have been the establishment of a national church, and perhaps the preference of one religious sect over another; but it was definitely not concerned about whether the Government might aid all religions evenhandedly. If one were to follow the advice of JUSTICE BRENNAN, concurring in *Abington School District v. Schempp,* at 236, and construe the Amendment in the light of what particular [100] "practices . . . challenged threaten those consequences which the Framers deeply feared; whether, in short, they tend to promote that type of interdependence between religion and state which the First Amendment was designed to prevent," one would have to say that the First Amendment Establishment Clause should be read no more broadly than to prevent the establishment of a national religion or the governmental preference of one religious sect over another.

The actions of the First Congress, which reenacted the Northwest Ordinance for the governance of the Northwest Territory in 1789, confirm the view that Congress did not mean that the Government should be neutral between religion and irreligion. The House of Representatives took up the Northwest Ordinance on the same day as Madison introduced his proposed amendments which became the Bill of Rights; while at that time the Federal Government was of course not bound by draft amendments to the Constitution which had not yet been proposed by Congress, say nothing of ratified by the States, it seems highly unlikely that the House of Representatives would simultaneously consider proposed amendments to the Constitution and enact an important piece of territorial legislation which conflicted with the intent of those proposals. The Northwest Ordinance, 1 Stat. 50, reenacted the Northwest Ordinance of 1787 and provided that "[religion], morality, and knowledge, being necessary to good government and the happiness of mankind, schools and the means of education shall forever be encouraged." *Id.,* at 52, n. (a). Land grants for schools in the Northwest Territory were not limited to public schools. It was not until 1845 that Congress limited land grants in the new States and Territories to nonsectarian schools.

On the day after the House of Representatives voted to adopt the form of the First Amendment Religion Clauses which was ultimately proposed and ratified, Representative [101] Elias Boudinot proposed a resolution asking President George Washington to issue a Thanksgiving Day proclamation. Boudinot said he "could not think of letting the session pass over without offering an opportunity to all the citizens of the United States of joining with one voice, in returning to Al-mighty G-d their sincere thanks for the many blessings he had poured down upon them." 1 Annals of Cong. 914 (1789). Representative Aedanas Burke objected to the resolution because he did not like "this mimicking of European customs"; Representative Thomas Tucker objected that whether or not the people had reason to be satisfied with the Constitution was something that the States knew better than the Congress, and in any event "it is a religious matter, and, as such, is proscribed to us." *Id.,* at 915. Representative Sherman supported the resolution "not only as a laudable one in itself, but as warranted by a number of precedents in Holy Writ: for instance, the solemn thanksgivings and rejoicings which took place in the time of Solomon, after the building of the temple, was a case in point. This example, he thought, worthy of Christian imitation on the present occasion. . . ." *Ibid.*

Boudinot's resolution was carried in the affirmative on September 25, 1789. Boudinot and Sherman, who favored the Thanksgiving Proclamation, voted in favor of the adoption of the proposed amendments to the Constitution, including the Religion Clauses; Tucker, who opposed the Thanksgiving Proclamation, voted against the adoption of the amendments which became the Bill of Rights.

Within two weeks of this action by the House, George Washington responded to the Joint Resolution which by now had been changed to include the language that the President "recommend to the people of the United States a day of public thanksgiving and prayer, to be observed by acknowledging with grateful hearts the many and signal favors of Almighty G-d, especially by affording them an opportunity peaceably to establish a form of government for their safety and happiness."

1 J. Richardson, *Messages and Papers of* [102] *the Presidents, 1789-1897*, p. 64 (1897). The Presidential Proclamation was couched in these words:

"Now, therefore, I do recommend and assign Thursday, the 26th day of November next, to be devoted by the people of these States to the service of that great and glorious Being who is the beneficent author of all the good that was, that is, or that will be; that we may then all unite in rendering unto Him our sincere and humble thanks for His kind care and protection of the people of this country previous to their becoming a nation; for the signal and manifold mercies and the favorable interpositions of His providence in the course and conclusion of the late war; for the great degree of tranquillity, union, and plenty which we have since enjoyed; for the peaceable and rational manner in which we have been enabled to establish constitutions of government for our safety and happiness, and particularly the national one now lately instituted; for the civil and religious liberty with which we are blessed, and the means we have of acquiring and diffusing useful knowledge; and, in general, for all the great and various favors which He has been pleased to confer upon us. And also that we may then unite in most humbly offering our prayers and supplications to the great L-rd

and Ruler of Nations, and beseech Him to pardon our national and other transgressions; to enable us all, whether in public or private stations, to perform our several and relative duties properly and punctually; to render our National Government a blessing to all the people by constantly being a Government of wise, just, and constitutional laws, discreetly and faithfully executed and obeyed; to protect and guide all, sovereigns and nations (especially such as have shown kindness to us), and to bless them with good governments, peace, and concord; to promote the knowledge and practice of true religion and virtue, and the increase of science among them and [103] us; and, generally, to grant unto all mankind such a degree of temporal prosperity as He alone knows to be best." Ibid.

George Washington, John Adams, and James Madison all issued Thanksgiving Proclamations; Thomas Jefferson did not, saying:

"Fasting and prayer are religious exercises; the enjoining them an act of discipline. Every religious society has a right to determine for itself the times for these exercises, and the objects proper for them, according to their own particular tenets; and this right can never be safer than in their own hands, where the Constitution has deposited it."

11 *Writings of Thomas Jefferson* 429 (A. Lipscomb ed. 1904).

As the United States moved from the 18th into the 19th century, Congress appropriated time and again public moneys in support of sectarian Indian education carried on by religious organizations. Typical of these was Jefferson's treaty with the Kaskaskia Indians, which provided annual cash support for the Tribe's Roman Catholic priest and church. It was not until 1897, when aid to sectarian education [104] for Indians had reached $500,000 annually, that Congress decided thereafter to cease appropriating money for education in sectarian schools. See generally R. Cord, *Separation of Church and State* 61-82 (1982). This history shows the fallacy of the notion found in *Everson* that "no tax in any amount" may be levied for religious activities in any form. 330 U.S., at 15-16.

From 1789 to 1823 the United States Congress had provided a trust endowment of up to 12,000 acres of land "for the Society of the United Brethren, for propagating the Gospel among the Heathen." See, *e.g.*, ch. 46, **1** Stat. 490. The Act creating this endowment was renewed periodically and the renewals were signed into law by Washington, Adams, and Jefferson.

Congressional grants for the aid of religion were not limited to Indians. In 1787 Congress provided land to the Ohio Company, including acreage for the support of religion. This grant was reauthorized in 1792. See 1 Stat. 257. In 1833 Congress authorized the State of Ohio to sell the land set aside for religion and use the proceeds "for the support of religion . . . and for no other use or purpose whatsoever. . . . " 4 Stat. 618-619.

Joseph Story, a Member of this Court from 1811 to 1845, and during much of that time a professor at the Harvard Law School, published by far the most comprehensive treatise on the United States Constitution that had then appeared. Volume 2 of Story's *Commentaries on the Constitution of the United States* 630-632 (5th ed. 1891) discussed the meaning of the Establishment Clause of the First Amendment this way:

"Probably at the time of the adoption of the Constitution, and of the amendment to it now under consideration [First Amendment], the general if not the universal sentiment in America was, that Christianity ought to receive encouragement from the State so far as was not incompatible with the private rights of conscience and the freedom of religious worship. An attempt to level all religions, and to make it a matter of state policy to hold all in utter indifference, would have created universal disapprobation, if not universal indignation. . . .

The real object of the [First] [Amendment] was not to countenance, much less to advance, Mahometanism, or Judaism, or infidelity, by prostrating Christianity; but to exclude all rivalry among Christian sects, and to prevent [105] any national ecclesiastical establishment which should give to a hierarchy the exclusive patronage of the national government. It thus cut off the means of religious persecution (the vice and pest of former ages), and of the subversion of the rights of conscience in matters of religion, which

had been trampled upon almost from the days of the Apostles to the present age. . . . "

Thomas Cooley's eminence as a legal authority rivaled that of Story. Cooley stated in his treatise entitled *Constitutional Limitations* that aid to a particular religious sect was prohibited by the United States Constitution, but he went on to say:

"But while thus careful to establish, protect, and defend religious freedom and equality, the American constitutions contain no provisions which prohibit the authorities from such solemn recognition of a superintending Providence in public transactions and exercises as the general religious sentiment of mankind inspires, and as seems meet and proper in finite and dependent beings. Whatever may be the shades of religious belief, all must acknowledge the fitness of recognizing in important human affairs the superintending care and control of the Great Governor of the Universe, and of acknowledging with thanksgiving his boundless favors, or bowing in contrition when visited with the penalties of his broken laws. No principle of constitutional law is violated when thanksgiving or fast days are appointed; when chaplains are designated for the army and navy; when legislative sessions are opened with prayer or the reading of the Scriptures, or when religious teaching is encouraged by a general exemption of the houses of religious worship from taxation for the support of State government. Undoubtedly the spirit of the Constitution will require, in all these cases, that care be taken to avoid discrimination [106] in favor of or against any one religious denomination or sect; but the power to do any of these things does not become unconstitutional simply because of its susceptibility to abuse. . . . " Id., at *470-*471.

Cooley added that

"[this] public recognition of religious worship, however, is not based entirely, perhaps not even mainly, upon a sense of what is due to the Supreme Being himself as the author of all good and of all law; but the same reasons of state policy which induce the government to aid institutions of charity and seminaries of instruction will incline it also to

foster religious worship and religious institutions, as conservators of the public morals and valuable, if not indispensable, assistants to the preservation of the public order." Id., at *470.

It would seem from this evidence that the Establishment Clause of the First Amendment had acquired a well-accepted meaning: it forbade establishment of a national religion, and forbade preference among religious sects or denominations. Indeed, the first American dictionary defined the word "establishment" as "the act of establishing, founding, ratifying or ordaining," such as in "[the] episcopal form of religion, so called, in England." 1 N. Webster, *American Dictionary of the English Language* (1st ed. 1828). The Establishment Clause did not require government neutrality between religion and irreligion nor did it prohibit the Federal Government from providing nondiscriminatory aid to religion. There is simply no historical foundation for the proposition that the Framers intended to build the "wall of separation" that was constitutionalized in *Everson.*

Notwithstanding the absence of a historical basis for this theory of rigid separation, the wall idea might well have served as a useful albeit misguided analytical concept, had it led this Court to unified and principled results in Establishment Clause cases. The opposite, unfortunately, has been [107] true; in the 38 years since *Everson* our Establishment Clause cases have been neither principled nor unified. Our recent opinions, many of them hopelessly divided pluralities, have with embarrassing candor conceded that the "wall of separation" is merely a "blurred, indistinct, and variable barrier," which "is not wholly accurate" and can only be "dimly perceived." *Lemon v. Kurtzman,* 403 U.S. 602, 614 (1971); *Tilton v. Richardson,* 403 U.S. 672, 677-678 (1971); *Wolman v. Walter,* 433 U.S. 229, 236 (1977); *Lynch v. Donnelly,* 465 U.S. 668, 673 (1984).

Many of our other Establishment Clause cases have been decided by bare 5-4 majorities. *Committee for Public Education & Religious Liberty v. Regan* (1980); *Larson v. Valente* (1982); *Mueller v. Allen* (1983); *Lynch v. Donnelly* (1984); cf. *Levitt v. Committee for Public Education & Religious Liberty* (1973).

Whether due to its lack of historical support or its practical unworkability, the *Everson* "wall" has proved all but useless as a guide to sound constitutional adjudication. It illustrates only too well the wisdom of Benjamin Cardozo's observation that "[metaphors] in law are to be narrowly watched, for starting as devices to liberate thought, they end often by enslaving it." *Berkey v. Third Avenue R. Co.,* 244 N.Y. 84, 94, 155 N. E. 58, 61 (1926).

But the greatest injury of the "wall" notion is its mischievous diversion of judges from the actual intentions of the drafters of the Bill of Rights. The "crucible of litigation," *ante,* at 52, is well adapted to adjudicating factual disputes on the basis of testimony presented in court, but no amount of repetition of historical errors in judicial opinions can make the errors true. The "wall of separation between church and State" is a metaphor based on bad history, a metaphor which has proved useless as a guide to judging. It should be frankly and explicitly abandoned.

[108] The Court has more recently attempted to add some mortar to *Everson's* wall through the three-part test of *Lemon v. Kurtzman,* at 614-615, which served at first to offer a more useful test for purposes of the Establishment Clause than did the "wall" metaphor. Generally stated, the *Lemon* test proscribes state action that has a sectarian purpose or effect, or causes an impermissible governmental entanglement with religion.

Lemon cited *Board of Education v. Allen,* 392 U.S. 236, 243 (1968), as the source of the "purpose" and "effect" prongs of the three-part test. The *Allen* opinion explains, however, how it inherited the purpose and effect elements from *Schempp* and *Everson,* both of which contain the historical errors described above. See *Allen,* at 243. Thus the purpose and effect prongs have the same historical deficiencies as the wall concept itself: they are in no way based on either the language or intent of the drafters.

The secular purpose prong has proved mercurial in application because it has never been fully defined, and we have never fully stated how the test is to operate. If the purpose prong is intended to void those aids to sectarian institutions accompanied by a stated legislative purpose to aid religion, the prong will condemn nothing so long as the legislature utters a secular purpose and says nothing about aiding religion. Thus the constitutionality of a statute may depend upon what the legislators put into the legislative history and, more importantly, what they leave out. The purpose prong means little if it only requires the legislature to express any secular purpose and omit all sectarian references, because legislators might do just that. Faced with a valid legislative secular purpose, we could not properly ignore that purpose without a factual basis for doing so.

However, if the purpose prong is aimed to void all statutes enacted with the intent to aid sectarian institutions, whether stated or not, then most statutes providing any aid, such as [109] textbooks or bus rides for sectarian school children, will fail because one of the purposes behind every statute, whether stated or not, is to aid the target of its largesse. In other words, if the purpose prong requires an absence of any intent to aid sectarian institutions, whether or not expressed, few state laws in this area could pass the test, and we would be required to void some state aids to religion which we have already upheld. *E.g., Allen, supra.*

The entanglement prong of the *Lemon* test came from *Walz v. Tax Comm'n*, 397 U.S. 664, 674 (1970). *Walz* involved a constitutional challenge to New York's time-honored practice of providing state property tax exemptions to church property used in worship. The *Walz* opinion refused to "undermine the ultimate constitutional objective [of the Establishment Clause] as illuminated by history," *id.*, at 671, and upheld the tax exemption. The Court examined the historical relationship between the State and church when church property was in issue, and determined that the challenged tax exemption did not so entangle New York with the church as to cause an intrusion or interference with religion. Interferences with religion should arguably be dealt with under the Free Exercise Clause, but the entanglement inquiry in *Walz* was consistent with that case's broad survey of the relationship between state taxation and religious property.

We have not always followed *Walz'* reflective inquiry into entanglement, however. *E.g., Wolman*, at 254. One of the difficulties with the entanglement prong is that, when divorced from the logic of *Walz*,

it creates an "insoluble paradox" in school aid cases: we have required aid to parochial schools to be closely watched lest it be put to sectarian use, yet this close supervision itself will create an entanglement. For example, in *Wolman*, the Court in part struck the State's nondiscriminatory provision of buses for parochial school field trips, because the state supervision [110] of sectarian officials in charge of field trips would be too onerous. This type of self-defeating result is certainly not required to ensure that States do not establish religions.

The entanglement test as applied in cases like *Wolman* also ignores the myriad state administrative regulations properly placed upon sectarian institutions such as curriculum, attendance, and certification requirements for sectarian schools, or fire and safety regulations for churches. Avoiding entanglement between church and State may be an important consideration in a case like *Walz*, but if the entanglement prong were applied to all state and church relations in the automatic manner in which it has been applied to school aid cases, the State could hardly require anything of church-related institutions as a condition for receipt of financial assistance.

These difficulties arise because the *Lemon* test has no more grounding in the history of the First Amendment than does the wall theory upon which it rests. The three-part test represents a determined effort to craft a workable rule from a historically faulty doctrine; but the rule can only be as sound as the doctrine it attempts to service. The three-part test has simply not provided adequate standards for deciding Establishment Clause cases, as this Court has slowly come to realize. Even worse, the *Lemon* test has caused this Court to fracture into unworkable plurality opinions depending upon how each of the three factors applies to a certain state action. The results from our school services cases show the difficulty we have encountered in making the *Lemon* test yield principled results.

For example, a State may lend to parochial school children geography textbooks[9] that contain maps of the United States, but the State may not lend maps of the United States for use in geography class.[10] A State may lend textbooks on American colonial history, but it may not lend a film on [111] George Washington, or a film projector to show it in history class. A State may lend classroom workbooks, but may not lend workbooks in which the parochial school children write, thus rendering them nonreusable.[11] A State may pay for bus transportation to religious schools[12] but may not pay for bus transportation from the parochial school to the public zoo or natural history museum for a field trip.[13] A State may pay for diagnostic services conducted in the parochial school but therapeutic services must be given in a different building; speech and hearing "services" conducted by the State inside the sectarian school are forbidden, *Meek v. Pittenger,* 421 U.S. 349, 367, 371 (1975), but the State may conduct speech and hearing diagnostic testing inside the sectarian school. *Wolman,* 433 U.S., at 241. Exceptional parochial school students may receive counseling, but it must take place outside of the parochial school,[14] such as in a trailer parked down the street. *Id.,* at 245. A State may give cash to a parochial school to pay for the administration of state-written tests and state-ordered reporting services,[15] but it may not provide funds for teacher-prepared tests on secular subjects.[16] Religious instruction may not be given in public school,[17] but the public school may release students during the day for religion classes elsewhere, and may enforce attendance at those classes with its truancy laws.[18]

These results violate the historically sound principle "that the Establishment Clause does not forbid governments . . . to [provide] general welfare under which benefits are distributed to private individuals, even though many of those individuals [112] may elect to use those benefits in ways that 'aid' religious instruction or worship." *Committee for Public Education & Religious Liberty v. Nyquist,* 413 U.S. 756, 799 (1973) (BURGER, C. J., concurring in part and dissenting in part). It is not surprising in the light of this record that our most recent opinions have expressed doubt on the usefulness of the *Lemon* test.

Although the test initially provided helpful assistance, *e.g., Tilton v. Richardson* (1971), we soon began describing the test as only a "guideline," *Committee for Public Education & Religious Liberty v. Nyquist,* and lately we have described it as "no more than [a] useful [signpost]." *Mueller v. Allen,* 463 U.S. 388, 394 (1983),

citing *Hunt v. McNair,* 413 U.S. 734, 741 (1973); *Larkin v. Grendel's Den, Inc.* (1982). We have noted that the *Lemon* test is "not easily applied," *Meek,* at 358, and as JUSTICE WHITE noted in *Committee for Public Education & Religious Liberty v. Regan* (1980), under the *Lemon* test we have "[sacrificed] clarity and predictability for flexibility." 444 U.S., at 662. In *Lynch* we reiterated that the *Lemon* test has never been binding on the Court, and we cited two cases where we had declined to apply it. 465 U.S., at 679, citing *Marsh v. Chambers* (1983); *Larson v. Valente* (1982).

If a constitutional theory has no basis in the history of the amendment it seeks to interpret, is difficult to apply and yields unprincipled results, I see little use in it. The "crucible of litigation," *ante,* at 52, has produced only consistent unpredictability, and today's effort is just a continuation of "the Sisyphean task of trying to patch together the 'blurred, indistinct and variable barrier' described in *Lemon v. Kurtzman.*" *Regan,* at 671 (STEVENS, J., dissenting). We have done much straining since 1947, but still we admit that we can only "dimly perceive" the *Everson* wall. *Tilton, supra.* Our perception has been clouded not by the Constitution but by the mists of an unnecessary metaphor.

[113] The true meaning of the Establishment Clause can only be seen in its history. As drafters of our Bill of Rights, the Framers inscribed the principles that control today. Any deviation from their intentions frustrates the permanence of that Charter and will only lead to the type of unprincipled decision-making that has plagued our Establishment Clause cases since *Everson.*

The Framers intended the Establishment Clause to prohibit the designation of any church as a "national" one. The Clause was also designed to stop the Federal Government from asserting a preference for one religious denomination or sect over others. Given the "incorporation" of the Establishment Clause as against the States via the Fourteenth Amendment in *Everson,* States are prohibited as well from establishing a religion or discriminating between sects. As its history abundantly shows, however, nothing in the Establishment Clause requires government to be strictly neutral between religion and irreligion, nor does that Clause prohibit Congress or the States from pursuing legitimate secular ends through nondiscriminatory sectarian means.

The Court strikes down the Alabama statute because the State wished to "characterize prayer as a favored practice." *Ante*, at 60. It would come as much of a shock to those who drafted the Bill of Rights as it will to a large number of thoughtful Americans today to learn that the Constitution, as construed by the majority, prohibits the Alabama Legislature from "endorsing" prayer. George Washington himself, at the request of the very Congress which passed the Bill of Rights, proclaimed a day of "public thanksgiving and prayer, to be observed by acknowledging with grateful hearts the many and signal favors of Al-mighty G-d." History must judge whether it was the Father of his Country in 1789, or a majority of the Court today, which has strayed from the meaning of the Establishment Clause.

The State surely has a secular interest in regulating the manner in which public schools are conducted. Nothing in [114] the Establishment Clause of the First Amendment, properly understood, prohibits any such generalized "endorsement" of prayer. I would therefore reverse the judgment of the Court of Appeals.

Vincent Phillip Munoz, *Religious Liberty and the American Supreme Court: The Essential Cases and Documents* (Lanham, Md.: Rowman & Littlefield, 2013), Ch. 36, p. 271ff.

Reprinted with permission of the publisher. All rights reserved.

Endnotes

1 The statement indicated, in pertinent part:
Gentlemen, by passage of this bill by the Alabama Legislature our children in this state will have the opportunity of sharing in the spiritual heritage of this state and this country. The United States as well as the State of Alabama was founded by people who believe in G-d. *I believe this effort to return voluntary prayer* to our public schools for its return to us to the original position of the writers of the Constitution, this local philosophies and beliefs hundreds of Alabamians have urged my continuous support for permitting school prayer. Since coming to the Alabama Senate I have worked hard *on this legislation to accomplish the return of voluntary prayer in our public schools and return to the basic moral fiber.* (Emphasis added.)
2 THE CHIEF JUSTICE suggests that one consequence of the Court's emphasis on the difference between § 16-1-20.1 and its predecessor statute might be to render the Pledge of Allegiance unconstitutional because Congress amended it in 1954 to add the words "under G-d."

Post, at 88. I disagree. In my view, the words "under G-d" in the Pledge, as codified at 36 U.S.C. § 172, serve as an acknowledgment of religion with "the legitimate secular purposes of solemnizing public occasions, [and] expressing confidence in the future." *Lynch v. Donnelly,* 465 U.S. 668, 693 (1984) (concurring opinion).
3 The House Report on the legislation amending the Pledge states that the purpose of the amendment was to affirm the principle that "our people and our Government [are dependent] upon the moral directions of the Creator." H. R. Rep. No. 1693, 83d Cong., 2d Sess., 2 (1954). If this is simply "acknowledgment," not "endorsement," of religion, see *ante,* at 78, n. 5 (O'CONNOR, J., concurring in judgment), the distinction is far too infinitesimal for me to grasp.
4 Horace, *Epistles,* bk. III (Ars Poetica), line 139.
5 *Reynolds* is the only authority cited as direct precedent for the "wall of separation theory." 330 U.S., at 16. *Reynolds* is truly inapt; it dealt with a Mormon's Free Exercise Clause challenge to a federal polygamy law.
6 The New York and Rhode Island proposals were quite similar. They stated that no particular "religious sect or society ought to be favored or established by law in preference to others."
7 In a letter he sent to Jefferson in France, Madison stated that he did not see much importance in a Bill of Rights but he planned to support it because it was "anxiously desired by others . . . [and] it might be of use, and if properly executed could not be of disservice." 5 *Writings of James Madison* 271 IG. Hunted. 1904).
8 State establishments were prevalent throughout the late 18th and early 19th centuries. See Mass. Const. of 1780, Part 1, Art. III; N. H. Const. of 1784, Art. VI; Md. Declaration of Rights of 1776, Art. XXXIII; R. I. Charter of 1633 (superseded 1842).
9 *Board of Education v. Allen,* 392 U.S. 236 (1968).
10 *Meek,* 421 U.S., at 362-366. A science book is permissible, a science kit is not. See *Wolman,* 433 U.S., at 249.
11 See *Meek,* supra, at 354-355, nn. 3, 4, 362-366.
12 *Everson v. Board of Education,* 330 U.S. 1 (1947).
13 *Wolman,* at 252-255.
14 *Wolman,* at 241-248; *Meek,* at 352, n. 2, 367-373.
15 *Regan,* 444 U.S., at 648, 657-659.
16 *Levitt,* 413 U.S., at 479-482.
17 Illinois *ex rei. McCollum v. Board of Education,* 333 U.S. 203(1948).
18 *Zorach v. Clauson,* 343 U.S. 306 (1952).

Acknowledgments

"Let justice flow as water, and righteousness as a mighty stream."

AMOS 5:24

Criminal justice policy affects the safety and peace of mind of all citizens, and has broad implications for crime victims, the accused, the convicted, and their families. With a growing consensus on both sides of the ideological divide that the United States requires criminal justice reform—either because the current system is unjust, inequitable, ineffective, or simply too expensive to taxpayers—the Rohr Jewish Learning Institute's offering of *Crime and Consequence* is a particularly timely and insightful illumination of the subject.

Beyond the extensive contributions of leading legal experts used to craft *Crime and Consequence*, this study leans on an oft overlooked but timeless resource of brilliant legal insight: the rich compilation of Jewish legal and moral scholarship preserved in the Talmud and its commentaries. The Talmud is well-positioned to shed light on modern ethical and legal dilemmas because it dares to question, to suppose, to imagine, and to test the boundaries of intellectual curiosity. Across six sessions, *Crime and Consequence* moves between Judaic and American legal doctrines, addressing pressing ethical concerns and sharing multiple perspectives on criminal justice reform.

We are sincerely grateful for the contributions of the following individuals in constructing this innovative course:

Rabbi Shmuel Super, course author, for his tireless investment in this project; **Rabbi Mordechai Dinerman**, course editor; **Rabbi Naftali Silberberg**, who, along with Rabbi Dinerman, directs the JLI Curriculum Department and the Flagship editorial team; **Rabbi Zalman Abraham**, for skillfully providing the vision for strategic branding and marketing of JLI course offerings.

Professor Steven Drizin (Northwestern Pritzker School of Law; Center on Wrongful Convictions), and author and attorney **Scott Turow** (who has sold thirty million copies of his fourteen books in forty languages), for sharing insights with the JLI curriculum team that inspired the launch of this project. We also thank the following experts for their indispensable input: **Professor Dan Ariely** (Duke University); **Professor Robert Blecker** (New York Law School); **Rahmiel Hayyim (Robert) Drizin** (public defender, Chicago, IL); **Professor Stephen Greenwald** (president of Association for Jewish Lawyers and Jurists); **Professor Samuel Levine** (Touro College; director of the Jewish Law Institute); **Professor Martin Pritikin** (dean and vice president at Concord Law School); and **Mr. David Sonn** (criminal solicitor, UK).

We are indebted to **Rabbi Yakov Gershon** for his Judaic research, and for the following additional contributors of research and writing: **Rabbis Avrohom Bergstein, Lazer Gurkow, Binyamin Walters, Boruch Werdiger, Yosi Wolf,** and **Nochum Zajac.** We thank **Mendy Katzman** for his research on American law.

Rabbi Menachem Feldman, Rabbi Yehuda Leib Heber, Rabbi Levi Mendelow, Rabbi Shalom Paltiel, and **Rabbi Avremel Sternberg**, members of the JLI Editorial Board, spent many hours reviewing the course materials. They provided useful suggestions that enhanced the course and ensured its suitability for a wide range of students.

Rivki Mockin streamlined the curriculum process and ensured the smoothness and timeliness of the product, and **Chana Dechter,** JLI Flagship's administrator and project manager, contributed immeasurably to the production and professionalism of the entire project. **Zelda Abelsky, Mushka Backman,** and **Rabbi Michoel Shapiro** provided editorial assistance, and **Mimi Palace, Shmuel Telsner, Ya'akovah Weber,** and **Rachel Witty** enhanced the quality and accuracy of the writing with their proofreading. **Shternie Zaltzman** designed the textbooks with taste and expertise, and the textbook images were researched and selected by **Rabbi Zalman Abraham**. **Rabbi Mendel Sirota** directed the book's publication and distribution.

Mushka Druk, Baila Pruss, and **Chany Tauber** designed the aesthetically pleasing PowerPoints, and **Moshe Raskin** and **Getzy Raskin** produced the videos; the video scripts were masterfully written by **Rabbi Yaakov Paley.**

We are immensely grateful for the encouragement of JLI's visionary chairman, and vice-chairman of *Merkos L'Inyonei Chinuch*—Lubavitch World Headquarters, **Rabbi Moshe Kotlarsky.** Rabbi Kotlarsky has been highly instrumental in building the infrastructure for the expansion of Chabad's international network and is also the architect of scores of initiatives and services to help Chabad representatives across the globe succeed in their mission. We are blessed to have the unwavering support of JLI's principal benefactor, **Mr. George Rohr,** who is fully invested in our work, continues to be instrumental in JLI's monumental growth and expansion, and is largely responsible for the Jewish renaissance that is being spearheaded by JLI and its affiliates across the globe.

The commitment and sage direction of JLI's dedicated Executive Board—**Rabbis Chaim Block, Hesh Epstein, Ronnie Fine, Yosef Gansburg, Shmuel Kaplan, Yisrael Rice,** and **Avrohom Sternberg**—and the countless hours they devote to the development of JLI are what drive the vision, growth, and tremendous success of the organization.

Finally, JLI represents an incredible partnership of more than 1,400 *shluchim* and *shluchot* in more than one thousand locations across the globe, who contribute their time and talent to further Jewish adult education. We thank them for generously sharing feedback and making suggestions that steer JLI's development and growth. They are our most valuable critics and our most cherished contributors.

Inspired by the call of the **Lubavitcher Rebbe,** of righteous memory, it is the mandate of the Rohr JLI to provide a community of learning for all Jews throughout the world where they can participate in their precious heritage of Torah study and experience its rewards. May this course succeed in fulfilling this sacred charge!

On behalf of the Rohr Jewish Learning Institute,

RABBI EFRAIM MINTZ
Executive Director

RABBI YISRAEL RICE
Chairman, Editorial Board

Erev Rosh Hashanah, 5779

The Rohr Jewish Learning Institute

AN AFFILIATE OF MERKOS L'INYONEI CHINUCH,
THE EDUCATIONAL ARM OF THE CHABAD-LUBAVITCH MOVEMENT
822 EASTERN PARKWAY, BROOKLYN, NY 11213

CHAIRMAN
Rabbi Moshe Kotlarsky
Lubavitch World Headquarters

PRINCIPAL BENEFACTOR
Mr. George Rohr
New York, NY

EXECUTIVE DIRECTOR
Rabbi Efraim Mintz

EXECUTIVE COMMITTEE
Rabbi Chaim Block
S. Antonio, TX

Rabbi Hesh Epstein
Columbia, SC

Rabbi Ronnie Fine
Montreal, QC

Rabbi Yosef Gansburg
Toronto, ON

Rabbi Shmuel Kaplan
Potomac, MD

Rabbi Yisrael Rice
S. Rafael, CA

Rabbi Avrohom Sternberg
New London, CT

ADMINISTRATION
Rabbi Mendel Kotlarsky

ADMINISTRATOR
Rabbi Dubi Rabinowitz

ADVISORY BOARD OF GOVERNORS

George Rohr
New York, NY

Yaacov and Karen Cohen
Potomac, MD

Yitzchok and Julie Gniwisch
Montreal, QC

Barbara Hines
Aspen, CO

Daniel B. Markson
S. Antonio, TX

Daniel and Rosie Mattio
Mercer Island, WA

David Mintz
Tenafly, NJ

Dr. Stephen F. Serbin
Columbia, SC

Leonard A. Wien, Jr.
Miami Beach, FL

ACADEMIC ADVISORY BOARD
Dr. Lewis Glinert
Professor of Hebraic Studies and Linguistics
Dartmouth College

Rabbi Edward Reichman, MD
Professor of Emergency Medicine
Albert Einstein College of Medicine

Dr. Jonathan Sarna
Professor of American Jewish History
Brandeis University

Dr. Lawrence H. Schiffman
Professor of Hebrew and Judaic Studies
New York University

EDUCATIONAL CONSULTANTS

Mr. Michael Brandwein
Lincolnshire, IL
Speech and Communication Expert

Dr. Andrew Effrat
Amherst, MA
Professor, School of Education
University of Massachusetts, Amherst

Dr. David Pelcovitz
New York, NY
Professor of Education and Psychology
Yeshiva University

Dr. Chana Silberstein
Ithaca, NY

Dr. Casey Skvorc
Washington, DC
National Institutes of Health

RABBINIC ADVISORY BOARD
Rabbi Yossi Shusterman
Beverly Hills, CA
CHAIRMAN

Rabbi Mordechai Farkash
Bellevue, WA

Rabbi Mendel Lipskier
Sherman Oaks, CA

Rabbi Avrohom Sternberg
New London, CT

CURRICULUM DEVELOPMENT

Rabbi Mordechai Dinerman
Rabbi Naftali Silberberg
EDITORS-IN-CHIEF

Rabbi Shmuel Klatzkin, PhD
Rabbi Yanki Tauber
SENIOR EDITORS

Rabbi Binyomin Bitton
Rabbi Eliezer Gurkow
Rabbi Michoel Lipskier
Rabbi Ahrele Loschak
Rabbi Zalman Margolin
Rabbi Berry Piekarski
Rabbi Mendel Rubin
Rabbi Michoel Shapiro
Rabbi Shmuel Super
Rabbi Benyomin Walters
Rabbi Boruch Werdiger
Rabbi Yosi Wolf
CURRICULUM TEAM

Mrs. Rivki Mockin
CONTENT COORDINATOR

MARKETING AND BRANDING

Rabbi Zalman Abraham
DIRECTOR

Ms. Mashie Feldman
ADMINISTRATOR

Mrs. Peninah Baumgarten
Mrs. Chaya Mushka Kanner
Mrs. Shevi Rivkin
Mrs. Shifra Tauber
Mrs. Rikkie Wolf
GRAPHIC DESIGN

Mrs. Rivky Fieldsteel
Rabbi Zalman Korf
Mrs. Shternie Zaltzman
Ms. Chany Tauber
PUBLICATION DESIGN

Lazer Cohen
SOCIAL MEDIA

Yisroel Beenstock
MARKETING FOR RESULTS

Rabbi Eli Block
Ms. Tonia Lazaroff
Rabbi Yaakov Paley
WRITERS

Rabbi Yossi Grossbaum
Rabbi Mendel Lifshitz
Rabbi Mendel Teldon
Rabbi Shraga Sherman
Rabbi Ari Sollish
MARKETING COMMITTEE

MARKETING CONSULTANTS

JJ Gross
Israel

Warren Modlin
MEDNETPRO, INC.
Orange County, CA

Alan Rosenspan
ALAN ROSENSPAN & ASSOCIATES
Sharon, MA

Gary Wexler
PASSION MARKETING
Los Angeles, CA

Joseph Jaffe
EVOL8TION
New York, NY

JLI CENTRAL

Ms. Rochel Karp
Ms. Aliza Landes
Ms. Adina Posner
Mrs. Mussie Sputz
ADMINISTRATION

Rabbi Mendel Sirota
AFFILIATE SUPPORT

Rabbi Shlomie Tenenbaum
PROJECT MANAGER

Mrs. Mindy Wallach
AFFILIATE ORIENTATION

Ms. Mushka Backman
Mrs. Bunia Chazan
Mrs. Mushka Druk
Mrs. Mushka Lisker
Ms. Baila Pruss
Getzy Raskin
Moshe Raskin
Ms. Chany Tauber
MULTIMEDIA DEVELOPMENT

Rabbi Sholom Cohen
Rabbi Mendy Elishevitz
Mrs. Rochie Rivkin
ONLINE DIVISION

Ms. Shterna Karp
Ms. Mimi Palace
Mrs. Ya'akovah Weber
Mrs. Rachel Witty
PROOFREADERS

Rabbi Mendel Sirota
PRINTING AND DISTRIBUTION

Mrs. Musie Liberow
Mrs. Shaina B. Mintz
Mrs. Shulamis Nadler
ACCOUNTING

Mr. Yehuda Wengrofsky
DEVELOPMENT

Mrs. Musie Liberow
Mrs. Mindy Wallach
CONTINUING EDUCATION

JLI FLAGSHIP

Rabbi Yisrael Rice
CHAIRMAN

Mrs. Chana Dechter
PROJECT MANAGER

Rabbi Yisroel Altein
Rabbi Hesh Epstein
Rabbi Sholom Raichik
Mrs. Michla Schanowitz
Rabbi Shraga Sherman
Mrs. Rivkah Slonim
Rabbi Ari Sollish
Rabbi Avraham Steinmetz
Rabbi Avrohom Sternberg
EDITORIAL BOARD

PAST FLAGSHIP AUTHORS

Rabbi Zalman Abraham
Brooklyn, NY

Rabbi Berel Bell
Montreal, QC

Rabbi Nissan D. Dubov
London, UK

Rabbi Tzvi Freeman
Toronto, ON

Rabbi Eliezer Gurkow
London, ON

Rabbi Aaron Herman
Pittsburgh, PA

Rabbi Simon Jacobson
New York, NY

Rabbi Dr. Chaim D. Kagan
Monsey, NY

Rabbi Yitschak M. Kagan
of blessed memory

Rabbi Shmuel Klatzkin, PhD
Dayton, OH

Rabbi Nochum Mangel
Dayton, OH

Rabbi Moshe Miller
Chicago, IL

Rabbi Yosef Paltiel
Brooklyn, NY

Rabbi Yehuda Pink
Solihull, UK

Rabbi Yisrael Rice
S. Rafael, CA

Rabbi Eli Silberstein
Ithaca, NY

Mrs. Rivkah Slonim
Binghamton, NY

Rabbi Avrohom Sternberg
New London, CT

Rabbi Shais Taub
Cedarhurst, NY

Rabbi Shlomo Yaffe
Longmeadow, MA

ROSH CHODESH SOCIETY

Rabbi Shmuel Kaplan
CHAIRMAN

Mrs. Shaindy Jacobson
DIRECTOR

Ms. Baila Pruss
ADMINISTRATOR

Mrs. Malky Bitton
Mrs. Shula Bryski
Mrs. Chanie Wilhelm
EDITORIAL BOARD

Mrs. Devorah Kornfeld
Mrs. Chana Lipskar
Mrs. Chana Alte Mangel
Mrs. Ahuva New
Mrs. Dinie Rapoport
Mrs. Sorah Shemtov
Mrs. Binie Tenenbaum
STEERING COMMITTEE

JLI TEENS
IN PARTNERSHIP WITH
CTEEN: CHABAD TEEN NETWORK

Rabbi Chaim Block
CHAIRMAN

Rabbi Mendel Rosenfeld
DIRECTOR

Ms. Aliza Landes
ADMINISTRATOR

TORAH STUDIES
Rabbi Yosef Gansburg
CHAIRMAN

Rabbi Yehoshua Karp
PROJECT MANAGER

Rabbi Ahrele Loschak
EDITOR

Rabbi Levi Fogelman
Rabbi Yaacov Halperin
Rabbi Nechemia Schusterman
Rabbi Ari Sollish
STEERING COMMITTEE

SINAI SCHOLARS SOCIETY
IN PARTNERSHIP WITH
CHABAD ON CAMPUS

Rabbi Menachem Schmidt
CHAIRMAN

Rabbi Dubi Rabinowitz
DIRECTOR

Ms. Gitty Wilhelm
COORDINATOR

Mrs. Devorah Zlatopolsky
ADMINISTRATOR

Rabbi Moshe Chaim Dubrowski
Rabbi Yossy Gordon
Rabbi Efraim Mintz
Rabbi Menachem Schmidt
Rabbi Avi Weinstein
EXECUTIVE COMMITTEE

Rabbi Chaim Shaul Brook
Rabbi Shlomie Chein
Rabbi Moshe Leib Gray
Rabbi Zev Johnson
Rabbi Yossi Lazaroff
Rabbi Shmuel Tiechtel
Rabbi Zalman Tiechtel
Rabbi Shmuli Weiss
Rabbi Yisroel Wilhelm
STEERING COMMITTEE

JLI INTERNATIONAL

Rabbi Avrohom Sternberg
CHAIRMAN

Rabbi Dubi Rabinowitz
DIRECTOR

Rabbi Berry Piekarski
ADMINISTRATOR

Rabbi Yosef Yitzchok Noyman
ADMINISTRATOR, JLI ISRAEL
IN PARTNERSHIP WITH
MIVTZA TORAH—ISRAEL

Rabbi Eli Wolf
ADMINISTRATOR, JLI IN THE CIS
IN PARTNERSHIP WITH
THE FEDERATION OF JEWISH
COMMUNITIES OF THE CIS

Rabbi Shevach Zlatopolsky
EDITOR, JLI IN THE CIS

Rabbi Nochum Schapiro
REGIONAL REPRESENTATIVE,
AUSTRALIA

Rabbi Avraham Golovacheov
REGIONAL REPRESENTATIVE,
GERMANY

Rabbi Shmuel Katzman
REGIONAL REPRESENTATIVE,
NETHERLANDS

Rabbi Avrohom Steinmetz
REGIONAL REPRESENTATIVE,
BRAZIL

Rabbi Bentzi Sudak
REGIONAL REPRESENTATIVE,
UNITED KINGDOM

Rabbi Mendel Edelman
LIAISON TO FRENCH-SPEAKING
COUNTRIES

NATIONAL JEWISH RETREAT

Rabbi Hesh Epstein
CHAIRMAN

Mrs. Shaina B. Mintz
DIRECTOR

Bruce Backman
HOTEL LIAISON

Rabbi Menachem Klein
PROGRAM COORDINATOR

Rabbi Shmuly Karp
SHLUCHIM LIAISON

Rabbi Mendel Rosenfeld
LOGISTIC COORDINATOR

Ms. Rochel Karp
Ms. Aliza Landes
Mrs. Mussie Sputz
SERVICE AND SUPPORT

JLI LAND & SPIRIT
ISRAEL EXPERIENCE

Rabbi Shmuly Karp
DIRECTOR

Mrs. Shaina B. Mintz
ADMINISTRATOR

Rabbi Yechiel Baitelman
Rabbi Dovid Flinkenstein
Rabbi Chanoch Kaplan
Rabbi Levi Klein
Rabbi Mendel Lifshitz
Rabbi Mendy Mangel
Rabbi Sholom Raichik
Rabbi Ephraim Silverman
STEERING COMMITTEE

SHABBAT IN THE HEIGHTS

Rabbi Shmuly Karp
DIRECTOR

Mrs. Shulamis Nadler
SERVICE AND SUPPORT

Rabbi Chaim Hanoka
CHAIRMAN

Rabbi Mordechai Dinerman
Rabbi Zalman Marcus
STEERING COMMITTEE

MYSHIUR
ADVANCED LEARNING INITIATIVE

Rabbi Shmuel Kaplan
CHAIRMAN

Rabbi Levi Kaplan
DIRECTOR

TORAHCAFE.COM
ONLINE LEARNING

Rabbi Mendy Elishevitz
WEBSITE DEVELOPMENT

Moshe Levin
CONTENT MANAGER

Avrohom Shimon Ezagui
FILMING

MACHON SHMUEL
THE SAMI ROHR RESEARCH INSTITUTE

Rabbi Avrohom Bergstein
DEAN

Rabbi Zalman Korf
ADMINISTRATOR

Rabbi Gedalya Oberlander
Rabbi Chaim Rapoport
Rabbi Levi Yitzchak Raskin
Rabbi Chaim Schapiro
Rabbi Moshe Miller
RABBINIC ADVISORY BOARD

Rabbi Yakov Gershon
RESEARCH FELLOW

FOUNDING DEPARTMENT HEADS

Rabbi Mendel Bell
Rabbi Zalman Charytan
Rabbi Mendel Druk
Rabbi Menachem Gansburg
Rabbi Meir Hecht
Rabbi Levi Kaplan
Rabbi Yoni Katz
Rabbi Chaim Zalman Levy
Rabbi Benny Rapoport
Dr. Chana Silberstein
Rabbi Elchonon Tenenbaum
Rabbi Mendy Weg

Faculty Directory

ALABAMA

BIRMINGHAM
Rabbi Yossi Friedman 205.970.0100

MOBILE
Rabbi Yosef Goldwasser 251.265.1213

ALASKA

ANCHORAGE
Rabbi Yosef Greenberg
Rabbi Mendy Greenberg 907.357.8770

ARIZONA

CHANDLER
Rabbi Mendy Deitsch 480.855.4333

FLAGSTAFF
Rabbi Dovie Shapiro 928.255.5756

FOUNTAIN HILLS
Rabbi Mendy Lipskier 480.776.4763

ORO VALLEY
Rabbi Ephraim Zimmerman 520.477.8672

PHOENIX
Rabbi Zalman Levertov
Rabbi Yossi Friedman 602.944.2753

SCOTTSDALE
Rabbi Yossi Levertov 480.998.1410

TUCSON
Rabbi Yehuda Ceitlin 520.881.7956

ARKANSAS

LITTLE ROCK
Rabbi Pinchus Ciment 501.217.0053

CALIFORNIA

AGOURA HILLS
Rabbi Moshe Bryski
Rabbi Yisroel Levine 818.991.0991

BAKERSFIELD
Rabbi Shmuli Schlanger
Mrs. Esther Schlanger 661.331.1695

BEL AIR
Rabbi Chaim Mentz 310.475.5311

BERKELEY
Rabbi Yosef Romano 510.396.4448

BURBANK
Rabbi Shmuly Kornfeld 818.954.0070

CARLSBAD
Rabbi Yeruchem Eilfort
Mrs. Nechama Eilfort 760.943.8891

CHATSWORTH
Rabbi Yossi Spritzer 818.718.0777

CONTRA COSTA
Rabbi Dovber Berkowitz 925.937.4101

CORONADO
Rabbi Eli Fradkin 619.365.4728

ENCINO
Rabbi Aryeh Herzog 818.784.9986
Chapter founded by Rabbi Joshua Gordon, OBM

FOLSOM
Rabbi Yossi Grossbaum 916.608.9811

FREMONT
Rabbi Moshe Fuss 510.300.4090

GLENDALE
Rabbi Simcha Backman 818.240.2750

HUNTINGTON BEACH
Rabbi Aron David Berkowitz 714.846.2285

LA JOLLA
Rabbi Baruch Shalom Ezagui 858.455.5433

LOMITA
Rabbi Eli Hecht
Rabbi Sholom Pinson 310.326.8234

LONG BEACH
Rabbi Abba Perelmuter 562.621.9828

LOS ANGELES
Rabbi Leibel Korf 323.660.5177

MALIBU
Rabbi Levi Cunin 310.456.6588

MARINA DEL REY
Rabbi Danny Yiftach-Hashem
Rabbi Dovid Yiftach 310.859.0770

NORTH HOLLYWOOD
Rabbi Nachman Abend 818.989.9539

NORTHRIDGE
Rabbi Eli Rivkin 818.368.3937

OJAI
Rabbi Mordechai Nemtzov 805.613.7181

PACIFIC PALISADES
Rabbi Zushe Cunin 310.454.7783

PALO ALTO
Rabbi Yosef Levin
Rabbi Ber Rosenblatt 650.424.9800

PASADENA
Rabbi Chaim Hanoka
Rabbi Sholom Stiefel 626.539.4578

PLEASANTON
Rabbi Josh Zebberman 925.846.0700

POWAY
Rabbi Mendel Goldstein 858.208.6613

RANCHO MIRAGE
Rabbi Shimon H. Posner 760.770.7785

RANCHO PALOS VERDES
Rabbi Yitzchok Magalnic 310.544.5544

RANCHO S. FE
Rabbi Levi Raskin 858.756.7571

REDONDO BEACH
Rabbi Yossi Mintz
Rabbi Zalman Gordon 310.214.4999

S. CLEMENTE
Rabbi Menachem M. Slavin 949.489.0723

S. CRUZ
Rabbi Yochanan Friedman 831.454.0101

S. DIEGO
Rabbi Rafi Andrusier 619.387.8770
Rabbi Motte Fradkin 858.547.0076

S. FRANCISCO
Rabbi Shlomo Zarchi 415.752.2866

S. LUIS OBISPO
Rabbi Chaim Leib Hilel 805.229.1836

S. MONICA
Rabbi Boruch Rabinowitz 310.394.5699

S. RAFAEL
Rabbi Yisrael Rice 415.492.1666

SACRAMENTO
Rabbi Mendy Cohen 916.455.1400

SOUTH LAKE TAHOE
Rabbi Mordechai Richler 530.314.7677

SUNNYVALE
Rabbi Yisroel Hecht 408.720.0553

TUSTIN
Rabbi Yehoshua Eliezrie 714.508.2150

VENTURA
Rabbi Yakov Latowicz 805.658.7441

WEST HOLLYWOOD
Rabbi Mordechai Kirschenbaum 310.275.1215

WEST LOS ANGELES
Rabbi Mordechai Zaetz 424.652.8742

YORBA LINDA
Rabbi Dovid Eliezrie 714.693.0770

COLORADO

ASPEN
Rabbi Mendel Mintz 970.544.3770

DENVER
Rabbi Yossi Serebryanski 303.744.9699

FORT COLLINS
Rabbi Yerachmiel Gorelik 970.407.1613

HIGHLANDS RANCH
Rabbi Avraham Mintz 303.694.9119

LONGMONT
Rabbi Yakov Borenstein 303.678.7595

VAIL
Rabbi Dovid Mintz 970.476.7887

WESTMINSTER
Rabbi Benjy Brackman 303.429.5177

CONNECTICUT

FAIRFIELD
Rabbi Shlame Landa 203.373.7551

GLASTONBURY
Rabbi Yosef Wolvovsky 860.659.2422

GREENWICH
Rabbi Yossi Deren
Rabbi Menachem Feldman 203.629.9059

MILFORD
Rabbi Schneur Wilhelm 203.887.7603

NEW LONDON
Rabbi Avrohom Sternberg 860.437.8000

STAMFORD
Rabbi Yisrael Deren
Rabbi Levi Mendelow 203.3.CHABAD

WEST HARTFORD
Rabbi Shaya Gopin 860.232.1116

WESTPORT
Rabbi Yehuda L. Kantor 203.226.8584

DELAWARE

WILMINGTON
Rabbi Chuni Vogel 302.529.9900

DISTRICT OF COLUMBIA

WASHINGTON
Rabbi Levi Shemtov
Rabbi Shua Hecht 202.332.5600

FLORIDA

ALTAMONTE SPRINGS
Rabbi Mendy Bronstein 407.280.0535

BAL HARBOUR
Rabbi Dov Schochet 305.868.1411

BOCA RATON
Rabbi Zalman Bukiet
Rabbi Arele Gopin 561.994.6257
Rabbi Moishe Denburg 561.526.5760
Rabbi Ruvi New 561.394.9770

BOYNTON BEACH
Rabbi Yosef Yitzchok Raichik 561.732.4633

BRADENTON
Rabbi Menachem Bukiet 941.388.9656

SOUTHWEST BROWARD COUNTY
Rabbi Aryeh Schwartz 954.252.1770

CAPE CORAL
Rabbi Yossi Labkowski 239.963.4770

CORAL GABLES
Rabbi Avrohom Stolik 305.490.7572

CORAL SPRINGS
Rabbi Yankie Denburg 954.471.8646

DELRAY BEACH
Rabbi Sholom Ber Korf 561.496.6228

FLEMING ISLAND
Rabbi Shmuly Feldman 904.290.1017

FORT LAUDERDALE
Rabbi Yitzchok Naparstek 954.568.1190

FORT MYERS
Rabbi Yitzchok Minkowicz
Mrs. Nechama Minkowicz 239.433.7708

HALLANDALE BEACH
Rabbi Mordy Feiner 954.458.1877

HOLLYWOOD
Rabbi Leizer Barash 954.965.9933
Rabbi Leibel Kudan 954.801.3367

KENDALL
Rabbi Yossi Harlig 305.234.5654

LAKELAND
Rabbi Moshe Lazaros 863.510.5968

LONGWOOD
Rabbi Yanky Majesky 407.636.5994

MAITLAND
Rabbi Sholom Dubov
Rabbi Levik Dubov 470.644.2500

MIAMI
Rabbi Yakov Fellig 305.445.5444

MIAMI BEACH
Rabbi Yisroel Frankforter 305.534.3895

N. MIAMI BEACH
Rabbi Eli Laufer 305.770.4412

OCALA
Rabbi Yossi Hecht 352.330.4466

ORLANDO
Rabbi Yosef Konikov 407.354.3660

ORMOND BEACH
Rabbi Asher Farkash 386.672.9300

PALM BEACH GARDENS
Rabbi Dovid Vigler 561.624.2223

PALM CITY
Rabbi Shlomo Uminer 772.288.0606

PALM HARBOR
Rabbi Pinchas Adler 727.789.0408

PALMETTO BAY
Rabbi Zalman Gansburg 786.282.0413

PARKLAND
Rabbi Mendy Gutnick 954.796.7330

PEMBROKE PINES
Rabbi Mordechai Andrusier 954.874.2280

PLANTATION
Rabbi Pinchas Taylor 954.644.9177

PONTE VEDRA BEACH
Rabbi Nochum Kurinsky 904.543.9301

S. AUGUSTINE
Rabbi Levi Vogel 904.521.8664

S. PETERSBURG
Rabbi Alter Korf 727.344.4900

SARASOTA
Rabbi Chaim Shaul Steinmetz 941.925.0770

SATELLITE BEACH
Rabbi Zvi Konikov 321.777.2770

SOUTH PALM BEACH
Rabbi Leibel Stolik 561.889.3499

SOUTH TAMPA
Rabbi Mendy Dubrowski 813.922.1723

SUNNY ISLES BEACH
Rabbi Alexander Kaller 305.803.5315

TALLAHASSEE
Rabbi Schneur Oirechman 850.523.9294

VENICE
Rabbi Sholom Ber Schmerling 941.493.2770

WELLINGTON
Rabbi Mendy Muskal 561.333.4663

WESLEY CHAPEL
Rabbi Mendy Yarmush
Rabbi Mendel Friedman 813.731.2977

WESTON
Rabbi Yisroel Spalter 954.349.6565

WEST PALM BEACH
Rabbi Yoel Gancz 561.659.7770

GEORGIA

ALPHARETTA
Rabbi Hirshy Minkowicz 770.410.9000

ATLANTA
Rabbi Yossi New
Rabbi Isser New 404.843.2464

ATLANTA: INTOWN
Rabbi Eliyahu Schusterman
Rabbi Ari Sollish 404.898.0434

CUMMING
Rabbi Levi Mentz 310.666.2218

GWINNETT
Rabbi Yossi Lerman 678.595.0196

MARIETTA
Rabbi Ephraim Silverman 770.565.4412

IDAHO

BOISE
Rabbi Mendel Lifshitz 208.853.9200

ILLINOIS

CHICAGO
Rabbi Mendy Benhiyoun 312.498.7704
Rabbi Meir Hecht 312.714.4655
Rabbi Dovid Kotlarsky 773.495.7127
Rabbi Yosef Moscowitz 773.772.3770
Rabbi Levi Notik 773.274.5123

DES PLAINES
Rabbi Lazer Hershkovich 224.392.4442

ELGIN
Rabbi Mendel Shemtov 847.440.4486

GLENVIEW
Rabbi Yishaya Benjaminson 847.910.1738

HIGHLAND PARK
Mrs. Michla Schanowitz 847.266.0770

NORTHBROOK
Rabbi Meir Moscowitz................847.564.8770

OAK PARK
Rabbi Yitzchok Bergstein 708.524.1530

PEORIA
Rabbi Eli Langsam................309.692.2250

ROCKFORD
Rabbi Yecheskel Rothman................815.596.0032

SKOKIE
Rabbi Yochanan Posner................847.677.1770

VERNON HILLS
Rabbi Shimmy Susskind 847.984.2919

WILMETTE
Rabbi Dovid Flinkenstein................847.251.7707

INDIANA

INDIANAPOLIS
Rabbi Avraham Grossbaum
Rabbi Dr. Shmuel Klatzkin 317.251.5573

IOWA

BETTENDORF
Rabbi Shneur Cadaner................563.355.1065

KANSAS

OVERLAND PARK
Rabbi Mendy Wineberg................913.649.4852

KENTUCKY

LOUISVILLE
Rabbi Avrohom Litvin................502.459.1770

LOUISIANA

BATON ROUGE
Rabbi Peretz Kazen................225.267.7047

METAIRIE
Rabbi Yossie Nemes
Rabbi Mendel Ceitlin................504.454.2910

MARYLAND

BALTIMORE
Rabbi Velvel Belinsky................410.764.5000
Classes in Russian

BEL AIR
Rabbi Kushi Schusterman 443.353.9718

BETHESDA
Rabbi Sender Geisinsky................301.913.9777

CHEVY CHASE
Rabbi Zalman Minkowitz................301.260.5000

CLARKSBURG
Rabbi Yehuda Glick................301.337.0514

COLUMBIA
Rabbi Hillel Baron
Rabbi Yosef Chaim Sufrin 410.740.2424

FREDERICK
Rabbi Boruch Labkowski................301.996.3659

GAITHERSBURG
Rabbi Sholom Raichik................301.926.3632

OLNEY
Rabbi Bentzy Stolik................301.660.6770

OWINGS MILLS
Rabbi Nochum H. Katsenelenbogen................410.356.5156

POTOMAC
Rabbi Mendel Bluming................301.983.4200
Rabbi Mendel Kaplan................301.983.1485

ROCKVILLE
Rabbi Moishe Kavka................301.836.1242

MASSACHUSETTS

ANDOVER
Rabbi Asher Bronstein................978.470.2288

BOSTON
Rabbi Yosef Zaklos................617.297.7282

BIGHTON
Rabbi Dan Rodkin................617.787.2200

CAPE COD
Rabbi Yekusiel Alperowitz................508.775.2324

HINGHAM
Rabbi Levi Lezell................617.862.2770

LONGMEADOW
Rabbi Yakov Wolff...413.567.8665

NEWTON
Rabbi Shalom Ber Prus..617.244.1200

SUDBURY
Rabbi Yisroel Freeman...978.443.0110

SWAMPSCOTT
Rabbi Yossi Lipsker
Rabbi Yisroel Baron...781.581.3833

MICHIGAN

ANN ARBOR
Rabbi Aharon Goldstein.......................................734.995.3276

BLOOMFIELD HILLS
Rabbi Levi Dubov..248.949.6210

GRAND RAPIDS
Rabbi Mordechai Haller.......................................616.957.0770

WEST BLOOMFIELD
Rabbi Elimelech Silberberg..................................248.855.6170

MINNESOTA

MINNETONKA
Rabbi Mordechai Grossbaum
Rabbi Shmuel Silberstein.....................................952.929.9922

S. PAUL
Rabbi Shneur Zalman Bendet...............................651.998.9298

MISSOURI

S. LOUIS
Rabbi Yosef Landa..314.725.0400

NEVADA

LAS VEGAS
Rabbi Yosef Rivkin...702.217.2170

SUMMERLIN
Rabbi Yisroel Schanowitz
Rabbi Tzvi Bronchtain...702.855.0770

NEW JERSEY

BASKING RIDGE
Rabbi Mendy Herson
Rabbi Mendel Shemtov..908.604.8844

CHERRY HILL
Rabbi Mendel Mangel...856.874.1500

CLINTON
Rabbi Eli Kornfeld..908.623.7000

FAIR LAWN
Rabbi Avrohom Bergstein....................................201.362.2712

FORT LEE
Rabbi Meir Konikov..201.886.1238

FRANKLIN LAKES
Rabbi Chanoch Kaplan.......................................201.848.0449

GREATER MERCER COUNTY
Rabbi Dovid Dubov
Rabbi Yaakov Chaiton...609.213.4136

HASKELL
Rabbi Mendy Gurkov..201.696.7609

HOLMDEL
Rabbi Shmaya Galperin......................................732.772.1998

MADISON
Rabbi Shalom Lubin...973.377.0707

MANALAPAN
Rabbi Boruch Chazanow
Rabbi Levi Wolosow...732.972.3687

MEDFORD
Rabbi Yitzchok Kahan..609.451.3522

MOUNTAIN LAKES
Rabbi Levi Dubinsky..973.551.1898

MULLICA HILL
Rabbi Avrohom Richler.......................................856.733.0770

OLD TAPPAN
Rabbi Mendy Lewis..201.767.4008

ROCKAWAY
Rabbi Asher Herson
Rabbi Mordechai Baumgarten.............................973.625.1525

RUTHERFORD
Rabbi Yitzchok Lerman.......................................347.834.7500

SCOTCH PLAINS
Rabbi Avrohom Blesofsky....................................908.790.0008

SHORT HILLS
Rabbi Mendel Solomon
Rabbi Avrohom Levin 973.725.7008

SOUTH BRUNSWICK
Rabbi Levi Azimov 732.398.9492

TEANECK
Rabbi Ephraim Simon 201.907.0686

TENAFLY
Rabbi Mordechai Shain 201.871.1152

TOMS RIVER
Rabbi Moshe Gourarie 732.349.4199

VENTNOR
Rabbi Avrohom Rapoport 609.822.8500

WAYNE
Rabbi Michel Gurkov 973.694.6274

WEST ORANGE
Rabbi Mendy Kasowitz 973.325.6311

WOODCLIFF LAKE
Rabbi Dov Drizin 201.476.0157

NEW MEXICO

LAS CRUCES
Rabbi Bery Schmukler 575.524.1330

NEW YORK

BAY SHORE
Rabbi Shimon Stillerman 631.913.8770

BEDFORD
Rabbi Arik Wolf 914.666.6065

BINGHAMTON
Mrs. Rivkah Slonim 607.797.0015

BRIGHTON BEACH
Rabbi Moshe Winner 718.946.9833

CEDARHURST
Rabbi Zalman Wolowik 516.295.2478

COMMACK
Rabbi Mendel Teldon 631.543.3343

DOBBS FERRY
Rabbi Benjy Silverman 914.693.6100

EAST HAMPTON
Rabbi Leibel Baumgarten
Rabbi Mendy Goldberg 631.329.5800

ELLENVILLE
Rabbi Shlomie Deren 845.647.4450

FOREST HILLS
Rabbi Yossi Mendelson 917.861.9726

GREAT NECK
Rabbi Yoseph Geisinsky 516.487.4554

KINGSTON
Rabbi Yitzchok Hecht 845.334.9044

LARCHMONT
Rabbi Mendel Silberstein 914.834.4321

LITTLE NECK
Rabbi Eli Shifrin 718.423.1235

LONG BEACH
Rabbi Eli Goodman 516.897.2473

NYC KEHILATH JESHURUN
Rabbi Elie Weinstock 212.774.5636

NYC UPPER EAST SIDE
Rabbi Uriel Vigler 212.369.7310

NYACK
Rabbi Chaim Zvi Ehrenreich 845.356.6686

OCEANSIDE
Rabbi Levi Gurkow 516.764.7385

OSSINING
Rabbi Dovid Labkowski 914.923.2522

OYSTER BAY
Rabbi Shmuel Lipszyc
Rabbi Shalom Lipszyc 347.853.9992

PARK SLOPE
Rabbi Menashe Wolf 347.957.1291

PORT WASHINGTON
Rabbi Shalom Paltiel 516.767.8672

PROSPECT HEIGHTS
Rabbi Mendy Hecht 347.622.3599

ROCHESTER
Rabbi Nechemia Vogel 585.271.0330

ROSLYN
Rabbi Yaakov Reiter 516.484.8185

SEA GATE
Rabbi Chaim Brikman 917.975.2792

SOUTHAMPTON
Rabbi Chaim Pape................................917.627.4865

STATEN ISLAND
Rabbi Mendy Katzman..........................718.370.8953

STONY BROOK
Rabbi Shalom Ber Cohen......................631.585.0521

SUFFERN
Rabbi Shmuel Gancz.............................845.368.1889

YORKTOWN HEIGHTS
Rabbi Yehuda Heber.............................914.962.1111

NORTH CAROLINA

ASHEVILLE
Rabbi Shaya Susskind...........................828.505.0746

CARY
Rabbi Yisroel Cotlar.............................919.651.9710

CHAPEL HILL
Rabbi Zalman Bluming..........................919.630.5129

CHARLOTTE
Rabbi Yossi Groner
Rabbi Shlomo Cohen............................704.366.3984

GREENSBORO
Rabbi Yosef Plotkin..............................336.617.8120

RALEIGH
Rabbi Pinchas Herman
Rabbi Lev Cotlar..................................919.637.6950

OHIO

BEACHWOOD
Rabbi Shmuli Friedman.........................216.282.0112

BLUE ASH
Rabbi Yisroel Mangel............................513.793.5200

COLUMBUS
Rabbi Yitzi Kaltmann............................614.294.3296

DAYTON
Rabbi Nochum Mangel
Rabbi Shmuel Klatzkin.........................937.643.0770

OKLAHOMA

OKLAHOMA CITY
Rabbi Ovadia Goldman..........................405.524.4800

TULSA
Rabbi Yehuda Weg................................918.492.4499

OREGON

PORTLAND
Rabbi Mordechai Wilhelm......................503.977.9947

SALEM
Rabbi Avrohom Yitzchok Perlstein...........503.383.9569

PENNSYLVANIA

AMBLER
Rabbi Shaya Deitsch..............................215.591.9310

BALA CYNWYD
Rabbi Shraga Sherman...........................610.660.9192

LAFAYETTE HILL
Rabbi Yisroel Kotlarsky.........................484.533.7009

LANCASTER
Rabbi Elazar Green...............................717.368.6565

MONROEVILLE
Rabbi Mendy Schapiro...........................412.372.1000

NEWTOWN
Rabbi Aryeh Weinstein..........................215.497.9925

PHILADELPHIA: CENTER CITY
Rabbi Yochonon Goldman......................215.238.2100

PITTSBURGH
Rabbi Yisroel Altein...................412.422.7300 EXT. 269

PITTSBURGH: SOUTH HILLS
Rabbi Mendy Rosenblum........................412.278.3693

RYDAL
Rabbi Zushe Gurevitz...........................267.536.5757

WYNNEWOOD
Rabbi Moishe Brennan..........................610.529.9011

PUERTO RICO

CAROLINA
Rabbi Mendel Zarchi.............................787.253.0894

RHODE ISLAND

WARWICK
Rabbi Yossi Laufer.................................401.884.7888

SOUTH CAROLINA

COLUMBIA
Rabbi Hesh Epstein
Rabbi Levi Marrus.................................803.782.1831

MYRTLE BEACH
Rabbi Doron Aizenman.........................843.448.0035

TENNESSEE

CHATTANOOGA
Rabbi Shaul Perlstein............................423.490.1106

MEMPHIS
Rabbi Levi Klein...................................901.754.0404

TEXAS

ARLINGTON
Rabbi Levi Gurevitch............................817.451.1171

BELLAIRE
Rabbi Yossi Zaklikofsky.......................713.839.8887

DALLAS
Rabbi Mendel Dubrawsky
Rabbi Moshe Naparstek........................972.818.0770

FORT WORTH
Rabbi Dov Mandel...............................817.263.7701

FRISCO
Rabbi Mendy Kesselman.......................214.460.7773

HOUSTON
Rabbi Dovid Goldstein
Rabbi Zally Lazarus..............................281.589.7188
Rabbi Moishe Traxler............................713.774.0300

HOUSTON: RICE UNIVERSITY AREA
Rabbi Eliezer Lazaroff...........................713.522.2004

LEAGUE CITY
Rabbi Yitzchok Schmukler.....................281.724.1554

MISSOURI CITY
Rabbi Mendel Feigenson.......................832.758.0685

PLANO
Rabbi Mendel Block
Rabbi Yehudah Horowitz.......................972.596.8270

S. ANTONIO
Rabbi Chaim Block
Rabbi Levi Teldon.................................210.492.1085

THE WOODLANDS
Rabbi Mendel Blecher...........................281.719.5213

UTAH

SALT LAKE CITY
Rabbi Benny Zippel..............................801.467.7777

VERMONT

BURLINGTON
Rabbi Yitzchok Raskin..........................802.658.5770

VIRGINIA

ALEXANDRIA/ARLINGTON
Rabbi Mordechai Newman.....................703.370.2774

FAIRFAX
Rabbi Leibel Fajnland...........................703.426.1980

GAINESVILLE
Rabbi Shmuel Perlstein.........................571.445.0342

NORFOLK
Rabbi Aaron Margolin
Rabbi Levi Brashevitzky........................757.616.0770

TYSONS CORNER
Rabbi Chezzy Deitsch...........................703.829.5770
Chapter founded by Rabbi Levi Deitsch, OBM

WASHINGTON

BELLINGHAM
Rabbi Yosef Truxton.............................617.640.8841

MERCER ISLAND
Rabbi Elazar Bogomilsky.......................206.527.1411

OLYMPIA
Rabbi Yosef Schtroks............................360.867.8804

SPOKANE COUNTY
Rabbi Yisroel Hahn..............................509.443.0770

WISCONSIN

BAYSIDE
Rabbi Cheski Edelman 414.439.5041

KENOSHA
Rabbi Tzali Wilschanski 262.359.0770

MADISON
Rabbi Avremel Matusof 608.231.3450

MILWAUKEE
Rabbi Mendel Shmotkin 414.961.6100

WAUKESHA
Rabbi Levi Brook 925.708.4203

ARGENTINA

BUENOS AIRES
Mrs. Chani Gorowitz 54.11.4865.0445
Rabbi Mendi Mizrahi 54.11.4963.1221
Rabbi Mendy Gurevitch 55.11.4545.7771
Rabbi Pinhas Sudry 54.1.4822.2285
Rabbi Shloimi Setton 54.11.4982.8637
Rabbi Shiele Plotka 54.11.4634.3111
Rabbi Yosef Levy 54.11.4504.1908

SALTA
Rabbi Rafael Tawil 54.387.421.4947

AUSTRALIA

NEW SOUTH WALES

DOUBLE BAY
Rabbi Yanky Berger
Rabbi Yisroel Dolnikov 612.9327.1644

QUEENSLAND

BRISBANE
Rabbi Levi Jaffe 617.3843.6770

DOVER HEIGHTS
Rabbi Motti Feldman 614.0400.8572

NORTH SHORE
Rabbi Nochum Schapiro
Mrs. Fruma Schapiro 612.9488.9548

VICTORIA

MOORABBIN
Rabbi Elisha Greenbaum 614.0349.0434

WESTERN AUSTRALIA

PERTH
Rabbi Shalom White 618.9275.2106

AZERBAIJAN

BAKU
Mrs. Chavi Segal 994.12.597.91.90

BELARUS

BOBRUISK
Mrs. Mina Hababo 375.29.104.3230

MINSK
Rabbi Shneur Deitsch
Mrs. Bassie Deitsch 375.29.330.6675

BRAZIL

CURITIBA
Rabbi Mendy Labkowski 55.41.3079.1338

S. PAULO
Rabbi Avraham Steinmetz 55.11.3081.3081

CANADA

ALBERTA

CALGARY
Rabbi Mordechai Groner 403.281.3770

EDMONTON
Rabbi Ari Drelich
Rabbi Mendy Blachman 780.200.5770

BRITISH COLUMBIA

KELOWNA
Rabbi Shmuly Hecht 250.575.5384

RICHMOND
Rabbi Yechiel Baitelman 604.277.6427

VANCOUVER
Rabbi Dovid Rosenfeld 604.266.1313

VICTORIA
Rabbi Meir Kaplan 250.595.7656

MANITOBA

WINNIPEG
Rabbi Shmuel Altein 204.339.8737

ONTARIO

LAWRENCE/EGLINTON
Rabbi Menachem Gansburg 416.546.8770

MAPLE
Rabbi Yechezkel Deren 647.883.6372

MISSISSAUGA
Rabbi Yitzchok Slavin 905.820.4432

NIAGARA FALLS
Rabbi Zalman Zaltzman 905.356.7200

OTTAWA
Rabbi Menachem M. Blum 613.843.7770

RICHMOND HILL
Rabbi Mendel Bernstein 905.770.7700

GREATER TORONTO REGIONAL OFFICE & THORNHILL
Rabbi Yossi Gansburg 905.731.7000

THORNHILL WOODS
Rabbi Chaim Hildeshaim 905.881.1919

WATERLOO
Rabbi Moshe Goldman 226.338.7770

WHITBY
Rabbi Tzali Borenstein 905.493.9007

YORK MILLS
Rabbi Levi Gansburg 416.551.9391

QUEBEC

HAMPSTEAD
Rabbi Moshe New
Rabbi Berel Bell 514.739.0770

MONTREAL
Rabbi Ronnie Fine
Pesach Nussbaum 514.738.3434

S. LAZARE
Rabbi Nochum Labkowski 514.436.7426

TOWN OF MOUNT ROYAL
Rabbi Moshe Krasnanski
Rabbi Shneur Zalman Rader 514.342.1770

WESTMOUNT
Rabbi Yossi Shanowitz
Mrs. Devorah Leah Shanowitz 514.937.4772

SASKATCHEWAN

REGINA
Rabbi Avrohom Simmonds 306.585.1359

SASKATOON
Rabbi Raphael Kats 306.384.4370

CAYMAN ISLANDS

GRAND CAYMAN
Rabbi Berel Pewzner 717.798.1040

COLOMBIA

BOGOTA
Rabbi Chanoch Piekarski 57.1.635.8251

COSTA RICA

S. JOSÉ
Rabbi Hershel Spalter
Rabbi Moshe Bitton 506.4010.1515

CROATIA

ZAGREB
Rabbi Pinchas Zaklas 385.1.4812227

DENMARK

COPENHAGEN
Rabbi Yitzchok Loewenthal 45.3316.1850

ESTONIA

TALLINN
Rabbi Shmuel Kot 372.662.30.50

FRANCE

BOULOGNE
Rabbi Michael Sojcher 33.1.46.99.87.85

DIJON
Rabbi Chaim Slonim 33.6.52.05.26.65

MARSEILLE
Rabbi Eliahou Altabe 33.6.11.60.03.05
Rabbi Menahem Mendel Assouline 33.6.64.88.25.04
Rabbi Emmanuel Taubenblatt 33.4.88.00.94.85

PARIS
Rabbi Avraham Barou'h Pevzner 33.6.99.64.07.70
Rabbi Asher Marciano 33.1.45.26.87.60

PONTAULT COMBAULT
Rabbi Yossi Amar 33.6.61.36.07.70

VILLIERS-SUR-MARNE
Rabbi Mendy Mergui 33.6.31.19.94.92

GEORGIA

TBILISI
Rabbi Meir Kozlovsky 995.32.2429770

GERMANY

BERLIN
Rabbi Yehuda Tiechtel 49.30.2128.0830

DUSSELDORF
Rabbi Chaim Barkahn 49.173.2871.770

HAMBURG
Rabbi Shlomo Bistritzky 49.40.4142.4190

HANNOVER
Rabbi Binyamin Wolff 49.511.811.2822

GREECE

ATHENS
Rabbi Mendel Hendel 30.210.323.3825

GUATEMALA

GUATEMALA CITY
Rabbi Shalom Pelman 502.2485.0770

ISRAEL

ASHKELON
Rabbi Shneor Lieberman 054.977.0512

BALFURYA
Rabbi Noam Bar-Tov 054.580.4770

CAESAREA
Rabbi Chaim Meir Lieberman 054.621.2586

EVEN YEHUDA
Rabbi Menachem Noyman 054.777.0707

GANEI TIKVA
Rabbi Gershon Shnur 054.524.2358

GIV'ATAYIM
Rabbi Pinchus Bitton 052.643.8770

KARMIEL
Rabbi Mendy Elishevitz 054.521.3073

KFAR SABA
Rabbi Yossi Baitch 054.445.5020

KIRYAT BIALIK
Rabbi Pinny Marton 050.661.1768

KIRYAT MOTZKIN
Rabbi Shimon Eizenbach 050.902.0770

KOCHAV YAIR
Rabbi Dovi Greenberg 054.332.6244

MACCABIM-RE'UT
Rabbi Yosef Yitzchak Noiman 054.977.0549

NES ZIYONA
Rabbi Menachem Feldman 054.497.7092

NETANYA
Rabbi Schneur Brod 054.579.7572

RAMAT GAN-KRINITZI
Rabbi Yisroel Gurevitz 052.743.2814

RAMAT GAN-MAROM NAVE
Rabbi Binyamin Meir Kali 050.476.0770

RAMAT YISHAI
Rabbi Shneor Zalman Wolosow 052.324.5475

RISHON LEZION
Rabbi Uri Keshet 050.722.4593

ROSH PINA
Rabbi Sholom Ber Hertzel 052.458.7600

TEL AVIV
Rabbi Shneur Piekarski 054.971.5568

JAPAN

TOKYO
Rabbi Mendi Sudakevich 81.3.5789.2846

KAZAKHSTAN

ALMATY
Rabbi Shevach Zlatopolsky......................7.7272.77.59.49

KYRGYZSTAN

BISHKEK
Rabbi Arye Raichman......................996.312.68.19.66

LATVIA

RIGA
Rabbi Shneur Zalman Kot
Mrs. Rivka Glazman......................371.6720.40.22

LITHUANIA

VILNIUS
Rabb Sholom Ber Krinsky......................370.6817.1367

LUXEMBOURG

LUXEMBOURG
Rabbi Mendel Edelman......................352.2877.7079

NETHERLANDS

ALMERE
Rabbi Moshe Stiefel......................31.36.744.0509

AMSTERDAM
Rabbi Yanki Jacobs......................31.644.988.627
Rabbi Jaacov Zwi Spiero......................31.652.328.065

EINDHOVEN
Rabbi Simcha Steinberg......................31.63.635.7593

HAGUE
Rabbi Shmuel Katzman......................31.70.347.0222

HEEMSTEDE-HAARLEM
Rabbi Shmuel Spiero......................31.23.532.0707

MAASTRICHT
Rabbi Avrohom Cohen......................32.48.549.6766

NIJMEGEN
Rabbi Menachem Mendel Levine......................31.621.586.575

ROTTERDAM
Rabbi Yehuda Vorst......................31.10.265.5530

PANAMA

PANAMA CITY
Rabbi Ari Laine
Rabbi Gabriel Benayon......................507.223.3383

RUSSIA

ASTRAKHAN
Rabbi Yisroel Melamed......................7.851.239.28.24

BRYANSK
Rabbi Menachem Mendel Zaklas......................7.483.264.55.15

CHELYABINSK
Rabbi Meir Kirsh......................7.351.263.24.68

MOSCOW: MARINA ROSHA
Rabbi Mordechai Weisberg......................7.495.645.50.00

NIZHNY NOVGOROD
Rabbi Shimon Bergman......................7.920.253.47.70

OMSK
Rabbi Osher Krichevsky......................7.381.231.33.07

PERM
Rabbi Zalman Deutch......................7.342.212.47.32

ROSTOV
Rabbi Chaim Danzinger......................7.8632.99.02.68

S. PETERSBURG
Rabbi Zvi Pinsky......................7.812.713.62.09

SAMARA
Rabbi Shlomo Deutch......................7.846.333.40.64

SARATOV
Rabbi Yaakov Kubitshek......................7.8452.21.58.00

TOGLIATTI
Rabbi Meier Fischer......................7.848.273.02.84

UFA
Rabbi Dan Krichevsky......................7.347.244.55.33

VORONEZH
Rabbi Levi Stiefel......................7.473.252.96.99

SINGAPORE

SINGAPORE
Rabbi Mordechai Abergel 656.337.2189
Rabbi Netanel Rivni 656.336.2127
Classes in Hebrew

SOUTH AFRICA

CAPE TOWN
Rabbi Levi Popack 27.21.434.3740

JOHANNESBURG
Rabbi Dovid Masinter
Rabbi Ari Kievman 27.11.440.6600

SWEDEN

MALMO
Rabbi Shneur Kesselman 46.707.366.770

STOCKHOLM
Rabbi Chaim Greisman 468.679.7067

SWITZERLAND

BASEL
Rabbi Zalmen Wishedsky 41.41.361.1770

LUZERN
Rabbi Chaim Drukman 41.41.361.1770

THAILAND

BANGKOK
Rabbi Yosef C. Kantor 6681.837.7618

UKRAINE

DNEPROPETROVSK
Rabbi Dan Makagon 380.504.51.13.18

NIKOLAYEV
Rabbi Sholom Gotlieb 380.512.37.37.71

ODESSA
Rabbi Avraham Wolf
Rabbi Yaakov Neiman .... 38.048.728.0770 EXT. 280

ZHITOMIR
Rabbi Shlomo Wilhelm 380.504.63.01.32

UNITED KINGDOM

BOURNEMOUTH
Rabbi Bentzion Alperowitz 44.749.456.7177

CHEADLE
Rabbi Peretz Chein 44.161.428.1818

LEEDS
Rabbi Eli Pink 44.113.266.3311

LONDON
Rabbi Mendel Cohen 44.777.261.2661
Rabbi Nissan D. Dubov 44.208.944.1581
Rabbi Dovid Katz 44.207.624.2770
Rabbi Yisroel Lew 44.207.060.9770
Rabbi Gershon Overlander
Rabbi Hillel Gruber 44.208.202.1600
Rabbi Shlomo Odze 44.791.757.3558
Rabbi Yossi Simon 44.208.458.0416
Rabbi Bentzi Sudak 44.207.078.7469

MANCHESTER
Rabbi Levi Cohen 44.161.792.6335
Rabbi Shmuli Jaffe 44.161.766.1812

JEWISH LEARNING INSTITUTE

THE JEWISH LEARNING MULTIPLEX
Brought to you by the Rohr Jewish Learning Institute

In fulfillment of the mandate of the Lubavitcher Rebbe, of blessed memory,
whose leadership guides every step of our work,
the mission of the Rohr Jewish Learning Institute is to transform
Jewish life and the greater community through the study of Torah,
connecting each Jew to our shared heritage of Jewish learning.

While our flagship program remains the cornerstone of our organization,
JLI is proud to feature additional divisions catering to specific populations,
in order to meet a wide array of educational needs.

THE ROHR JEWISH LEARNING INSTITUTE,
a subsidiary of *Merkos L'Inyonei Chinuch*,
is the adult education arm of the Chabad-Lubavitch Movement.

Torah Studies provides a rich and nuanced encounter with the weekly Torah reading.

MyShiur courses are designed to assist students in developing the skills needed to study Talmud independently.

This rigorous fellowship program invites select college students to explore the fundamentals of Judaism.

Jewish teens forge their identity as they engage in Torah study, social interaction, and serious fun.

The Rosh Chodesh Society gathers Jewish women together once a month for intensive textual study.

TorahCafe.com provides an exclusive selection of top-rated Jewish educational videos.

This yearly event rejuvenates mind, body, and spirit with a powerful synthesis of Jewish learning and community.

Participants delve into our nation's rich past while exploring the Holy Land's relevance and meaning today.

Select affiliates are invited to partner with peers and noted professionals, as leaders of innovation and excellence.

Machon Shmuel is an institute providing Torah research in the service of educators worldwide.